Stories, Stats and Stuff
About Texas A&M™ Football

By Sam Blair
Foreword by Roger Staubach

Printed in the United States of America by
Mennonite Press, Inc.

ISBN 1-880652-77-3

PHOTO CREDITS All photographs were supplied
by Barbara Ridgway, Sam Blair, John Rhodes,
Eliot Kamenitz and Texas A&M University.

INTRODUCTION

Unique is an adjective that is greatly over-used and rarely merited, but it applies to Texas A&M.

I have written about college football and visited

Sam Blair

campuses all over America for 45 years and I guarantee you there's no place else like A&M and the spirit of Aggieland. Sure, I'm a native Texan and remember first listening to an Aggie football game in 1939, when I was 7 and Homer Norton's powerhouse was winning the national championship. But I'm sure not biased.

I earned my bachelor of journalism from the University of Texas in 1954. In those days you didn't have to add "at Austin." There was only one UT. And then as now, as both schools move into the new Big 12 Conference, the Longhorns are the oldest and staunchest rivals of the Aggies. But I checked my allegiances at the door when I got into this business. I forever have thrived on writing special stories about special places and special people.

That's why I was delighted when I was offered the opportunity to write this book. Texas A&M is a special place, and Aggies are special people. This one has been fun, and enlightening, and inspiring. My goal was to capture the essence of a unique institution and its football program as they pass an historic milestone. I hope I chalked up some wins. I know I got some grins.

The A&M campus is a lovely place today, a booming coed school of 43,000 enrollment sprawling across 5,000 lush acres. It is the product of a tremendous transition: from a remote all-male, land-grant military college to one of the nation's largest and most diversified universities. Interestingly, a few years after the first female students enrolled at A&M, the Aggies entered their most sustained period of football success. With Coach R.C. Slocum, who knows and loves A&M as well as anyone, the Aggies should continue to field impact teams in the Big 12.

But way back in the days of Uncle Charley Moran, D.X. Bible, Homer Norton and Bear Bryant — when the campus was plain and ugly — there still were some fine football players and that wonderful spirit.

Bryant expressed it well in his autobiography, *Bear*, noting that his wife, Mary Harmon, "turned white" at her first sight of A&M when they moved there from Kentucky in 1954. They stayed four years, a period when Bryant made an indelible mark on the school and Aggie football. Bryant wrote:

"Dr. Thom Harrington, the chancellor, told me, 'Paul, this place will grow on you,' and he was right. Mary Harmon cried her eyes out that first night. And when we left, she cried all over again."

That unique school on the Brazos River bottoms has touched countless Aggies in a way only Aggies can understand. Karen Arrington Jordan is an Aggie as well as my old friend and colleague at the *Dallas Morning News*, where I happily closed out 41 years last December with a neat early-retirement-bonus buyout. She said it so well.

"Once the spirit of Aggieland touches your heart, it's with you forever."

I'll try to show you why in the pages ahead.

— *Sam Blair*

My thanks to Wilbur Evans, Jones Ramsey, Spec Gammon, Ralph Carpenter, Alan Cannon, H.B. McElroy, Dub King, Margaret Rudder, Randy Matson, Tom O'Dwyer, Walter Robertson and Dave Smith, plus numerous members of the Dallas Morning News *family, for their help and guidance along the way. And my special thanks to Roger Staubach, who's still the master of the 2-minute offense.*

— *Sam Blair*

FOREWORD

Roger Staubach won the Heisman Trophy as a Navy quarterback. After four years of active duty as a Naval officer, including one year in Vietnam, he joined the Dallas Cowboys in 1969. He led the Cowboys to five Super Bowls and two championships during his 11-year career. In 1985, his first year of eligibility, he was elected to the Pro Football Hall of Fame. He lives in Dallas and is chairman and CEO of The Staubach Company, a national real estate firm. He and his wife, Marianne, have five children and two grandchildren.

Texas A&M first became a part of my life on Thanksgiving Day 1963 when I was a junior at the Naval Academy. The Aggies were playing a nationally televised game with Texas, which was unbeaten and ranked No. 1 nationally. Since Navy was No. 2, our team watched that game with keen interest.

Naturally, we were rooting real hard for A&M, and it looked like the Aggies had the game won until right at the end. An A&M linebacker intercepted a pass and tried to lateral it, but the ball bounced loose and Texas recovered. If he had just fallen on the ball, A&M would have won.

Texas drove downfield, and then an Aggie defensive back intercepted in the end zone. We thought for sure A&M had won. But the official ruled the Aggie stepped out of the end zone before he had possession of the ball. Texas scored with a few seconds left to win, 15-13, and then beat us in the Cotton Bowl on New Year's Day, 28-6.

For years that was my only knowledge of A&M. But once I joined the Cowboys in 1969, the fever of the Southwest Conference got my attention. Naturally, I noticed the great spirit of A&M.

Shortly after I retired from football, about 1980, I spoke at Aggie Muster in Fort Worth and I was very moved by the Aggies' loyalty to their school and each other. I have been very aware of A&M, and Aggies, since then.

Today A&M is a large coed university but it still has those special qualities of friendship, camaraderie and pride that originated when it was a small, all-male military college. Its spirit reminds me of a smaller, close-knit school like the Naval Academy, where 4,000 midshipmen lived together in one dormitory.

Now we have that A&M spirit in our family because our daughter, Amy, is an Aggie. She told us early in her high school years that she really liked the idea of going to A&M. She thought she wanted to be a veterinarian and knew A&M was a good school for that. Later she changed her mind about being a vet but she still was excited about A&M. She didn't even want to visit any other schools, but Marianne and I thought she should at least look at some others.

Before we could visit any other schools, I received an award at Texas A&M's School of Business and we took Amy to College Station for the luncheon. Some of the students showed her around the campus and that just solidified her feelings. Amy was hooked on A&M.

She applied for early admission and she was so

excited when she got the letter telling her she was in, that she started screaming. Amy is an Aggie, for sure.

Amy Staubach at Kyle Field in 1996.

She has a little bit of the cowgirl mentality anyway — loves rodeo, riding horses and C&W music — and A&M kind of goes to the roots of Texas.

Each of our children has gone to different schools. Jennifer went to Incarnate Word in San Antonio; Michelle to Catholic University in Washington, D.C., where she also attended law shool; Stephanie to Vanderbilt and then law school at SMU; and Jeff is entering his senior year at Duke.

Now, Amy is ready for her sophomore year at A&M and the school is a big part of our lives.

Last fall we went to the bonfire the night before the Texas game and it was an amazing experience. Some people had come a couple of days earlier and parked their campers on the street near the bonfire. I couldn't believe the pride and preparation that went into it. That's the heart of A&M.

A lot of schools have pride and spirit, but I don't know any other that has the long-term bonding with its traditions like A&M. I'm just glad we have an Aggie in our family.

— *Roger Staubach*
June 1996

TABLE OF CONTENTS

Earl Rudder
The Greatest Aggie Hero

Earl Rudder

Romanticists would believe that destiny led John Tarleton Agricultural College Coach W.J. Wisdom to that drugstore in the little West Texas town of Eden on a hot, dusty afternoon in the summer of 1927. Realists would figure he was just thirsty.

Wisdom wiped his sweaty brow with a handkerchief and looked around until he found the case of ice cold soft drinks. He pulled out a bottle, popped the cap and drank deeply. Refreshed, he handed the store owner a nickel and smiled.

"You got any football players in this town?" Wisdom asked. The store owner grinned and nodded across the store.

"Just that fat boy behind the soda fountain," he said.

Earl Rudder, newly graduated from Eden High School and delighted to have a summer job that took him away from grueling work on the family ranch and allowed him to eat ice cream for free, smiled as Wisdom took a stool at his counter. They talked awhile, then Wisdom went to visit with the local high school football coach and discuss Earl's ability. By the time Wisdom left town he had offered the 17-year-old from a large, poor family something he never dreamed he might have — an opportunity to attend college.

Earl was eager to accept a modest scholarship to play football at Tarleton, a junior college in Stephenville and a member of the Texas A&M College System, a group of schools which emphasized agricultural and engineering studies and compulsory military training in ROTC. He still would have to pay some expenses and his father, who had worked hard simply to get Earl and his siblings through high school, had no interest in college education for his children.

AGGIE QUIZ

1. How many games did the Aggies play with Texas before they won?

Earl's mother encouraged him to enroll at Tarleton, however, and gave him $5 from her butter-and-egg money. Soon Earl was off to Stephenville, unaware that he was starting a journey that would change dramatically not only his life but ultimately the course of World War II, the state of Texas and Texas A&M.

It almost ended a few weeks later, though. By the middle of football season, Earl was broke and went to Wisdom's office to tell him he was leaving school. But the coach was hurrying to his weekly service club luncheon and cut off the downcast freshman as soon as he announced he was quitting.

"Rudder, I don't have time to talk to you now," Wisdom said. "Meet me here before practice this afternoon."

When Earl returned to continue his farewell speech, his coach had arranged a deal that would enable him to stay at Tarleton. At lunch, Wisdom explained his young athlete's plight to his fellow club members and asked for

FACT BOX: JAMES EARL RUDDER

BORN May 6, 1910, at Eden, Concho County, Texas.

DIED March 23, 1970, at Houston, Texas.

WIFE Margaret Williamson Rudder (married June 12, 1937).

CHILDREN James Earl Jr., Anne, Linda, Jane (died 1983) and Robert.

EDUCATION Graduated from Eden High School, 1927; John Tarleton Agricultural College, 1930; Texas A&M, 1932; graduate school, TCU, 1939.

FOOTBALL Lettered as center on Eden High School's first football team, 1926; Tarleton, 1927-29; A&M, 1931. Named to the *Sports Illustrated* first Silver Anniversary All-America team, 1956. Coached at Brady High School, 1933-37; and Tarleton, 1938-40.

MILITARY HIGHLIGHTS
Commissioned as 2nd lieutenant in U.S. Army Reserve upon graduation from A&M in 1932 and rose to rank of colonel while on active duty, 1941-45. Remained active in Army Reserve after World War II and retired as major general in 1967.

GOVERNMENT Mayor of Brady, 1946-52; Texas Land Commissioner, 1955-58.

The Earl Rudder statue.

TEXAS A&M ADMINISTRATION
Appointed A&M vice president, 1958; promoted to president, 1959; named president of Texas A&M University System, consolidating offices of chancellor and university president, 1965.

Margaret Rudder helped unveil this life-size bronze statue of her husband, Earl Rudder, in ceremonies on Oct. 15, 1994, on the Texas A&M campus.

2. When was the Aggies' first perfect season?

their help. At Wisdom's suggestion, the club voted to buy a cow and let it graze on the campus near the football field. Wisdom told Earl he could milk the cow daily, sell the milk to the manager of the campus dining hall and use the money for his college expenses.

Earl, delighted by his change of fortune, quickly accepted. But disappointment soon followed. When he arrived at the dining hall the next morning with less than a full pail of milk, the manager reduced his payment.

Earl was walking dejectedly back to his dorm when he noticed a water faucet outside the fieldhouse. He was paid for a full pail of milk thereafter.

So he stayed at Tarleton, played center on the football team and became a popular campus leader. In 1930, he transferred to Texas A&M. Earl was just happy to be playing football and finishing his education at remote, rural College Station.

He worked hard and grew into a personable young man eager to get on with his life. But when he graduated from A&M in 1932, no one could sense that Earl Rudder would become the greatest Aggie hero. That chapter would not begin for another dozen years.

By then he was a lieutenant colonel in the U.S. Army, charged with one of the most difficult missions of World War II.

RUDDER'S RANGERS For Rudder's Rangers, D-Day at Normandy was their Day of Destiny.

And Rudder always remembered June 6, 1944, as the strongest day for him and the men of his 2nd Ranger Battalion.

At the most important moment of the biggest and worst war in history, Lt. Col. Rudder and his Rangers climbed the sheer 100-foot cliff to Pointe de Hoc for the first battle of D-Day, one on which the Allies' invasion of France would turn. Once on top, they defeated the German soldiers who had leaned over the edge of the cliff, blasting away with machine guns, throwing grenades down at them and cutting their ropes, determined to kill them or drive them back into the English Channel.

Most significantly, Rudder's Rangers knocked out five 155mm guns, powerful artillery pieces with a 17-mile range with which the Germans would have opened fire on Omaha and Utah beaches once they filled with men and equipment later that morning.

After the war, James Earl Rudder went on to become a mayor, Texas Land Commissioner and Texas A&M University president. But to the men of Rudder's Rangers, he would always remain the man who led them up the cliff at Pointe du Hoc.

"Colonel Rudder has always been my hero," said Len Lomell, who was a 24-year-old Ranger from New Jersey on D-Day whose alertness and daringness enabled him to destroy the German guns. "What I did was just plain, dumb luck. I was in the right place at the right time, and I did the right thing because that was how he trained all of us. We were unstoppable under his command because we just knew we could do it.

"He talked to you softly but firmly, like a big brother. He inspired you to do your best. You just wanted to die for him," said Lomell, now a retired attorney in Toms River, N.J.

That the German guns on Point de Hoc never fired that fateful morning was due to Sgt. Maj. Lomell's fast, furious search. He had just been promoted to platoon leader by Col. Rudder because the leading officers in Company D had been knocked out of action.

Lomell discovered the huge guns hidden in camouflage in an apple orchard. They were 700 yards

AGGIE QUIZ

3. When was the Aggies' last perfect season?

AGGIE QUIZ

4. When did Texas A&M record its worst record?

5. Which school did the Aggies tie in 1948, a winless season?

Margaret Rudder plays the organ in her home during the 1996 Rangers Reunion. A photo of her husband, Earl Rudder, is on the music stand.

back from the primary gun emplacement site that advance intelligence reports had made the first goal of the Rangers' D-Day mission. There he had found emplacements containing only telephone poles, which appeared to be guns in aerial reconnaissance photos.

Certain that the guns were somewhere on Pointe du Hoc, Lomell moved inland with his platoon to secure the coastal highway that served as the main transportation artery between the villages of Vierville and Grandcamp. Then he and Staff Sgt. Jack Kuhn went in search of the missing guns, and finally found them. Another 100 yards beyond the guns, he saw about 100 German soldiers apparently in a briefing with commanders.

Unknown to Lomell, the artillery unit was meeting to plan new strategy for its counter-attack. The men were confused by the mysterious lack of communication from their comrades in the forward observation post, which had been wiped out by the Rangers.

At that moment, Lomell knew only that he had an opportunity, and he seized it. While Kuhn peered over a hedgerow and covered him with a Tommy gun, Lomell scurried 200 yards across the orchard to the guns and destroyed them with silent Thermite grenades, whose intense heat melted the moving parts in the firing mechanism.

"We had to knock out those guns and, by God, we did," Lomell said.

Lomell ignored a wound he suffered as soon as he

charged off his boat. He was the first American hit by German machine gun fire when Rudder's Rangers jumped from their assault landing craft and invaded the beach at Pointe du Hoc. He recalls shrugging off the bleeding wound in his side and charging on, inspired, he said, by the example of his leader.

Rudder's Rangers fought on alone at Pointe du Hoc for two days and nights, their original force of 225 men reduced to 90 with no food and dwindling arms and ammunition. They repulsed five counter-attacks by Germans outnumbering them 10-to-1 until reinforcements arrived.

Lomell said his fellow Rangers fought and died so well because they knew that Col. Rudder, Texas A&M '32, also was willing to die for them and his country.

Margaret Rudder hosts a Rangers Reunion every year.

Rudder was wounded twice, first in the leg and then in the arm, while leading his men of the 2nd Battalion, Companies D, E and F in combat after refusing an order to stay behind on the headquarters ship.

Maj. Gen. Clarence Huebner, the 1st Division commander, wanted Rudder removed from the action to direct the overall Ranger operation, which also involved other Ranger units elsewhere on Normandy beaches.

But Rudder insisted on leading, and fighting, after his newly promoted executive officer, a major designated to lead the assault on Pointe du Hoc, got drunk on the holding ship Prince Charles on the night of June 4 and began telling young Rangers that theirs was a suicide mission. The major, besides being drunk, was distraught and disillusioned by a new, top-secret intelligence report that there were no guns on Pointe du Hoc.

Rudder, who maintained the guns were there, relieved the officer of his Ranger assignment and decided he would bolster the sagging morale of his men by climbing the nine-story cliff and leading them into battle.

"I can't let you do that," Gen. Huebner told him. "You can't risk getting knocked out in the first round."

Rudder replied, "I'm sorry, sir, but I'm going to have to disobey you. If I don't take it, it may not go."

Demolition officer Elmer (Dutch) Vermeer, who for years attended the Ranger reunions that Margaret Rudder has hosted at her Bryan, Texas, home since her husband's death in 1970, once wrote: "One of the Rangers' mottos was, 'The impossible can be done immediately. Miracles take a little while.' With Colonel Rudder, anything seemed possible."

AGGIE QUIZ

6. Who was the Aggies' opponent in their 300th win?

THE REST OF THE STORY What he achieved with his Rangers when destiny took charge was a far cry from his prewar life.

The 6-foot, 220-pound Rudder had been content as a

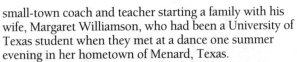

7. *Who was the A&M's opponent in its 400th win?*

small-town coach and teacher starting a family with his wife, Margaret Williamson, who had been a University of Texas student when they met at a dance one summer evening in her hometown of Menard, Texas.

As a college graduate in the depths of the Great Depression, he dug ditches to earn a meager living after earning a bachelor of science degree in industrial education, an A&M football letter as a center and a second lieutenant's commission in the U.S. Army Reserve.

He was happy to drop his pick and shovel and pursue coaching and teaching, first at Brady High School and then at John Tarleton Agricultural College, where he had begun his pursuit of higher learning in 1927 after his fortunate meeting with Coach W.J. Wisdom at that drugstore soda fountain in Eden.

He was called to active duty with the Army and promoted to first lieutenant in June 1941, six months before the United States entered World War II. He was promoted to captain and then to major in June 1943, when he was assigned to Camp Forrest, Tenn., to organize and train the 2nd Ranger Battalion. Other officers had failed in this assignment.

"When he learned I was the only guy from Texas in the outfit, he called me in and asked me what was wrong," said James (Ike) Eikner, the 2nd Battalion's communications officer who now lives in Austin and each April attends the Ranger reunion hosted by Margaret Rudder. "I told him we were bored and needed a firm hand of discipline. Well, he certainly knew what to do."

The new commander told his Rangers: "I'm going to work you harder than you've ever worked. In a shorter time than you can imagine, you're going to be the best fighting unit in this man's army."

Rudder's Rangers proved themselves on D-Day at Pointe du Hoc. It was a mission so foreboding that Gen. Omar Bradley, commander of U.S. forces in Europe, wrote in his autobiography, *A Soldier's Story*, "No soldier in my command has ever been wished a more difficult task than that which befell the 34-year-old commander of this Ranger force, James Earl Rudder."

8. *Who was the Aggies' opponent in their 500th win?*

The mission started out badly. Rudder's Rangers had to overcome a critical 40-minute delay caused by an error in navigation by the British boatswain in the guide boat leading them across the dark and choppy English Channel in their 10 small assault landing craft.

At daylight, just as the bombardment of German posts on the cliffs ended as scheduled five minutes before H-Hour of 6:30 a.m., Col. Rudder saw that his force was approaching Pointe et Raz de la Percee, three miles east of Pointe du Hoc. He immediately ordered all boats to turn 90 degrees right and follow a dangerous route to

Pointe du Hoc parallel to the coastline, leaving them open to machine gun fire from Germans who had emerged from underground tunnels.

"Earl always believed if they had hit the beach on time, they could have taken Pointe du Hoc without firing a shot," Margaret Rudder said. "But no matter how much went wrong, he and his men still succeeded. I think what he went through there gave him the confidence to do all that he did later in life."

Earl Rudder's performance on D-Day proved forever that he was born to lead. He pursued that mission with courage and calmness the rest of his life.

He came home with the rank of full colonel and a chest full of medals, including the Distinguished Service Cross, Silver Star, Bronze Star, Purple Heart and French Legion of Honor with Croix de Guerre and Palm. He became successful in ranching and business in Brady and served as mayor six years, 1946-52.

In January 1955, Rudder accepted Texas Governor Allan Shivers' request to become Texas Land Commissioner in the wake of the Texas veterans land

AGGIE QUIZ

9. The Aggies posted the highest winning percentage in the last 10 seasons of Southwest Conference play. What was it?

FIGHTIN' TEXAS AGGIE BAND

The Texas A&M band, famous for its musicianship and precision marching, has grown from 13 members in 1894 to more than 300 today. A major unit within the Corps of Cadets, the band devotes seven to 10 hours per week to intense rehearsals — and that dedication shows when it marches into Kyle Field.

The band plays continuously from the first strains of "Hullabaloo, Caneck! Caneck!," the beginning of "Aggie War Hymn" until the traditional block T that stretches almost half the length of the football field dissolves. Then, as the crowd cheers, the musicians whoop and race for their section in the stands.

The Aggie Band in 1894. Today's band, thanks to the work of Earl Rudder, includes women and men.

AGGIE QUIZ

10. Name the Aggie kicker who became the only player in college football history to kick two 60-yard field goals in one game, as well as the opponent and season in which he did it.

scandal, which had allowed promoters to buy state land set aside for veterans at low prices and sell it for huge profits. Bascom Giles, the incumbent commissioner, soon would be sentenced to six years in prison for his role in the scandal.

Commissioner Rudder, selected by Shivers because of his record of leadership and reputation for integrity, reorganized the land department and in 1956 won election to the office. So distinguished was his service that today a state office building near the Capitol in Austin bears his name.

If Rudder had responded to the urging of Texas Democratic Party leaders, his portrait might now hang in the Capitol Rotunda along with other Texas governors like Sam Houston and Ann Richards. He became so admired for his service as Texas Land Commissioner and his charismatic personality that he loomed as the logical successor to Shivers in the Governor's office. But his political future was overshadowed by an opportunity to return to his alma mater.

HIS A&M LEGACY Rudder resigned as Land Commissioner in 1958 and moved to Texas A&M as vice president. He was elevated to president in 1959 and in that role led the university into an era of growth in the '60s, opening the school to female students, eliminating compulsory military training and broadening its educational mission.

But first he had to bring the tradition-bound Corps of Cadets and grudging old grads kicking and screaming into the 20th century. These forces believed A&M should remain forever an all-male institution and they reacted angrily when Rudder announced that A&M would admit female students starting with the fall semester in 1963.

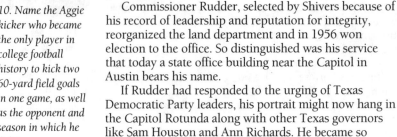

Earl Rudder as president of A&M.

In fact, the Corps of Cadets, in a shameful act of rudeness and immaturity, booed the greatest Aggie hero when he announced the new policy of co-education approved by the regents. But on that April day in 1963, the man who overcame staggering odds on D-Day, stood calmly before the Corps in a packed G. Rollie White Coliseum and explained that this change was inevitable. Military schools like A&M had fallen into disfavor across America because of the country's growing and unpopular role in the Vietnam War. And legal action by potential female students inevitably would force A&M to change its admission policy. With the first wave of postwar Baby Boomers about to engulf U.S. colleges and universities, A&M leaders knew it was time for a drastic change.

AGGIE QUIZ

11. How many 100-yard rushing games did All-American fullback John Kimbrough have for the national champion Aggies in 1939?

"If Texas A&M goes on fighting and resisting this, we'll find 10 years from now that we are still about the same size and the two major public universities in this state will be the University of Texas and Texas Tech,"

Rudder said. "Now is the time to change and move on."

His was the voice of prophecy. A&M's enrollment had been static for years, about 7,000 male students in a school with compulsory military training. In 1996, A&M had an enrollment of more than 43,000, ranking behind only Ohio State and the University of Texas among the nation's largest public universities. And since the early '70s, when a rapidly-growing student body became 50 percent female, football recruiting has flourished. So has winning.

As much as the Corps and old grads hated it, the change Earl Rudder announced that day in G. Rollie White Coliseum now looks like the best thing that has happened in Texas A&M's 120 years.

Sallie Sheppard, one of the first women to enroll at A&M.

"Earl Rudder was a very insightful man," said Dr. Sallie Sheppard, one of those first female Aggies to enroll in 1963, and now A&M's associate provost for undergraduate programs and academic services. "He had a vision and knew how to get things done. You always can speculate on what might have happened to A&M if he hadn't been here. From A&M's standpoint, he was the right person at the right time."

Like the Rangers saw their commander on D-Day, so did the A&M Board of Regents see Earl Rudder as the ideal leader at that point in the school's history. In September 1965, the board members expanded his role and named him president of the Texas A&M University System. As such, Rudder oversaw the operation of all branches of the A&M System, including his other beloved alma mater, Tarleton State at Stephenville. He worked for progress and improvement in all areas until he suffered a cerebral hemorrhage in January 1970.

The greatest Aggie hero died in a Houston hospital March 23, 1970, just six weeks short of his 60th birthday, leaving behind a history of leadership, service and inspiration.

Rudder is still in the hearts of all living Rangers who served under him on D-Day. Many of them say they still tingle with the memory of struggling up the cliff with him and winning the battle that had to be won at Pointe du Hoc.

As countless Aggies since have learned, great things happened with Earl Rudder in charge.

Different Name,
Different Game

There was no hint of future greatness for Texas A&M's first football team. This bunch was called Farmers, not Aggies, and the abbreviated two-game season ended in such disappointment that Coach Frank Dudley Perkins wasn't the only one who failed to return the next season.

The team didn't show up either.

The Farmers were so frustrated by a 38-0 loss to Varsity, as the University of Texas was called in those days, that A&M decided to take a year off to re-think its approach to this strange new game. If current Aggies think 38-0 was bad, consider this: Varsity scored eight touchdowns but they were worth only four points each then and a conversion kick two. By today's scoring system, Texas would have won 51-0.

AGGIE QUIZ

12. Name the first season the Aggies had two 100-yard rushers in the same game.

A&M's FIRST COACH Frank Dudley Perkins was an ambitious student who played fullback and served as trainer in 1894, as well as coach. When the team re-formed in 1896, Perkins turned the coaching over to two professors, A.M. Soule and H.W. South, and stuck to playing fullback the next two seasons.

So the Farmers started over, still seeking their first victory against a college team. They had beaten Ball High in Galveston, 14-6, before Varsity rudely reminded them they still had much to learn. And there was no let-up. The Varsity rascals outscored them, 138-0, in five games, all played in either Austin or San Antonio.

Not every game was lopsided, however. In 1899, Varsity recorded a disputed 6-0 decision at San Antonio. The game ended 28 minutes early when A&M captain Hal Moseley took his team off the field because Texas was awarded possession on the A&M 2-yard line after a scramble for a loose ball. The Farmers already were steamed because they had been denied a touchdown on a controversial ruling by an official.

Hal Mosley

The breakthrough came in 1902. A&M outbid Ohio State for Coach J.E. Platt of Lafayette College, and he produced a team that not only beat Texas, 11-0, at Austin but finished the season 7-0-2 and was proclaimed Champions of the Southwest. A&M football was moving up in class. And in the 1908 game with the hated Longhorns, the Aggies really moved up in clash.

A&M had another new coach, M.A. Merriam, in 1908, and the Aggies sagged to their first losing season

The 1894 football team, the school's first.

(3-5) since 1901. Two more losses to Texas ran the A&M series record to 1-14-2, and Aggie fans' frustration erupted into an ugly scene on the field at halftime at the No-Tsu-Oh Carnival in West End Park at Houston. (No-Tsu-Oh is Houston spelled backward.)

Texas led 14-0, and some of the 1,200 UT students at the game paraded on the field with brooms on their shoulders like rifles. A&M fans thought the Longhorns were inplying they would sweep the Aggies when it actually was part of a traditional snake dance. Some cadets were so incensed they rushed on the field and tore

The 1900 team played to a 2-2-1 record, with both defeats coming against Texas.

Charley Moran

into the celebrants. One Texas student was stabbed three times, but no arrests were made. Peace was restored in the second half, and the Longhorns won, 24-8. After Texas won again, 28-12, in the season finale at Austin, the Aggies were desperate to change their fortunes.

MORAN STEPS IN A&M hired controversial Coach Charley Moran in 1909 and he promptly changed everything. When a faculty member asked the new head coach if he would teach his players to be good losers, Moran snapped, "Hell, I didn't come here to lose."

Tough and outspoken, Moran inspired fierce loyalty from the Aggies and bitter hatred from their opponents. His six-year record of 38-8-4 (.800) stood as the highest winning percentage by an A&M coach for 80 years.

Rivals charged that Moran brought in professional players, but this was never proved. They also accused him of ordering his players to use dirty, brutal tactics, particularly against Texas. Moran's Aggies beat the Longhorns three times his first two seasons, 23-0 at Houston and 5-0 at Austin in 1909 and 14-8 at Houston in 1910.

When the two state schools met again at Houston in 1911, A&M was a heavy favorite. The Aggies had outscored their first four opponents (Southwestern, Austin College, Auburn, Ole Miss) 88-0 and were 21-1 in their last 22 games. But the Longhorns and their fans were intent on finally beating a Moran-coached team. UT students swarmed across the No-Tsu-Oh Carnival grounds and into the stands singing this verse:

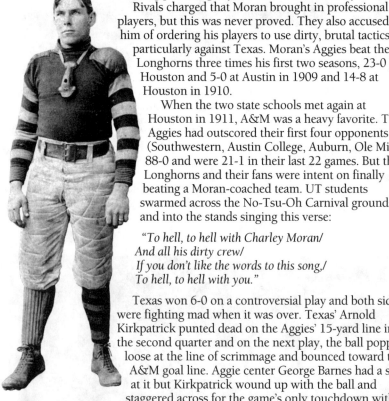

Earl Schultz (1900-03) was one of the first Aggies to experience beating Texas, when the Aggie's won 11-0 in 1902.

"To hell, to hell with Charley Moran/
And all his dirty crew/
If you don't like the words to this song,/
To hell, to hell with you."

Texas won 6-0 on a controversial play and both sides were fighting mad when it was over. Texas' Arnold Kirkpatrick punted dead on the Aggies' 15-yard line in the second quarter and on the next play, the ball popped loose at the line of scrimmage and bounced toward the A&M goal line. Aggie center George Barnes had a shot at it but Kirkpatrick wound up with the ball and staggered across for the game's only touchdown with Barnes hanging on. Some Aggies insisted Kirkpatrick fouled Barnes in the fight for the ball but no penalty was called. Thus, the Longhorns broke Moran's dominance.

Pushing, shoving and cursing were so rampant when fans swarmed onto the field after the game that the traditional downtown victory parade that night was canceled. The next day, UT officials announced they

were breaking off athletic relations with A&M starting in 1912.

Although Moran was not mentioned, Texas clearly was sick of him. The Aggies and Longhorns did not play the next three years while Uncle Charley continued at A&M, but in time A&M officials realized they valued a healthy rivalry with Texas and other schools more than their controversial coach.

A CONFERENCE FORMS In 1914, Texas Athletic Director L. (Leo) Theo Bellmont and athletic council chairman W.T. Mather became the catalysts in organizing a conference of major Southwest schools interested in abiding by rules governing eligibility and sportsmanship. A&M officials gladly accepted an invitation to attend the organizational meetings at Dallas in May of 1914 and at Houston the following December.

When Southwest Conference football kicked off the

Above left, Bill Carlin (1909) helped A&M beat Texas twice in one season — the only time that has happened in school history.

Darrace Burns, above right, was a three-year standout from 1914-16.

The 1915 team, the first to compete in the Southwest Conference.

The first Bevo, shown branded with the final score of the 1915 Aggies victory.

new league in the fall of 1915, the Aggies were in and Uncle Charley Moran was out.

His spirit hovered over Kyle Field, however, as many of his old stars played that first SWC season under E.H. Harlan, a well-regarded coach from Pittsburgh. And Moran's influence on his "boys" peaked when Texas visited College Station for the first time to launch a home-and-home series that has endured since. Moran, from his home in Horse Cave, Ky., wrote every Aggie player, "If you still love me, beat those people

from Austin."

The inspired Aggies, led by Rip Collins' remarkable punting and tremendous defense that forced 12 Texas fumbles, blanked the Longhorns 13-0.

Before the schools played at Austin in 1916, some A&M students managed to brand that score on the side of Texas' new longhorn mascot. When UT students saw that, they added their own ingenious branding, redesigning the 13-0 to make the word Bevo. UT's mascot has been called Bevo ever since.

The students behind the prank.

A few days later, as Bevo grazed contentedly at Clark Field, Texas beat A&M, 21-7, and the Longhorns finished first in the seven-school SWC standings with a 5-1 record. The Aggies finished 2-1 in the SWC (tied for third place with 1915 champion Oklahoma) and 6-3 overall. That game at Austin ended Coach E.H. Harlan's stay at A&M, where he was 12-5 for two seasons. A&M officials decided to offer the head job to an impressive young man who had served as freshmen coach at Aggieland before taking over at LSU in mid-season and guiding the Tigers to a 3-0-2 finish.

That man was D.X. Bible, who would lead the Aggies through one of the greatest eras in their football history.

D.X. Bible
As Inspiring As His Name

Dana Bible

Dana Xenophon Bible's role in Southwest Conference football history is as unique as his name.

The only man to serve as head football coach at both Texas A&M and the University of Texas, his integrity, personality, knowledge and leadership left a tremendous imprint on each school. This short, bald man with a resounding bass voice always walked his talk.

"Mr. Bible did not have to demand respect," Joel Hunt, the Aggies' legendary halfback of 1925-27, once said. "You could not keep from respecting him. He was a man who stood above, and you had to look up to him. And you sought him. He was the type of man you could go to talk about either football or personal matters."

Bible was only 25 when he became A&M's head coach in 1917, after brief but successful stops at Mississippi College and LSU. But Bible promptly produced some marvelous numbers at A&M. That first team was unbeaten (8-0), unscored-on (270-0) and won

Lineman Cap Murrah (1918-21), left, earned All-SWC honors three straight seasons.

Rosey Higginbotham, right, a star for Dana Bible from 1917-20.

the first of the school's five SWC titles under Bible.

Inspirational and intelligent, the graduate of little Carson Newman College in Tennessee clearly did things in a big way.

After that first season in 1917, Bible left for World War I duty but returned to College Station in 1919 after his service as an Army Air Corps pursuit pilot. He coached the Aggies 10 more years with distinction and imagination.

Generations of Aggies have taken rare pride in the 11-year record of 72-19-9 Bible posted before moving to Nebraska in 1929, but they glow at the thought of Bible's greatest legacy: the 12th Man.

A&M's proudest tradition was born on a bright but chilling January day in 1921 at Dallas' Fair Park Stadium, when Bible's Aggies upset heavily favored Centre College 22-14 in the Dixie Classic, forerunner to the Cotton Bowl Classic. Several critical first half injuries left Bible with such thin reserves that he sent a manager into the stands to summon E. King Gill, a substitute end he had excused from football in December to join the basketball team.

Bible asked Gill to go under the stands and put on the uniform of an injured player, who in turn put on Gill's

Rosey Higginbotham carries the ball in the Aggies' final game of 1917, an undefeated season. A&M won the game, 10-0, against Rice.

1921   1921

TEXAS AGGIES

A. & M. 22 - CENTRE 14

SOUTHERN CHAMPIONS

NAPOLEON BELIEVED IN THE "BIBLE" SO DOES THE WORLD

The victory over Centre College on Jan. 2, 1922, in which the 12th Man tradition was born, stirred enthusiasm. This is a souvenir postcard created after the game.

The original 12th Man, King Gill.

A&M's original colors were red and white, but a sporting goods company erred in the late '20s and delivered maroon and white jerseys. A&M officials decided to keep the jerseys, figuring too many schools already wore red and white.

clothes. Once Gill was suited up and ready to play, Bible asked him to stand beside him throughout a pulsating second half in case he was needed.

It was an unforgettable stroke of Bible genius, a magnificent mixture of logic, drama and psychology. To this day, A&M students stand throughout all games, saluting the spirit and loyalty of King Gill, the original 12th Man whose statue stands outside Kyle Field.

A&M's inspired play in that Dixie Classic earned a rave review from Tiny Maxwell, who worked the game as an umpire and as a sports-writer for the Philadelphia Evening Public Ledger and for whom the Maxwell Trophy was named.

"The Aggies would have beaten any team in the country, barring none," Maxwell wrote. "I can not give too much praise to Coach Bible and members of the team. Football critics and fans over the nation can not help but recognize in them one of the greatest football teams ever assembled."

TOUGH ON TEXAS Bible's prestige and reputation also grew to heroic proportions during his later career at Texas (1937-46), but when he coached the Aggies he often was bad news for the Longhorns. Texas failed to score against A&M at Kyle Field until a tough 6-0 victory in 1923, and even then the Longhorns were driven to avenge the Aggies' 14-7 upset of a heavily-favored Texas team at Clark Field in Austin in 1922.

This was a rebuilding season for Bible and his Aggies had a modest 4-4 record as they hit the road for the Thanksgiving Day showdown with their arch rivals.

"To me, this game proved what a masterful strategist Coach Bible was," said A.B. "Bugs" Morris, then a senior who kicked two extra points in the surprising victory. "Prior to that game we worked out behind closed doors, and just before we left for Austin he told us the story of David and Goliath. I think Coach Bible felt the general public thought the odds against A&M were about the same as against David. I distinctly remember entering Clark Field through an opening in the wooden fence which was made possible by removing a couple of boards. I think the idea was not to be exposed to the fans prior to the game."

One of A&M's stars that day was King Gill, the 12th Man who stood in readiness at the Dixie Classic the previous January. This time Gill was a gamer, catching a 25-yard touchdown pass from T.L. Miller for the Aggies' first points and later grabbing a 25-yarder from Miller on the Texas 4-yard line to set up the winning touchdown.

BIBLE'S FIFTH TITLE The Aggies won the last of their five SWC titles under Bible in 1927. The legendary Joel Hunt climaxed his spectacular career by scoring two touchdowns in a 28-7 victory over Texas, giving him an SWC season record 128 points, a mark which stood for 62 years. The only frustration for Bible in that game was caused by fullback Harold Burgess slowing down in an open field and being tackled one yard short of the goal line, denying him a touchdown on a trick play Bible had designed: Hunt passing to J.V. Sikes, who flipped a perfectly-timed lateral to Burgess running at full speed.

Joel Hunt scored 19 touchdowns and came up with 128 points in his senior season, 1927.

When Burgess returned to the sideline, his coach asked why he slowed down. "I thought I was across the goal line," the fullback said.

In his booming voice, Bible replied, "Burgess, you do all right until you start thinking. Then you blow it completely."

At the end of the 1928 season, Bible received an attractive offer from Nebraska, inspired by a recommendation from Notre Dame legend Knute Rockne. "I consider Dana X. Bible the finest young coach in America," Rockne told Nebraska officials. "If you can get him, he is your man."

Cornhusker fans often toasted Rockne's words over the next eight seasons. Bible made Nebraska the power of the Midlands, winning the Big Six title six times while posting a 50-15-7 record. He was so impressive that Texas lured him back to the SWC with a whopping contract in 1937. This sent countless A&M loyalists into an emotional mixmaster for the next 10 seasons.

They still admired Bible tremendously, but they hated to see him on the opposite sideline during the biggest game of the year.

The Aggies' 1927 backfield is considered one of the best in school history. Shown here, left to right, P.C. Colgin, Joel Hunt, Al Simmons, Herschel Burgess and Jelly Woodman.

Brilliant Coaches,
Dark Endings

Matty Bell

Tommy Mills

AGGIE QUIZ

13. Name the quarterback and receiver who teamed for the longest pass play in A&M history, as well as the yardage, opponent and year.

Matty Bell and Homer Norton, like D.X. Bible before them, became Hall of Fame coaches. But unlike Bible, neither was a happy camper when he left Texas A&M.

Bell came to Aggieland in 1929, a handsome, personable and knowledgeable young coach whom Bible had recommended as his successor when he left for Nebraska. He resigned as head coach of a promising program at TCU to make his second of three stops in the Southwest Conference, eager to rebuild a depleted A&M team to the greatness the Aggies had achieved under Bible.

Even a positive, energetic coach like Bell had to be disillusioned by what he found at College Station.

While his old school, TCU, won the 1929 SWC title, Bell struggled through a 5-4 season. The Aggies, led by All-SWC quarterback Tommy Mills, won those five games by a total of 15 points with an undersized team that did not have a player weighing more than 180 pounds. Worse yet, the football operating budget was undersized, leaving Bell with a bleak recruiting outlook.

Rival schools had increased financial assistance to athletes by offering them campus jobs. A&M offered jobs to only a few, hiring them to work in the program and pillow concessions and in night mail collection. Little wonder the Aggies finished 2-7 in 1930, losing all five SWC games by a combined 62-7. The Aggies suffered five shutouts, including a 13-0 loss to Bible's Cornhuskers at Lincoln.

But Bell's coaching ability lifted the 1931 Aggies to a 7-3 record. Renowned for his defensive tactics, Bell masterminded five shutouts while the Aggies doubled their scoring from the previous season. A&M's three losses were close shutouts by outstanding teams — 7-0 at Rose Bowl-bound Tulane, 6-0 at TCU, and 8-0 against SWC champion SMU. Another highlight: A&M and Baylor resumed athletic relations after a five-year break. The breakoff followed a tragic fight at halftime of the Bears' 20-9 victory at Waco's Cotton Palace field in 1925, when senior cadet Charles M. Sessums of Dallas died of his injuries. With Baylor back on the schedule, the Aggies played a full SWC round-robin.

Were better days ahead for the Aggies? Nope.

In 1932 America was in the depths of the Great Depression and the Aggies were strapped even more. Bell managed a .500 season (4-4-2) with a weak team but A&M scored only 14 points while going 1-4-1 in SWC games. As '33 approached, the natives were restless, regardless of the problems that had confronted Bell since his arrival. They wanted the Aggies to win big.

A 4-0 start in non-conference play raised hopes, but TCU punctured them with its 10th straight victory over the Aggies — 13-7 at Fort Worth. A&M could win only two SWC games, one a 27-0 licking of Rice after rumors leaked out that Bell would be fired. The players, knowing Bell had given much more than he received at A&M, threatened a mutiny before the Rice game. But Bell quelled it, asking them to play hard the last two games.

The final game was against Texas at Kyle Field and the inspired Aggies were too tightly wound. Texas kicked a last-minute field goal for a 10-10 tie. This was no consolation for Longhorn Coach Clyde Littlefield, who also was dismissed as football coach. That left Littlefield with more time to concentrate on track and field, where he developed the Texas Relays into a national event and earned international fame as a U.S. Olympic coach.

James Aston

The change worked out even better for Bell. He moved to SMU as assistant to Ray Morrison in 1934 and was promoted to head coach a year later when Morrison left for Vanderbilt. Bell's 1935 Mustangs will be SWC legends forever, the first league school to win the national championship and the only one to have a 12-0 regular season.

Bell won two more SWC championships (1947-48) in the pulsating Doak Walker era and shared the 1940 title with A&M. Years later, after retiring with a career record of 155-86-17, he spoke warmly of his five years with the Aggies.

"I coached some great people at A&M and was associated with a lot of great folks," he said. "Those players down there have a great incentive. Gosh, they don't want to let down those students. That student body was the greatest asset we had at A&M. I don't guess there is one in the country that can compare with them for support."

NORTON'S TIME The hard times of the Depression did Matty Bell in at Aggieland, never allowing him to prove how good a coach he actually was. In contrast, Homer Norton reached the mountaintop, guiding the 1939 Aggies to the school's only national championship, then came crashing down after World War II, a victim of his good and faithful heart. Still, he left with the best record in A&M history: 82-53-9.

Willie Zapalac, a star halfback for Norton in 1940 and '41, missed four years for military service before playing his senior year in '46. He regrets that Norton didn't deal

Homer Norton

Halfback Dick Todd earned All-SWC honors in 1937 and '38.

sternly with his old players who returned to college football with a casual, sometimes sloppy attitude. But Norton, the son of a Methodist minister, lived and coached by the Golden Rule. Unfortunately, this was forgotten by A&M officials in the postwar uproar over a disappointing football team. Once one of his sport's most celebrated names, Norton was fired in 1947 after successive records of 4-6 and 3-5-1.

"Homer Norton was a fine coach, but his loyalty to his old players killed him," Zapalac said. "He gave all the war veterans scholarships when they returned to school, but our priorities had changed and we didn't put out for him like we did before the war. He should have told a lot of old guys to go on and played the kids."

In his prime, however, Norton contributed a tremendous chapter to A&M's football history. He pulled a busted program out of debt, recruited better than anyone dreamed possible and built a nationally-

Two-time All-American running back "Jarrin" John Kimbrough led the Aggies to the national title in 1939.

renowned team with creativity, drive and emotion.

"Coach Norton was great with one-liners: 'Showing up at the showdown is what counts,' " said Jimmie Parker, student manager for the 1939 national champions. "He could cry and tears would hang on his cheekbones."

In the best of times, no one dreamed that Norton's final tears at A&M would be shed after his own firing. But he still loved the school. "I will not even consider an offer from another school," he said. After a few years in the motel business in Galveston and Rosenberg, he came home to College Station and opened a popular restaurant. And he remained close to the sport, writing a football commentary column for the Houston Post.

A program from the Aggies' game against Manhattan College at New York's Polo Grounds.

His columns were insightful and colorful and Norton developed a large readership. A generation of football fans still appreciated his great years at A&M.

Norton already was a marquee name when he arrived at Aggieland in 1934. In 10 seasons at Centenary, his teams were 60-19-9 with three perfect seasons. And they barely missed a fourth in 1930 when they suffered a 7-6 loss to Bell's Aggies at Kyle Field. The 1932-33 Gents won 20 straight, so Norton was peaking at the Shreveport, La., school when Bell was in the pits at Aggieland.

Norton, blessed with a clever mind and easy-going style, earned respect and instilled discipline in his own way. Once he got his program rolling, he produced impressively with a gang of Depression-era players who realized they were lucky to be getting an education at A&M rather than in the School of Hard Knocks as laborers in the WPA. That was the Works Progress Administration, a key program in President Franklin Delano Roosevelt's New Deal that annually provided work for an average of 2 million Americans without jobs from 1935-41.

Meanwhile, Norton had his own new deal humming at College Station.

AGGIE QUIZ

14. Name the Aggie receiver who holds the single-season receiving record and his number of catches.

Guard Joe Routt became the Aggies' first All-American in 1936. He was named to the All-America team again in '37.

A program from the 1940 Sugar Bowl Classic, in which A&M beat Tulane, 14-13, for the school's only national championship.

He laid the foundation for a powerhouse with great recruiting. In 1937, A&M — already far behind in paying off the indebtedness on Kyle Field — received a $25,000 loan from a Dallas bank and used the money to improve the football scholarship program. Norton and his staff pursued a "Wanted Forty" list of top Texas high school players and landed 37.

Of those 37 players, 23 played on the 1939 national champions, a group that ultimately won 20 straight games before a 7-0 loss to Bible's improving young Texas team at Austin on Thanksgiving Day 1940 cost the Aggies a Rose Bowl bid. The Aggies then won another nine straight, leaving Norton 29-1 in a 30-game span from 1938-41.

Guard Marshall Robnett, named an All-American in 1940, paved the way for "Jarrin" John Kimbrough.

A&M football clearly was a hot ticket in Norton's best years, so hot the school paid off the debts on its stadium as well as that $25,000 loan for scholarships. The 1940 team, stunned by Texas, at first voted to reject an invitation to play Fordham in the Cotton Bowl but then decided to accept the trip to Dallas, where they won a dandy, 13-12. The Aggies trailed at halftime, 6-0, but stunned the Rams early in the third quarter when Norton used his pet "hideout pass."

Earl "Bama" Smith, who broke a scoreless tie on the same play against Texas in 1939 that triggered a 20-0 victory, trotted toward the east sideline while his teammates rushed to their huddle after the second half kickoff. The Rams never saw him. When the ball was snapped to Marion Pugh, Smith raced downfield and grabbed a 62-yard touchdown pass. Back in New York, a young high school coach and former Fordham lineman named Vince Lombardi, one of the Rams' famed Seven Blocks of Granite in the '30s, heard the play described on the radio and stomped the floor in disgust. In time,

AGGIE QUIZ

15. Name the Aggie receiver who holds the school career touchdown record and the number of touchdowns.

AGGIE QUIZ

16. Since the national champions of 1939, which A&M team achieved the highest national ranking?

Lombardi would call a few big plays himself during the Green Bay Packers' golden era in the '60s.

This Aggie team, more seasoned than the 1939 national champions, might have been the best in school history. There were stars throughout the lineup, led by two-time All-American fullback John Kimbrough and All-American guard Marshall Robnett, a wondrous athlete described by Jimmie Parker, later business manager for the Dallas Cowboys, as "the greatest football player I ever was around, including pro players."

Kimbrough, a thunderous 220-pounder, finished second to Michigan 's Tom Harmon in voting for the 1940 Heisman Trophy, but he was unimpressed by the news.

A DOG SHALL LEAD THEM

Reveille, Texas A&M's beloved mascot, came to Aggieland by accident.

In 1931, some cadets were headed back to campus from the A&M-Rice game at Houston in their Model T Ford when they accidentally ran over a black and white dog. It was late night so they carried the injured dog to their dormitory, planning to take it to the vet for treatment the next day.

When the bugler sounded reveille the next morning, the dog began barking. Thus A&M's mascot was christened.

Reveille quickly was adopted by the entire Corps, but there was a special bond with the band. She followed the band to all formations and led them when they marched. At the first football game she took the field with the band and officially became the Aggies' mascot.

Reveille died in 1944 and was buried at the north entrance to Kyle Field, later joined there by Reveille II, Reveille III and Reveille IV. A crowd of 35,000 attended funeral services for Reveille IV.

Reveille V was retired at ceremonies Nov. 13, 1993, at Kyle Field before the A&M-Louisville game. Reveille VI, a full-bred American Collie like the four previous mascots, has thrived after starting her career on a scary note.

A few days before the Aggies played Notre Dame in the Mobil Cotton Bowl Classic on Jan. 1, 1994, the 4-month-old puppy disappeared from the backyard of her handler's North Dallas home. Later, an anonymous caller claiming to be a University of Texas student told *The Dallas Morning News* and the *Austin American* that he was spokesman for a group of some 30 UT students that plotted the dognapping after reading Reveille's handler boast that the A&M mascot never had been stolen. Bevo, UT's Longhorn mascot, has been stolen three times by the Aggies through the years.

The dognappers insisted that Reveille VI would not be returned until Texas A&M officials declared UT superior and the Aggies quarterback flashed the UT "Hook 'Em Horns" sign on national TV during the Notre Dame game. UT president Robert Berdahl denounced the incident as "a

"Hell, I didn't even know what the Heisman Trophy was," said Kimbrough, who grew up on a ranch at Haskell in West Texas. "We had tremendous loyalty and friendship on those teams. We played for A&M and each other, not for individual honors. For many years after we finished school, the guys from that '39 team got together twice a year — once for deer hunting in the Big Bend and once for dove hunting at my place. We always were loyal to A&M. In the '50s, I wore out two cars in four years helping Bear Bryant get boys to play there."

The 1941 Aggies won the SWC title after Bible's own Rose Bowl hopes for his best Texas team were ruined by a 7-7 tie with Baylor and 14-7 loss to TCU. Texas rallied to beat A&M, 23-0, but the Aggies won the league

AGGIE QUIZ

17. Name the opponent, score and year of the Aggies' most lopsided victory.

---

stupid, puerile act. If it was perpetrated by UT students, as allgeged, it has achieved nothing except to embarrass UT."

Neither ransom demand was met and Reveille VI was found unharmed near Lake Travis outside of Austin before the game.

While the young mascot was missing, 9-year-old Haley Duggan of Sugar Land composed a handwritten plea for the dog's release.

"Please take good care of Reveille. We love her very much," Haley wrote. She described herself as a collie owner and member of the "future Aggie class of 2008.

Reveille I (1931-44)

The official program from A&M's 1941 game at New York University.

The 1941 Aggies, SWC champions.

championship by a half game with a 5-1 record and accepted a return bid to the Cotton Bowl on New Year's Day. They finished the regular season with a 7-0 win over Washington State at Tacoma on Dec. 6.

"The next day our train stopped at Sun Valley, Idaho, when we heard the news that the Japanese had bombed Pearl Harbor," Parker said. "We knew we were in another world war."

The Aggies, ranked No. 9 nationally, lost the Cotton Bowl to No. 20 Alabama, 29-21, in one of the strangest games ever. The Crimson Tide made only one first down to A&M's 13 and was outgained in total offense, 309-75. But the Aggies suffered 12 turnovers on seven pass interceptions and five lost fumbles. Norton knew his players' hearts and minds were elsewhere.

AGGIES GO TO WAR A&M, an outstanding military school, would send more commissioned officers into World War II than the U.S. Military Academy at West Point. A lot of them had played football for Norton and they served their country as they had A&M — with pride, courage and honor. Some of them, like Joe Routt,

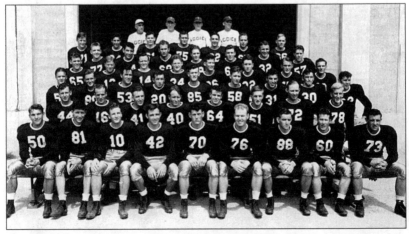

*Joe Routt (1935-37)
died in World War II.*

died the same way.

Routt was a tough, quick and keenly competitive guard who became the Aggies' first All-American in 1936 and '37 as he cleared the way for remarkable running back Dick Todd. As an infantry captain in 1944, Routt and his troops advanced on German tanks in the Battle of the Bulge when he was killed in a flurry of gunfire. He was posthumously awarded the Bronze Star for his bravery.

King Gill, the original 12th Man at A&M, said that Routt's commanding officer called him "the most courageous man I have known." When Routt was elected to the National Football Foundation Hall of Fame in 1962, Norton said, "Joe Routt had the biggest heart and was one of the best fighters I ever saw."

It figured. Routt learned from one of the best.

*18. Name the
opponent, score and
year of the Aggies'
most lopsided loss.*

1948-53
Searching for A Winner

Harry Stiteler

Bob Goode

Aggie football was a roller-coaster ride for the six years between Homer Norton's sad exit and Bear Bryant's wildly celebrated arrival. There were a few thrilling highs but a lot more depressing lows.

Harry Stiteler, a Norton assistant in 1947, had a lot going for him when he was promoted to head coach the next season. Sure, he was following a legend but this trim, silver-haired man brought his own special qualities to the job.

He truly loved the school. Stiteler was an Aggie, a track star who also lettered as a quarterback on Matty Bell's 1930 team, and he was one of the most successful Texas high school coaches of his era. Stiteler won state championships at Corpus Christi and Waco and, adding his earlier stops at Bellville and Smithville, his 14-year head coaching record was 138-29-4. Blessed with a keen football mind, Stiteler appeared capable of returning A&M to national prominence once he had time to rebuild. As a past president of the Texas High School Coaches Association, he had the contacts and the savvy to recruit successfully.

Few were surprised that Stiteler's first Aggie team finished 0-9-1, the worst record in A&M history. Those Aggies, prolific on offense but porous on defense, still achieved one great distinction. They finished that terrible season on Thanksgiving Day with halfback Bob Goode leading a startling 14-14 tie against a good Texas team at Austin, the first time A&M did not lose this classic grudge game in Memorial Stadium. Considering the high quality of Stiteler's first recruiting class, old Aggies figured their football team would win big again once these youngsters matured.

Wartime eligibility rules had been rescinded, so blue-chip running backs Bob Smith, Glenn Lippman, Billy Tidwell and Yale Lary were limited to playing a 5-game freshman schedule in 1948. The young Aggies struggled through a 1-8-1 season in 1949 but there was another impressive recruiting class, led by fast, rangy tackle Jack Little. As the Aggies and college football passed the halfway point of the game's first full century, A&M fans hoped the school's return to glory was near.

The 1950 Aggies held great promise but they also had problems. Stiteler's talented young recruits formed the nucleus of the team but a remaining handful of war veterans, led by rugged, free-spirited end Andy

Harry Stiteler, center, replaced Homer Norton after the 1947 season. Here Stiteler is shown with assistants Bill DuBose, left, and Charles DeWare.

Hillhouse, shrugged off the coach's attempts to instill discipline and camaraderie.

"Stiteler recruited all the top players we had — enough for two or three good teams in the years ahead," said Darrow Hooper, a sophomore that season who ranks among the most versatile athletes in A&M history. "He was the reason I played football at A&M. He had a brilliant offensive mind and he utilized his talent, but we were not a team that year.

"The veterans were so old they seemed like our daddies or uncles. We didn't have any senior leaders, and we had rotating quarterbacks."

The 1950 Aggies had so many talented runners like Smith, Lippman, Tidwell and Lary (later an all-pro defensive back and punter for the Detroit Lions) that a gifted athlete like Hooper was strictly a supporting player. They scored 162 points in their four opening non-conference games and only a last-minute 34-28 loss to powerful Oklahoma at Norman marred their record. And the Aggies played so brilliantly against the Sooners that their fans considered it a moral victory.

That gave them confidence but not consistency.

"As the season wore on, Harry's high school mentality exposed his short-comings," Hooper said. "We had awesome offensive statistics (scoring 55 touch-downs while averaging 30.4 points and 336.7 yards per game) but he didn't develop the game plan like more experienced coaches did."

The flaws became obvious against tough, experienced teams like

All-American Bob Smith was a terrific broken field runner. He still holds the A&M record for most rushing yards in a single game, with 297 yards against SMU in 1950.

Yale Lary

The 1950 backfield shown left to right: right halfback Billy Tidwell, quarterback Dick Gardemal, fullback Bob Smith and left halfback Glenn Lippman.

Baylor, which won a bruising 27-20 battle at Waco that left Smith with a broken nose. But Smith, a junior fullback blessed with power and speed, roared into Dallas the next Saturday for a showdown with No. 7 SMU. Players did not have face bars on their helmets then, so Smith wore a black leather-and-steel mask for protection.

When it was over, the Mustangs were asking, "Who was that masked man?" Smith exploded for 297 yards on 29 carries and the Aggies won a whizbang, 25-20 contest that left a sellout Cotton Bowl crowd of 75,504 limp and hoarse. Smith still holds the A&M single-game rushing record, no Aggie having come within 20 yards of it since.

Stiteler's team slipped badly in its final two SWC games, however, suffering a 21-13 loss to a so-so Rice team at Kyle Field and a 17-0 shutout by No. 3 Texas at Austin. Far worse, Stiteler was plagued by personal problems then and there were serious doubts that he would return for the 1951 season. The Aggies still closed the year on a high note, however, with a spectacular 40-20 win over Georgia in the Presidential Cup at College Park, Md. Their 7-4 record was the best by an A&M team since 1944 and their 344 points the most since Uncle Charley Moran's 1912 Aggies scored 366 in an 8-1 season.

For awhile it appeared Stiteler might weather his personal storm, but he was forced to resign in the spring. Suddenly all of those Aggie stars who had grown and matured under Stiteler had a new head coach named Ray George.

CURIOUS GEORGE Ray George, a highly-regarded line coach at Southern Cal and once an All-Pacific Coast Conference tackle for the Trojans, had joined Stiteler's staff just a few weeks before. He was named head coach after A&M Athletic Director Barlow "Bones" Irvin, once an outstanding high school coach at San Antonio Jefferson, turned down the job.

Ray George

"If Stiteler had been there in 1951 we would have been dynamite," Hooper said. "Ray George wasn't a head coach and we didn't have a quarterback. We had no passing threat and as the season wore on we found ourselves trying to run against 9-man defensive lines."

Hooper shared the job with Dick Gardemal and Ray Graves and the Aggies, after rousing early victories over UCLA (21-14) and Oklahoma (14-7) stumbled through the season until Texas came to Kyle Field on Thanksgiving Day needing to win to earn an Orange Bowl bid. Smith was knocked out of the game with a broken jaw on the opening kickoff, and the Aggies responded to the loss by outplaying the Longhorns in a free-wheeling, free-swinging 22-21 upset.

Lippman became a raging runner at fullback when Smith was sidelined and raced for 174 yards. "That was the best game of my career," he said years later. Lary and Hooper, the old North Side teammates, also proved game-breakers in a 15-point third quarter. Lary sped 68 yards for a touchdown, Hooper kicked a 31-yard field goal and both were involved in a weird play that wound

Coach Ray George shows players Bob Smith, Yale Lary, Glenn Lippman and Jack Little how to protect the ball. George took over in 1951.

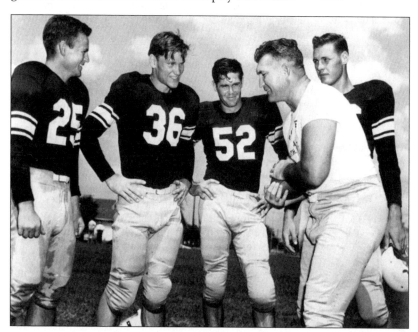

VERSATILE AGGIES

Any discusssion of versatile athletes at Texas A&M must include Darrow Hooper with Bill "Jitterbug" Henderson and Randy Matson.

In football, Hooper was good at everything he tried. He played quarterback and end and also was the regular kicker. In track and field, he was a superstar weight man.

At Fort Worth North Side, Hooper had excelled in football and basketball as well as track and field, where he set a national high school records in the shot put and discus throw. As a college shot putter, he was one of the best in the world, dominating the Southwest Conference and winning an Olympic silver medal at the 1952 Helsinki Games, where U.S. teammate Parry O'Brien edged him for the gold medal by five-eighths of an inch.

Henderson and Matson, in their own ways, were just as gifted.

Henderson earned a total of 11 letters in five sports at A&M — three each in football, basketball and track, one each in baseball and swimming. He once caught eight straight passes in a 25-0 win over Rice in 1940.

Matson was a world record shot putter and Olympic gold medalist at the 1968 Mexico City Games who also starred in basketball at A&M. He also boasted so much potential as a fullback and tight end based on his Pampa High School career that he was drafted by the NFL Atlanta

Bill "Jitterbug" Henderson was one of A&M's most versatile athletes. He picked up the nickname after winning a dance contest.

up as a 37-yard touchdown pass.

"I lined up at left halfback and swung out as sort of a safety valve receiver for Gardemal, who threw downfield for Darrow," Lary said. "The throw was high and both Darrow and a Texas defensive back went up for the ball. I was trailing the play and they deflected the ball into my hands. I ran into the end zone untouched."

Lary ended his Aggie football career a happy man. "I had a big hand in our beating Texas for the first time in 13 games, and I was voted MVP for the season," he said. He later played 11 seasons with the Detroit Lions and helped them win three NFL championships. Lary was an all-pro defensive back and still holds the club record punting averages for career (44.29 yards) and season (48.9).

Although he figured in scoring some vital points, Hooper always has been proudest of his play at tight end that day, repeatedly throwing big blocks on the Texas middle linebacker to spring runners like Lippman and Lary into the secondary.

AGGIE QUIZ

19. What is R.C. Slocum's full name?

Falcons. He never played pro football, but competed several years on the Professional Track and Field Tour. He later returned to his alma mater to become executive director of the Association of Former Students.

Darrow Hooper in 1996.

That victory allowed George to finish his first year as head coach with a 5-3-2 record, but the Aggies won only seven more games the next two years. The A&M brass realized their attempt to throw an unknown assistant into the top job had failed. This time they were determined to hire the biggest name available.

Paul W. Bryant
Roar of The Bear

Bear Bryant

Texas A&M records a 13-2 win over SMU in 1955.

Paul "Bear" Bryant was so determined to escape Kentucky and the shadow of basketball coaching legend Adolph Rupp that he accepted the Texas A&M job sight unseen in February of 1954. That proved a blessing for the Aggies.

Bryant, frustrated by his football program's second-class status at Kentucky despite his eight-year record of 60-23-5, also arrived at A&M in the dark of night. A second blessing.

The campus was a stark, remote outpost on the Brazos bottoms then, all male, all military, no girls, no fun. But Bryant didn't realize that until the next morning. Fortunately for the Aggies, the Bear's first impression of Aggieland was emotional, not visual.

Thousands of cadets roared at Easterwood Field when he stepped off that little two-engine airliner. Tall, rangy and handsome, Bryant exuded leadership, authority and determination. The Aggies had waited years for someone like Bryant. Now he was Texas A&M's new head coach and athletic director, the man who was going to straighten out this mess of a football program.

Years later in *Bear*, the autobiography he authored

with John Underwood, Bryant described the electricity of that evening. Hundreds of cadets escorted him to the Memorial Student Center, where he was to check into the hotel before heading to his first yell practice at The Grove outdoor theater.

"They were crowding around and I made several false starts with the pen. The 'address' part threw me," Bryant said. "Finally, I put down, 'Paul W. Bryant, Texas A&M, College Station, Texas.' The Aggies loved it."

It got better. As he waited to be introduced to 5,000 Aggies at The Grove, Bryant received some marvelous advice from A&M sports publicity director Jones Ramsey.

"Coach, when you walk out on that stage, pull off your coat and stomp on it," Ramsey said. "Then yank off your tie and stomp on it. Then roll up your sleeves. They'll eat it up."

Willie Zapalac, the only member of Ray George's staff Bryant would retain, smiled at the memory of that moment. "Coach Bryant grabbed the microphone and in that deep, rumbling voice of his, said, 'I'm ready to go to work!' He knew how to talk to those Aggies."

"It was like voodoo," Bryant said. "Those Aggies went crazy. I was awed, I tell you. Ten Aggies can yell louder than a hundred of anybody else."

Zapalac knew the new coach was inheriting a program at rock bottom, but he quickly learned what Bryant's goal was when he interviewed for a staff position. "I said, 'Coach, I think we can get it done here.' And he snapped back, 'Think, hell! We *will* get it done!'

"He was a great organizer, a great motivator, a great football coach. I thought I knew football until he came around. Shoot, I didn't know anything."

Bum Phillips, who coached for Bryant at Aggieland and became quite a legend himself, described the Bear's rare talents another way. "Others might know more about football, but I think, *I know*, I've never been around anyone who knew more about people. Like Jake Gaither used to say, Bryant could take his'n and beat your'n, and take your'n and beat his'n."

Jack Pardee, a sophomore fullback in 1954, grew from a 6-man football star in the West Texas hamlet of Cristoval to an All-American in 1956 and went on to play and coach in the NFL, where he won Coach of the Year honors, as well as in the WFL and USFL. Playing for Bryant inspired him to make coaching his profession.

"He had a great knack for instilling the work ethic and team spirit," Pardee said. "Today there is so much 'me' in the game. When you played for Bear Bryant, it was a 'we' game."

AGGIE QUIZ

20. Who was the Aggies' first All-American player?

GETTING DOWN TO WORK Bryant was determined that he, his coaches and players would work harder, play harder and believe in each other, and this rare bond ultimately would pay off. That made a tremendous difference in 1954, when he laid the foundation for a championship program with a handful of hitters who survived the notorious Junction fall training camp. The result wasn't immediately obvious, of course. Those Aggies struggled through a 1-9 season.

"Those ten days at Junction seemed like three months," Pardee said. "Players quit in hordes. My favorite pastime at night was lying on my bed in my tent and watching screen doors open as guys slipped out to the highway to hitch a ride home. In 10 days I played eight different positions.

"A tackle would quit and he'd move me there for practice. One day I was playing tight end and Bill Schroeder, the tackle, rolled over on me. He'd had a heat stroke. We moved him over on the edge of the field and the trainer worked on him while we went on scrimmaging. I thought he was the luckiest guy in the world, getting ice and water. We never got water on the practice field in those days. One day I lost 20 pounds. We're lucky we didn't have some guys die out there."

All-American guard Dennis Goehring helped A&M to its first SWC title since 1941.

The type of program Bryant would establish emerged from the misery of Junction and that 1-9 season.

The 1955 Aggies, blessed with brilliant young talent like running back John David Crow and tackle Charlie Krueger, played with lots of energy and pizzazz but still were too raw to win it all. They opened with a 21-0 loss at powerful UCLA and closed with a 21-6 upset by Texas at Kyle Field which enabled a mediocre Longhorn team to finish 5-5. Texas played inspired football that day, seemingly far more aware of the history and tradition of this rivalry than the young Aggies. "They handled us like children," said Bryant, never one for sugar-coating.

Bryant's third Aggie team was his best, the 1956 bunch captained by Pardee, Gene Stallings and Lloyd Hale. A 14-14 tie at Houston was the only blemish on a 9-0-1 record, climaxed by a 34-21 win over a 1-9 Texas team that broke the Memorial Stadium jinx.

On the field, these Aggies could cope with almost anything, including a 7-6 victory over powerful TCU at Kyle Field. That was the historic Hurricane Game, where a furious strorm swept inland from the Gulf of Mexico with blinding rain and wicked winds that left the light standards at Kyle Field swaying like stalks of bamboo.

Off the field, however, the Aggies were stung by a two-year probation dealt them by Southwest Conference faculty representatives, who in the spring of 1955 ruled A&M and some influential supporters guilty of illegal recruiting. This meant the splendid 1956 SWC championship team was ineligible to represent the league as host in the Cotton Bowl Classic on New Year's Day. Instead, the honor went to runner-up TCU, which edged Syracuse and future Hall of Fame fullback Jim Brown, 28-27.

Bryant still wanted to reward his team, which included eight seniors who stuck with him from the Junction training camp, with a nice trip so he scheduled an early December game with the University of Hawaii. Other schools had done this without its counting against the 10-game regular-season limit of that era. He told his players before the Texas game, "If they don't want us to go to a bowl, we'll have our own bowl."

But once SWC officials learned of his plan, they shot it down. The Aggies' best season since the 1939 national championship ended on Thanksgiving Day in Austin.

During his A&M years, Bryant always insisted that his program was victimized by over-zealous supporters. Years later, well into his legendary career as a national championship coach at Alabama, he said he knew what was happening in the recruiting of some players at A&M and endorsed it.

"I know now that we should have been put on probation," he said in the book, *Bear.* "I know, too, I was not just trying to justify it in my mind when I said that if we were paying players, then other schools were doing it twice as bad, which some were. I'm not going soft on that point.

"I'm not sure how many of our boys got something; I guess about four or five did. I didn't know what they got, and I didn't want to know, but they got something because they had other offers and I told my alumni to meet the competition. It was my program and I'm

21. Name the NCAA bowl record set by Mike Mosley, with the year and the opponent.

Young talent like tackle Charlie Krueger made an immediate impact in 1955.

responsible."

Eight games into his final season at A&M, Bryant's 1957 team seemed destined to join the 1939 national championship Aggies at the peak of college football. They were unbeaten, untied, ranked No. 1 nationally and solid favorites to beat Rice and Texas to wrap up a 10-0 regular-season record and repeat as SWC champions. This time, however, the Aggies were eligible to play in the Cotton Bowl Classic.

The dream season fell apart in Houston on Nov. 16.

That morning, *Houston Post* writer Jack Gallagher reported that Bryant would leave A&M at season's end to become head coach at his alma mater, Alabama. That afternoon, the distracted Aggies lost to No. 20 Rice, 7-6, before a sellout crowd of 72,000. A&M fell from No. 1 the next week, and no Aggie team would be ranked that high again during the school's remaining 38 years in the SWC.

Twelve days later, on Thanksgiving, Bryant coached his last game at Kyle Field. In a dismal finale to an historic career at Aggieland, his still-dazed team was upset again. This time it was more bitter — a 9-7 loss to Texas in the debut season under Darrell Royal, another coach destined to become a legend. It was the

John David Crow (44), Ken Hall (30) and Dennis Goehring (62) are carried off the field by Aggies Cadets following the one-point win over TCU in 1956.

The undefeated 1956 Aggies, Southwest Conference champions.

first of Royal's 17 wins over A&M in his 20 years as Longhorn coach.

Bryant and his Aggies finished their slide with a 3-0 loss to Tennessee in the Gator Bowl, then he was off to Alabama and A&M was in the market for a new coach. His four-year record of 25-14-2 wasn't too impressive, but his imprint on A&M and the SWC was. Bear Bryant won a place in every Aggie's heart, but the spirit of Aggieland captured his heart, too.

"Leaving A&M was the most difficult thing I ever had to do," he said. "But Mama called me home."

Battered, But Unbowed
Bryant's Junction Gang

On a lovely May evening in 1979, a crowd of proud Aggies celebrated a reunion with their old coach at the Junction training camp site where all of them made history in 1954. They won only one game that fall under Bear Bryant, but they forever will be Aggie legends because they survived what has been called college football's version of the Bataan Death March.

The last time most of them had seen this place was a scorching September day in 1954. They were scratched, bruised and limping from endless scrimmaging amid cactus and cockleburs, but they were still there to make the 150-mile trip back to College Station.

That scraggly bunch of Texas A&M football players didn't know what was ahead that season, but they knew it couldn't be as bad as what they were leaving behind in the dust of that solitary bus.

"When we left here, we were confident," Dennis Goehring said. "We knew we could survive in any endeavor."

It wasn't immediately apparent what the training camp meant to the players. That thin team of Bryant's first autumn at A&M managed only a 6-0 victory over Georgia, but the bad times of Junction toughened and tempered them and became the bedrock on which they would build their lives and careers.

They returned happily for their reunion, eager to reminisce and relive a lot of experiences that were a lot more fun to talk about a quarter-century later.

There at the '79 reunion to greet the players was Bryant, a coaching legend who gladly made a sentimental journey back to this little town in the Hill Country of Southwest Texas to visit with the players who presented him with the only losing season of his illustrious career.

He was 42 when they last met there, a tall, rangy man with an easy manner of speech but a hard edge to his football. Now he was 67, a trifle gray and paunchy. He was one of the game's marquee names, mellowed by the years and six national championships at Alabama. Compared to those mountaintop experiences, these '54 Aggies were the pits. But on this balmy evening, as a breeze rustled the trees, there clearly was no place else Paul William Bryant would rather be.

"I've never had a team I respected more," he

Aggies Off For Camp

COLLEGE STATION, Texas (*Æ*).—Forty Texas A&M football candidates left at noon Monday for the preschool practice training camp at Junction.

Coach Paul Bryant said three junior college transfers were on the trip. They are Joe Rowell, guard from Citronelli, Ala.; George Johnson, tackle from Ellisville, Miss., and Back Gene Henderson of San Angelo.

Varsity candidates making the trip were Joe Boring, Ray Barrett, Fred Broussard, Henry Clark, Darrell Brown, James Burkhart, Bob Thley, Dennis Goehring, Billy Granberry, Ivan Greenhaw, Walker Griffin, Lloyd Hale, Charles Hall, Billy Huddleston, Don Kachtik, Bobby Drake Keith, Paul Kennon, Elwood Kettler, Bobby Lockett, Billy McGowan, Russell Moake, Charles Moore, Norbert Ohlendorf, Jack Pardee, W. D. Powell, Donald Robbins, Joe Schero, Charles Scott, Bill Schroeder, Bennie Sinclair, Eugene Stallings, Tommy Strait, Marvin Tate, Foster Teague, Sid Theriot, Richard Vick, Don Watson, Lawrence Winkler, Herb Wolf.

said, echoing the tribute he had paid his "Junction Boys" repeatedly through the years. "I think I learned something about winning here and about people. It's important what people think about you and how much you care."

The Aggies of '54 cared enough to stick it out, taking all the torture that Bryant and his coaching staff dealt them with practices that began and ended each day in darkness.

Of course, a lot of others didn't. When the team opened the season with Texas Tech, there were only 29 players left. And injuries cut into those scrawny ranks as the year wore on. For some games, as few as 23 players suited up.

Bear Bryant at the Junction Reunion in May of 1979.

"I was the only publicity man in the country," recalled Jones Ramsey, the Aggie sports information director then, "who could type his football roster on a piece of 8 1/2-by-11 paper sideways."

The Junction experience earned a permanent place in the history of Texas A&M and Southwest Conference football because it established the hard-nosed style that Bryant felt was imperative to a winning program when he left Kentucky and took charge of the Aggies. The ability to survive paid off on the field for the younger players when they compiled a 7-2-1 record in '55 and went 9-0-1 in '56 to win the SWC championship. It also left lasting memories of the awesome attrition of that first fall training camp under the Bear.

"We went to Junction in two buses," said Gene Stallings, a sophomore end in '54, "and came back in one."

Gene Stallings always has been glad he stuck around for the ride back to College Station. When Bryant returned to coach at his alma mater — the University of Alabama — in '58, he took Stallings with him as an assistant. Then Stallings returned to his alma mater as the Aggies' head coach from 1965-71. Since then Stallings served as assistant coach for the Dallas Cowboys, head coach of the Cardinals in St. Louis and Phoenix, and then became head coach at Alabama, winning the National Championship in 1992.

AGGIE QUIZ

22. Name the two team-defense NCAA bowl records the Aggies set against Alabama in the 1942 Cotton Bowl.

The impresssion Bryant made upon him in his youth never left Stallings. The Bear had a similar impact on other young Aggies like Jack Pardee, a sophomore fullback in 1954 who grew into an All-American in '56 and later became head coach of the NFL's Washington Redskins and Houston Oilers and the SWC's University of Houston.

THE GANG'S ALL HERE The Junction reunion at the old campsite, hosted by the Kimble County Chamber of Commerce, was an evening of barbecue, band music and backslapping. A total of 22 players made it back. So did

Bear Bryant accepts the Field Scovell Award from former player and coaching assistant Gene Stallings in 1982.

Bryant, Pat James, Troy Summerlin and Billy Pickard. James was an assistant coach then, Summerlin the student manager who put on a uniform and snapped the ball for punts when bodies began to get thin, and Pickard, the student trainer who vowed that someday he would become the Aggies' head trainer, which he did.

Jack Pardee, a sophomore fullback in '54 who survived Junction and a 1-9 record that season to become an All-American as senior in '56.

In his own way, each man at the reunion had special memories of that training camp but they were unanimous on one point: The training site was far more attractive than it was 25 years earlier.

In 1954 the training site was known as Texas A&M Adjunct, a place normally used for field trips by students and professors, but Bryant selected it sight-unseen because of its remoteness.

It consisted of a few tents and a dining hall, which wasn't air-conditioned. Then, as now, there was a swimming pool and a nice grove of pecan trees behind the camp, but the players saw little of them. There was no football field, so the players used their helmets to beat down cactus and cockleburs and scratch out an open place where they scrimmaged during those burning hot drought days.

Twenty-five years later, the training site was the Texas Tech Center, having changed ownership in 1971. There were lots of attractive, modern dorms and meeting buildings. The tents now had permanent roofs and looked rather comfortable in this setting. And there was plenty of lush grass and trees.

A gentle breeze swept the camp and Bear and his old boys gathered there again. In one of the fields where they once blocked, tackled, bled and cussed, a group of female and male students happily played softball.

"This place," said Marvin Tate, who had become athletic director at A&M, "looks like what Coach Bryant described to us before he brought us here in '54."

Norbert Ohlendorf, a co-captain, recalled: "He told us we were going to a resort with lots of fishing."

Bennie Sinclair, the other co-captain, stood there silently with his old coach for a minute, soaking it in. "This looks like a fun place," he said. "It sure has changed."

Bryant also could joke about Junction now.

"Whoever I talked to at A&M before we came here exaggerated the beauty of the place," he said. "When we drove in that front gate I wanted to puke. The facilities were bad, all right, but we had to get to work. One thing we did have was delicious food. But we were usually too tired to eat it."

Bryant looked at his old players. All of them were established in their chosen fields. Bankers, engineers, architects, coaches, educators, salesmen, farmers, ranchers, builders, fast-food wheeler-dealers. But they listened as intently as when his word was law 25 years ago.

"Those who left, I don't blame 'em at all," he said. "Those who stayed, I appreciate 'em because I didn't have any place to go.

"I'll never know if what I did here was right or not but I'd do it again because I'm still surviving."

Elwood Kettler, the quarterback, has always idolized Bryant. He later coached under him at Alabama and after several other stops as a college assistant he settled in as head coach and athletic director at Texas City High School. But he didn't agree with everything that happened at Junction in '54.

"One thing I've never done is get a team up before dawn to work out," he said. "We would slip on those old pads still filled with sweat from the night before and go out on that field and we couldn't see."

"Yeah, the first morning they got us up at 4 and told us to hurry up," said Darnell Brown, a sophomore guard on that team. "We got out there in the dark and there was Coach Bryant standing there, staring at the sky. He was waiting for the sun to come up."

Kettler noted, "What made it so tough was that we had a practice schedule set up for a hundred players and pretty soon there were just 30 of us. You never got a breather while someone else took a turn. You went at it all the time."

"I was the taxi driver," said Summerlin, the manager who became a center. "When somebody was leaving I got the car keys from Coach Bryant and drove 'em in to town. Finally there wasn't anyone left to take. I think the assistant coaches wanted to leave but Coach Bryant

AGGIE QUIZ

23. *What was the final score of A&M's 1942 Cotton Bowl game against Bama?*

Years later, Bear Bryant said, "I'll never know if what I did here was right or not but I'd do it again because I'm still surviving."

The 1954 staff: (from left) Top row: Babe Parilli, Phil Cutchins, Elmer Smith, Willie Zapalac, Jim Owens. Bottom row: Tom Tipps, Jerry Clairborne, Bear Bryant, and Pat James.

locked 'em in at night."

Pat James, who left coaching to open a restaurant in Birmingham, grinned.

"I'm delighted to be here, but I was wondering if anyone would speak to me," he said. He shot a glance at Bryant and deadpanned: "It was such an intelligent approach to coaching."

SOME QUIT, SOME COULDN'T The most famous player who quit the team was All-SWC center Fred Broussard, who stalked off the field in disgust during one of the early practices. Broussard, a senior, asked Bryant a few hours later if he could rejoin the team but Bryant refused. He felt he would be bending the rules and discipline he demanded of everyone else if he allowed Broussard back. Even in the agony they were experiencing at the moment, the players were impressed.

Broussard's loss caused sophomore Lloyd Hale to move from guard to center. He was shaky on those snaps to the punter for awhile but he eventually made All-SWC.

Broussard's exit attracted a lot of attention, but many other players simply vanished in the night. "I remember one guy I was bunking with swearing he wouldn't quit," Brown said. "He was saying that when I fell asleep. When I got up the next morning he was gone."

Kettler recalled, "There were eight of us in my tent and the first day we started playing Hearts. By the third day there was no more game. I was the only one in the tent."

Don Watson was a sophomore halfback who later coached at A&M with Stallings. He made it clear he wanted to quit but just couldn't because he was a small-

AGGIE QUIZ

24. How many turnovers did the Aggies commit in the 1942 Cotton Bowl game against Bama?

town boy.

"If I had been from Houston or Dallas or San Antonio I could have quit and gone home and nobody would have noticed me," he said. "If you go back to Franklin, Texas, and stand on the corner, everyone knows you. I couldn't quit!"

But all the memories and what had happened since made those 10 terrible days an invaluable experience.

"This," said Tate, "was the beginning of something truly great for everyone here."

"I don't think I'll ever sit down again and weep about what happened," Bryant said. "All of you have done so well I'm not going to change anything I'm doing."

All the old players shared an affection for A&M that was touching to see and hear. Many of them mentioned they now had children enrolled there, and it seemed more of them were girls than boys. That also spoke strongly of the change at A&M since '54, when it was an all-male military school with very few diversions. But 10 days in Junction made them appreciate it more.

"When we got on the bus to leave," Brown recalled, "I guarantee you College Station really seemed uptown."

The hard work didn't immediately pay off. But after a dismal 1954 season, the '55 team (whose senior captains are shown here with Bryant) went 7-2-1, the school's best since 1943.

John David Crow
One of A Kind

At 6-foot-2, 218 pounds, halfback John David Crow was blessed with game-breaking speed.

The 1957 Aggies featuring John David Crow, second from the right on the back row.

Like Bear Bryant, his legendary coach, John David Crow was a backwoods boy who made it really big in college football.

So big that he won the Heisman Trophy for his superlative senior season at Texas A&M in 1957. This is an award that will be toasted forever at Aggieland, a school steeped in tradition and spirit. It also had a special place in Bryant's heart until his death in January of 1983.

Surprisingly, John David was Bryant's only Heisman Trophy winner in his historic 37-year head coaching career at Maryland, Kentucky, Texas A&M and Alabama, his alma mater and a place where he produced six national championship teams in 25 seasons. And Crow also remains the Aggies' only Heisman winner, surpassing John Kimbrough's second-place finish to Tom Harmon of Michigan in the 1940 voting.

Like Bryant, Crow as a college player was a big, rugged athlete who thrived on competition. Unlike Bryant, who was "the other end" opposite legendary pass receiver Don Hutson on Alabama's 1935 Rose Bowl championship team, the 6-foot-2, 218-pound A&M halfback was blessed with game-breaking speed. But both were drawling, personable men proud of the work ethic they learned early in life growing up in small rural communities.

Bryant hailed from Moro Bottom, Ark.; Crow came to A&M from Springhill, La., which he said was so far back in the woods "that they have to pipe in sunshine."

THE RECRUITMENT Elmer Smith knew the way to Springhill, La., and the A&M assistant coach spent three months in a little motel there in the spring of 1954 on orders from Bryant, who made signing Crow the No. 1 priority in his first recruiting year at A&M. Bryant had just moved to A&M from Kentucky and hired Smith

John David Crow, shown here with the 1957 award, is the only Aggie to win the Heisman Trophy.

AGGIE QUIZ

25. Legendary Aggie halfback Joel Hunt had the best game of his college career against SMU in 1927. Can you name his key stats?

from a small Arkansas college, Southern State at Magnolia, where Smith once coached Raymond Crow, John David's older brother. Even though he was on friendly terms with the Crow family, Smith figured he might have worn out his welcome with them long before he signed John David to a Southwest Conference letter of intent to enroll at A&M.

As Smith once recalled, "John David got so disgusted with me hanging around so much he said, 'Coach, I don't know whether I'll be able to finish high school or not.'"

On signing day, Smith's down-home personality and familiarity with the Crow family paid off for the Aggies. No coaches could have a letter of intent in their possession until signing day, and Bryant knew SMU and TCU recruiters would also be racing to Springhill to try and sign Crow as soon as they could leave their schools with a letter. So he told Smith to stay in Springhill until early that morning, then drive to the Shreveport airport, where a letter ready for Crow's signature would be delivered to him. Smith then sped back to Springhill and signed Crow an hour before the rival coaches arrived.

Throughout an intense recruiting season with so many schools vying for him, John David always liked the idea of playing at A&M because of Smith.

"I didn't know Coach Bryant," said Crow, who returned to his alma mater in 1981 and since has served

John David Crow was the go-to guy for A&M from 1955-57.

Coach Bear Bryant with several of the players in 1957, including John David Crow, second from bottom.

as athletic director, assistant AD and fund-raiser. "Newspaper and radio coverage wasn't what it is now. But I knew Elmer and knew him to be an honest, decent man. Elmer Smith recruited me, and Elmer Smith is the reason I came to Texas A&M. "

BREAKING 'EM IN John David soon knew Coach Bryant very well. The Aggies' new coach realized the future of his program rested with his talented freshmen team, so he worked the newcomers long and hard that fall. In fact, you had to be there to know how long and how hard.

"I remember a long, long scrimmage we had one day," John David said. "Afterward, I was sitting in a metal folding chair under the shower when the manager came in and yelled, 'Put 'em back on!' I said, 'What? You're crazy!' He said, 'Nope. The man said put 'em back on.' We did, and went back outside. Coach Bryant told us to grab a knee, but I knew if I went down to one knee, I'd never get up. Then he started telling us what we were

26. A&M halfback Joel Hunt later was a head college coach at two major schools. Name them.

John David Crow running against LSU in 1955. Crow scored two touchdowns and the Aggies won, 28-0.

going to accomplish.

"I looked at him, framed by the tunnel at the north end of the stadium, and I listened. I don't recall what he said, but I said to myself, 'By God, you might kill me, but you're not going to run me off!'

"And he almost did. I woke up three hours later in the infirmary, holding an orange drink, with my wife Carolyn standing at the side of the bed and Coach Bryant standing down at the end. I'd had a heat stroke.

"Coach Bryant looked at me and said, 'John, why didn't you tell me you were tired?' "

John David survived and thrived, becoming fiercely proud to be an Aggie and good enough to play Bryant's hard-nosed style of football. As a sophomore in '55, he was instrumental in A&M improving to 7-2-1 from the 1-9 a scrawny varsity managed in '54. Folks were calling him the best all-around back in the SWC since Doak Walker. For John David, hearing that was better than listening to the "Aggie War Hymn."

"Doak Walker was my idol when I was in junior high, and I wanted to follow him to SMU," he said. "But by the time I got to senior high, everyone was interested in Oklahoma. Then just as I was getting ready for college, I liked Elmer Smith so much I followed him to A&M. I knew that Coach Bryant would be building and that I could learn faster under him because he'd be concentrating on the freshmen. In fact, we had such a good freshman team that we beat the varsity whenever we scrimmaged."

No matter how many big plays John David made on offense and defense, he dreaded how Bryant might react if he messed up. As a sophomore against SMU, he found out.

"I was supposed to catch the ball on punts and they kicked to us on our 40. When I got tackled I was back on our 10. I tried to get around the wave and lost 30 yards.

"We ran a couple of plays and kicked, and then we got the ball back. On first down I was supposed to go around end, and I thought I could give ground and get around the corner man. I didn't make it and lost about five yards. When I got on my feet, I saw Bill Dendy trotting on the field. He was my substitute.

"I thought, 'Uh-oh, here's where I catch it.' As I came off I didn't even look at Coach Bryant. I kept my head down and headed for the opposite end of the bench, as far from him as I could get. I was scared to death and knew what was coming.

"I sat on the bench and never looked up. I kept looking at the ground, and all of a sudden I saw Coach Bryant's shoes. I kinda braced myself, and he put a hand on my knee. I looked up then, and he pointed out toward the field. All he said was, 'John, our goal is *thataway!*'"

JUNIOR SEASON By his junior season, John David not only ran in the right direction, he ran over plenty of guys who got in his way. The Aggies finished 9-0-1 and were unbeaten in the SWC but were denied the host school's spot in the Cotton Bowl Classic in Dallas on New Year's Day because of recruiting violations. Instead, he and his teammates savored their victories over their two toughest rivals — 7-6 over TCU in a roaring rainstorm that reached hurricane proportions and 19-13 over Baylor at Waco the following Saturday.

Against TCU, the Aggies managed to hold the visitors to a 6-0 lead in the fourth quarter after staving off a half dozen scoring threats. Then, just as the sun came out, the Aggies got possession on their 20 after Don Watson's end zone interception. John David bolted 21 yards to ignite A&M's best drive of the day, and soon Watson raced 37 to the TCU 20. John David banged it to the 8-yard line, then caught Watson's option pass on the goal line for the touchdown. Loyd Taylor kicked the extra point and the Aggies survived a wild, wet, weird afternoon.

In a locker room interview, Bryant was asked if the game went according to plan. "No," he said, "it went

AGGIE QUIZ

27. Name the Aggie who wrote the "Aggie War Hymn," as well as where he wrote it.

AGGIE QUIZ

28. How many straight passes did Bill "Jitterbug" Henderson catch in the Aggies' 20-0 win over Rice in 1940?

AGGIE QUIZ

29. What rare distinction did Aggie fullback Jack Pardee achieve in 1956?

according to prayer."

One week later came a Baylor game which Bryant always called, "the bloodiest, meanest and toughest game I've ever seen." Again the Aggies came from behind to win in the fourth quarter and again Crow produced in the clutch.

On fourth down and with all the marbles riding on it, Crow said, "Give me the cockeyed ball and I'll put it in there." Well, they gave him the ball and he put it in there from about six yards out.

SENIOR SEASON As a senior in '57, Crow made championship plays all year long on offense and defense. The Aggies, less explosive and talented than the '56 team, were 8-0 and ranked No. 1 nationally when they went to Houston to play Rice on Nov. 16. The morning of the game, the *Houston Post* ran a story speculating that Bryant would be going to Alabama in 1958, a move he confirmed less than a week later on Thanksgiving night. By then, the Aggies had lost 7-6 to Rice; 9-7 to Texas; and instead of taking a perfect record to the Cotton Bowl Classic, they settled for a trip to the Gator Bowl, where they lost to Tennessee, 3-0.

It was a down time for A&M, but John David picked it up when he won the Heisman Trophy, outscoring Alex Karras, Iowa's star lineman, by almost 500 points in the national voting. Before he headed for Alabama to start recruiting, Bryant campaigned hard for his greatest Aggie star to win the Heisman.

The 1957 A&M backfield included Loyd Taylor, Richard Gay, John David Crow and, kneeling, Roddy Osborne.

"John David is the greatest athlete who ever lived, for my money," Bryant said. "He had a burning desire for the team to win. If he doesn't get the Heisman, they ought to quit giving it."

In a final class act to wrap up his A&M years, Bryant sent Elmer Smith, the faithful assistant who landed Crow for the Aggies, to New York to celebrate with John David and his family at the award dinner. Smith beamed as John David stood at the dais, ran his hand down the handsome black and gold trophy and made perhaps the shortest acceptance speech in Heisman history.

"It all seems like a dream," John David said, "and I want to sit down before I make a racket that might wake me up."

AGGIE QUIZ

30. The Sugar Land Express, Ken Hall, was a prize in Bear Bryant's first A&M recruiting class in 1954. What was the most notable record of Hall's Aggie career?

The Bad, The Worst &
The Beautiful

From 1958 to 1971, Jim Myers, Hank Foldberg and Junction legend Gene Stallings struggled to return the Aggies to glory. The cumulative bottom line: 13 losing seasons and one mountaintop experience.

Except for seven wondrous weeks in 1967, the season Stallings' third A&M team rallied from an 0-4 start to win the SWC title and then score a 20-16 upset of Alabama in an emotional reunion with Bear Bryant in the Cotton Bowl, the Aggies too often played like Joe Zilch drew their game plans. Delete that 7-4 record in 1967 when Stallings was SWC Coach of the Year and was lifted off the muddy Cotton Bowl turf in an affectionate Bear hug by his old coach, and the Myers-Foldberg-Stallings record for the other 13 years was 38-88-6.

Each coach was fired but each left with a special feeling for A&M.

Jim Myers

JIM MYERS Myers, the only non-Aggie of the three, had the toughest act to follow, but today he reflects fondly on his four years as head coach after Bryant left for Alabama.

"The two best breaks in my coaching career were going to Texas A&M and leaving Texas A&M," Myers said.

He held up a 6-inch thick roll of yellowed Western Union paper. It bore the names of the entire A&M enrollment of 7,000 students in early 1958. They sent him a telegram urging him to leave Iowa State for A&M. "The spirit of the Aggies is just great. The only thing I kept from my A&M years is this roll of Western Union paper. All the names on it are why I never regretted leaving Iowa State, where I had been given a new contract and the future was bright. But the day after I was fired at A&M, Tom Landry hired me for his Dallas Cowboys staff and my career took a new direction."

Myers worked on Landry's staff 25 seasons, rising to assistant head coach. During those years the Cowboys became the most popular team in professional football, playing in five Super Bowls and winning two.

A&M officials had conducted a bizarre, highly-publicized search for Bryant's successor by the time Myers reconsidered his first refusal of the job and moved to Aggieland. Three high-profile coaches of that era — UCLA's Red Sanders, Navy's Eddie Erdelatz and former Notre Dame Coach Frank Leahy — were mentioned as strong candidates but all eventually faded from the picture.

"Everyone thought the A&M job was the plum of

college football," Myers said, "but it wasn't. Nearly all of the good players from the Bryant teams had graduated and we needed some time to build a new program. In 1958, we had the best recruiting class of the years I was there, but some of them left. Five outstanding freshmen were recruited off the campus by other schools. That was a major setback for a team as thin as ours."

Myers changed the Aggie offense from the T-formation to single wing and spread formations and converted junior Charlie Milstead from a T quarterback to a tailback. It was a masterful move.

Quarterback Charlie Milstead was captain of the 1959 team. In 1958, he ranked fourth nationally in passing.

Milstead wasn't fast but he was a strong passer, gutty runner and outstanding leader. Milstead teamed with senior end John Tracey to form one of the nation's best passing attacks — Milstead ranked fourth nationally in passing, Tracey fourth in receiving.

The Aggies finished 4-6 in 1958, the offense overcoming a weak defense for an occasional exciting game. The best one, and one of the best comebacks in A&M history, came at Baylor. The Bears led 27-7 entering the fourth quarter, but Milstead rallied the Aggies to win, 33-27.

The record slid to 3-7 in 1959 but Milstead closed his career with a brilliant effort against Cotton Bowl-bound Texas before the Longhorns finally won, 20-17. The Aggies won only five more games in Myers' final two seasons, but he still laughs when he remembers one headline in *The Battalion* late in 1960.

"We had tied Texas Tech, TCU and SMU, so *The Battalion* ran a banner headline : 'Tie The Hell Out Of Rice!' "

The Aggies lost, 21-14, and then lost to Texas by the same score to finish 1-6-3. There was improvement in 1961 but not enough. Myers was fired at the end of a 4-5-1 year, and left wondering how much better his four seasons might have been with deeper talent. Of his 24 losses at A&M, 10 were by a touchdown or less.

HANK FOLDBERG The Aggies then turned to Foldberg, who lettered as an end and tackle at A&M in 1942 before entering military service. Best known as an All-America end on Earl "Red" Blaik's great West Point teams in 1945-46, Foldberg had returned to A&M in 1951 as an assistant to Ray George before joining Bob Woodruff's staff at Florida for eight years. He had enjoyed brief success as a head coach at Wichita State in 1960-61 before coming to A&M for a third time in 1962.

It was a bad trip. Foldberg's Aggie teams usually looked out of synch and his plodding offense never scored more than 90 points in any of his three seasons.

The one highlight was a nationally-televised

Hank Foldberg

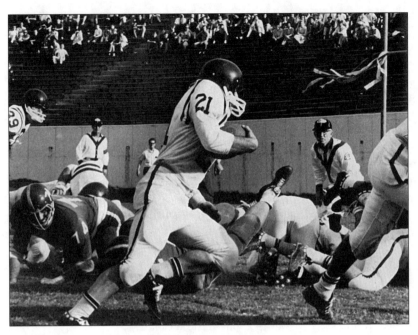

Travis Reagan, who lettered from 1961-63, makes a dash for the goal line.

Against Texas in 1964, the Aggies' Jim Kauffmann threw a 91-yard pass to Ken "Dude" McLean on a trick play that came to be called the "Texas Special."

Thanksgiving Day thriller against No. 1 Texas in 1963. Americans everywhere were in a state of shock and mourning after President John F. Kennedy's assassination in Dallas six days earlier, but the Aggies played with impressive zeal that day at Kyle Field.

They carried a 13-3 lead into the fourth quarter and still led late in the game, 13-9. But A&M defenders missed two great chances to end Texas' last drive. John Brotherton intercepted Tommy Wade's pass at midfield but Texas got the ball back after an excited Brotherton tried to lateral to a teammate, who fumbled. With 2:24 left, Jim Willenborg appeared to intercept Wade's pass deep in the end zone but an official ruled he did not have possession of the ball before he fell out of the end zone.

Texas still had the ball and scored with 1:19 left to pull out a scary 15-13 victory. The Longhorns went on to beat Navy and Heisman Trophy quarterback Roger Staubach, 28-6, in the Cotton Bowl Classic on New Year's Day to clinch UT's first national championship under Darrell Royal.

GENE STALLINGS Foldberg was out after a 1-9 season in 1964 and old Aggies cheered Stallings' return. At 29, he boasted an excellent coaching background, having risen to defensive coordinator during his seven years on Bryant's Alabama staff. But now it was 1965 and the proud, driven Stallings found A&M's situation had changed drastically during his absence. His alma mater was in the early stages of becoming a coed institution, having admitted its first few female students in 1963, but it still was a predominately male military school. It was not viewed favorably by a lot of young people angry and alarmed about escalating U.S. involvement in the Vietnam War.

"It was tough recruiting at A&M when I came back," he said. "Texas and Arkansas had become national powers and were by far the strongest schools in the Southwest Conference and there was a non-military mood around the country. But I was excited about coming back to a school I have always loved.

"A&M still had that wonderful spirit and I enjoyed my years there. We played hard. We just didn't have enough players."

Stallings still became the only Aggie coach to win a

Gene Stallings

Curley Hallman came up with an interception to help the Aggies beat Alabama, 20-16, in the 1968 Cotton Bowl. The game matched Gene Stallings against his former A&M coach, Bear Bryant.

Gene Stallings, in his days as captain and sure-handed end for the '56 Aggies.

AGGIE QUIZ

31. When and where did John Kimbrough achieve his greatest single-game rushing total? How many yards did he gain, and did he score?

AGGIE QUIZ

32. At which college did Earl Rudder play football before he transferred to Texas A&M?

clear SWC title between Bryant's 1956 champions, which he captained, and Jackie Sherrill's 1985 team. And he did it with perhaps the most dramatic turnaround in school history.

Stunned by a last-second, 20-17 opening loss to underdog SMU on national television, the 1967 Aggies stumbled to 0-4 before pulling out a 28-24 victory at Texas Tech. Then they won their five remaining SWC games, climaxed by Edd Hargett's 80-yard touchdown pass to Bob Long in the fourth quarter to beat Texas, 10-7, at Kyle Field.

That earned Stallings and his Aggies a classic pupil versus teacher matchup with Bryant and Alabama in the Cotton Bowl on New Year's Day. It was a swell game that delighted a sellout crowd, a national television audience and Aggies everywhere. A&M wiped out two Alabama leads and played a strong fourth quarter to win, 20-16. At the final gun, Bryant strode to midfield grinning like a proud daddy, wrapped his arms around Stallings and

Bear Bryant, then the Alabama coach, carries Gene Stallings off the field after Stallings' Aggies beat Bama, 20-16, in the 1968 Cotton Bowl.

lifted his old Junction boy off his feet in a wonderful moment of celebration.

It was the perfect gesture at the perfect time, and everyone loved it. Like Bum Phillips said, no one ever knew more about people than Bear Bryant.

Stallings never again approached the glory of that moment at A&M. He was fired after a 5-6 season in 1971 but, like Myers 10 years earlier, his coaching career was rejuvenated quickly when he joined Landry's Cowboy staff. He became one of Landry's most valuable assistants and a top NFL defensive coach over the next 14 years, then moved up to head coach of the Cardinals in St. Louis and Phoenix. Next he returned to college football as head coach at Bryant's alma mater, Alabama. In the finest tradition of his old coach, Stallings led the Crimson Tide to the 1992 national championship.

"I've been lucky," Stallings said. "I've coached at two great schools."

AGGIE QUIZ

33. What current tie does the Aggie football team have with Stephenville, Texas?

Bellard, Wilson & Sherrill
Three For The Road

Emory Bellard, Tom Wilson and Jackie Sherrill had two things in common. Each was elated when he got his turn at the wheel of the Aggie Express. Each was deflated when he surrendered it.

The reasons for their parting emotions varied greatly, but there was one consistent condition at the time of their exits — turmoil.

AGGIE QUIZ

34. Which coach represented Texas A&M when John David Crow received the Heisman Trophy at New York's Downtown Athletic Club in December 1957?

Each left Aggieland with a winning record. Each beat Texas at least twice. Each took the Aggies to bowl games. But each man left the head coaching job under pressure.

Their combined record for 1972-88 (121-76-1, .615) was far superior to the 14 previous seasons under Jim Myers, Hank Foldberg and Gene Stallings (45-92-6, .325). But it took more than that to keep the A&M job in this era.

It was like Elvis was out there somewhere choreographing the show. There was a whole lot of shakin' goin' on.

Maybe it went with the territory during a time of incredible growth for a school that no longer was a small, remote all-male college with compulsory military training.

Thanks to the visionary leadership of President Earl Rudder in the '60s, Texas A&M was a booming co-educational university whose enrollment was soaring beyond all projections. Integration, in both ethnicity and gender, was moving along rapidly. The school's academic personality was changing dramatically. A&M in the '70s and '80s was high-energy and full of surprises.

And for Bellard, Wilson and Sherrill they weren't all good.

EMORY BELLARD In an era that would hold so many changes for A&M, the hiring of Bellard was the first. A prime assistant on Darrell Royal's Texas staff and the developer of the celebrated Wishbone offense that was key to UT's national championships in '69 and '70, Bellard clearly possessed a brilliant football mind. His five years on Royal's staff comprised his entire college coaching experience, but he was a famous Texas high school coaching figure who took an assistant's job under Royal to better position himself for a major college head coaching job.

Emory Bellard

When A&M decided to fire Stallings with one year left on his contract, Aggie officials soon decided Bellard was the right choice to build a new program. He had

Emory Bellard and the Aggies prepare for their game against Wichitia State in 1972. The Aggies won 36-12, but struggled to a 3-8 record in Bellard's first season.

climbed the ladder of Texas high school coaching impressively, with a 139-34-3 record in 15 years at Ingleside, Breckenridge and San Angelo that included two state championships and a share of a third. As past president of the Texas High School Coaches Association, Bellard boasted a thorough knowledge of the coaches and schools in the state where the Aggies must sign a lot of blue-chip recruits to succeed.

Bellard and his staff, full of coaches with strong Texas high school roots including a young R.C. Slocum, signed two of the best recruiting classes in A&M and Southwest Conference history in 1972 and '73. These were the first two years since 1947 that freshmen were eligible to play

Two-time All-SWC fullback Bubba Bean starred on the 1974 and '75 teams. Here, he eludes the Rice defense in a 37-7 Aggie victory in '74.

Coach Emory Bellard wasn't afraid to use freshman David Walker as the team's regular quarterback in 1973.

varsity football in the SWC and this enabled Bellard's young talent to mature sooner. Over the next four seasons, 1974-77, A&M averaged nine wins a year and was a consistent title contender.

"We had a good commodity to sell," Bellard said. "We had to convince the top kids they could build their own winning tradition at A&M. We sold the future of football at A&M and the value of a degree from a respected university. And parents liked the conservative nature of the school.

"It was an exciting time around A&M. The school had gone through a great transition, from an all-male student body to 50 percent female enrollment. The Bryan-College Station area had gone from a small community to one of the fastest-growing areas in the nation."

Aggie rosters were filled with big-play guys in those

years. Athletes like Bubba Bean, Pat Thomas, Richard Osborne, Carl Roaches, George Woodard, Tim Gray, Tony Franklin, Ed Simonini, Lester "The Molester" Hayes, Edgar Fields and Curtis Dickey would move on to strong NFL careers. And as the won-lost record improved so did alumni financial support and attendance at Kyle Field.

"A&M was averaging 26,000 for home games and the A&M Club was pledging $70,000 for the football program when I came there," said Bellard, who also proved an innovative athletic director. "Three years later, pledges were up to $1 million a year and we were drawing 5,000 over capacity in a 48,000-seat stadium. We seated the overflow in chairs on the track and asked everyone to stick with us until we could enlarge the stadium."

Enlargement to 70,210 permanent seats came in 1980 but Bellard wasn't there to see it.

He resigned abruptly in October of '78 in a move that shocked nearly everyone at A&M.

The Aggies had loomed as national contenders when they opened that season 4-0, outscoring Kansas, Boston College, Memphis State and Texas Tech 170-21. Then, hit hard by injuries, they suffered lopsided losses at Houston, 33-0, and to Baylor at Kyle Field, 24-6. Three days after the Baylor game, Bellard met with new A&M President Jarvis Miller in Miller's office. When Bellard left, he no longer was A&M's football coach and athletic director.

Bellard still prefers to say little about his decision except that he sensed a drastic change in his relationship with the new president. He had enjoyed a good relationship with the previous president, Jack Williams, but Williams was replaced after he suffered a heart attack. Bellard found his conversation with Miller that day so dissatisfying that he decided to resign on the spot.

Bellard, 4-2 in 1978, left A&M with a 48-27 record, a winning percentage of .640.

"We had some good years," Bellard said. "A&M's football program came from way back to one of the better ones. It was a much better place when I left there."

TOM WILSON Marvin Tate, an Aggie and Junction survivor whom Rudder hired as associate athletic director in 1967, was promoted to athletic director that afternoon by Miller, who promptly asked Tate's recommendation for interim head coach. Tate believed offensive coordinator Tom Wilson was best qualified among the current staff, so Wilson took charge at practice.

The former Texas Tech quarterback had been A&M's offensive coordinator for three and a half seasons but once he became head coach he quickly junked Bellard's Wishbone for a power-I attack. He made another strong

AGGIE QUIZ

35. How did Aggie coach D.X. Bible spend the 1918 season?

Tom Wilson

Tom Wilson took over for Emory Bellard in the middle of the 1978 season. The Aggies went 4-2 in games under Wilson that season, including a Hall of Fame Bowl victory. That led to a contract for Wilson to become the permanent coach.

impression in his first game as head coach. On the Aggies' first offensive play, quarterback Mike Mosley connected with Gerald Carter for a 52-yard touchdown pass. A&M went on to win, 38-21.

The Aggies finished 4-2 under Wilson, capped by a 28-12 victory over Iowa State in the Hall of Fame Bowl. It was a good performance and Wilson received a new contract as head coach.

The Aggies weren't spectacular but they had some good moments the next three years. The '79 Aggies scored one of the greatest intersectional victories in school history — a 27-14 upset at Penn State. And Wilson matched Bellard's feat by beating Texas two straight, 13-7 at Kyle Field in '79 and 24-14 at Memorial Stadium in '80. Until Bellard and Wilson, no Aggie coach had won two straight against Texas since Uncle Charley Moran did it twice in 1909, 23-0 at Houston and 5-0 at Austin.

The Aggies were 7-5 in 1981, finishing with a 33-16 win over Oklahoma State in the Independence Bowl, but there already had been upheaval in the A&M program.

Regents chairman H.R. "Bum" Bright was intent on making sweeping changes in A&M football and wanted to offer a million-dollar package to a big name to become head coach and athletic director. The first bombshell was the firing of Tate after the Aggies' second game of the season. It left Tate and others close to the program stunned and bitter, but that was just the beginning.

By January of 1982, Bright's determined campaign

to hire a marquee coach was big news. Wilson still was on the job, and meeting with his players, while Bright was hiring Sherrill as head coach-athletic director, a job Michigan's Bo Schembechler had declined several days earlier.

Suddenly Wilson, 21-19 and .525 in three and a half seasons, was out. Sherrill, whose 50-9-1 in five seasons at Pitt was the best in Pitt history, was in. Boy, was he ever!

JACKIE SHERRILL A former Alabama player who helped the Crimson Tide win two national championships under Bear Bryant in the mid-60s, Sherrill was dissatisfied with his limited authority at Pitt. At A&M, he wanted autonomy in the athletic department and total support from the top of the administration. Bright, who in 1984 would purchase the Dallas Cowboys from club founder Clint Murchison Jr., made sure Sherrill had it.

Jackie Sherrill

In another development that ultimately proved more important to A&M's football future, Bright also was instrumental in Slocum's returning to A&M as defensive coordinator after one year in that position on the Southern Cal staff.

Sherrill came to A&M with the goal of building a national championship program but his first three Aggie teams made a lot of fans yearn for Bellard or maybe even Wilson. The coach with the big budget and big plans went 5-6, 5-5-1 and 6-5. That last record, in 1984, looks like a marginal winning season but the final two games indicated a breakthrough could be near. The Aggies upset TCU, 35-21, at Kyle Field, killing the Frogs' shot at the Cotton Bowl. Then they finished with a 37-12 whipping of Texas at Austin.

His greatest contribution of those first years was more psychological than athletic. Sherrill, seizing on A&M's greatest tradition, founded the 12th Man kickoff team. He invited walk-on players from the student body to try

In his first season, Coach Jackie Sherrill teaches tight end Mark Lewis a passing route.

A freshman, Bucky Richardson, above left, took over as A&M's quarterback in 1987.

Two-time All-American end Ray Childress, above right, led the Aggies defense from 1981-84.

out for the team, creating great excitement on campus and generating media coverage across the U.S. The 12th Man kickoff team became a fixture at home games and frequently played well.

Sherrill had some quality players in those first three years. Defensive tackle Ray Childress and safety Billy Cannon Jr. became No. 1 draft choices by the Houston Oilers and Dallas Cowboys, but the Aggies didn't achieve a combination of quality, quantity and consistency until 1985. Then stars like Kevin Murray, Roger Vick, John Roper and Johnny Holland led big-play teams that thrived on clutch situations. The Aggies won three straight SWC titles and went 2-1 in three Cotton Bowl Classics, sandwiching 36-16 and 35-10 wins over Auburn and Notre Dame around a 28-12 loss to Ohio State. From 1985-87 the Aggies were 10-2, 9-3 and 10-2.

After six years, however, Sherrill had won a lot more games than friends. His personality and his tactics had turned off lots of people.

"Some people grow," said Tate, the former athletic director forced out to make room for Sherrill and who became a successful realtor as well as mayor of Bryan. "Others swell."

A&M was under severe scrutiny by the NCAA and in September of 1988 would be sanctioned and ruled ineligible for a postseason bowl game that season. The NCAA cited A&M for lack of administrative control of the school's NCAA compliance procedures and announced that having Sherrill serve as both athletic director and head football coach was a problem. The most serious violation was the school not suspending quarterback Murray, the SWC Offensive Player of the Year in '85 and '86, when evidence was uncovered that Murray received illegal payments from a booster in 1983-84.

The penalty cost A&M its share of SWC bowl

WHEN THE CLOCK STRIKES 12, THEY YELL

Midnight Yell Practice evolved years ago when several uppperclasssmen sent some freshmen snaking around the campus to the YMCA Building, where they held an impromptu yell practice. The Fish (Aggie freshmen) had such fun they asked two senior yell leaders to lead them the next time.

The seniors said they could not authorize a yell practice but they could "manage to be" at the Y at midnight. Flares were planted, the Corps woke up and the band turned out. Midnight Yell Practice was born and later moved to Kyle Field, where it is held each Friday night before a home game.

The band starts the parade at the Quadrangle near the Corps dorms and marches to Kyle Field led by torch-bearing yell leaders. As many as 20,000 students fall in behind the band, yells are practiced and everyone sings those golden oldies, "Aggies War Hymn" and "Spirit of Aggieland." Then comes "lights out" and the after-touchdown kiss is practiced.

A&M Yell Leaders.

With Kevin Murray at quarterback, A&M scored 747 points and won 19 games through 1985 and '86.

revenues — between $250,000 and $500,000. Sherrill said A&M also had spent approximately $2 million responding to the allegations. The NCAA ordered A&M to place Sherrill under "administrative probation" for the next two years.

Penn State Coach Joe Paterno was approaching 60 but said he planned to remain in coaching indefinitely. "Someone has to keep college football safe from Jackie Sherrill and Barry Switzer," he said.

Paterno later said he called Switzer and told him he was just kidding when he mentioned his name. He apparently stuck by his comment about Sherrill, whom he had disliked since Sherrill's Pitt days.

The '88 season became the slide that sent Sherrill down the chute at A&M. Former A&M player George Smith charged that he had received illegal payments while he was an Aggie and later received "hush money" from Sherrill and an associate so he wouldn't talk to NCAA investigators.

This got the attention of the NCAA, which could have given A&M football the "death penalty" for a second violation within a five-year period, sidelining the Aggies as it had SMU.

It's possible A&M was saved this blow to its football program and embarrassment as an institution by Sherrill's resigning under pressure on Dec. 12, 1988. A&M President William Mobley announced Sherrill's resignation and said an internal investigation would continue.

Mobley also made two promotions: John David Crow to athletic director from associate athletic director, and R.C. Slocum to head coach from defensive coordinator and assistant head coach.

A&M was returning to its roots with Crow, its only Heisman Trophy winner; and Slocum, who had spent 17 of his last 18 years on the Aggie football staff. Now came the opportunity for new growth.

AGGIE QUIZ

37. Hank Foldberg, A&M head coach in 1962-64, was best known as an end on the powerful Army teams in 1945-46, but he previously had lettered as an end and tackle at A&M. Which year?

R.C. Slocum
Their Kind Of Coach

Two coaches in the history of Texas A&M football have achieved the ideal blending of school, players, traditions and winning effort. You only have to mention their initials and everyone knows you're talking about someone special.

D.X. and R.C.

Just as Dana Xenophon Bible raised the Aggies to a new plateau of pride and success from 1917-28, so has Richard Copeland Slocum from 1989-96.

As A&M roared into the new Big 12 Conference, his

When Greg Hill rushed for 100 yards or more, the Aggies racked up a 17-1 record in his three-year career.

winning percentage of .812 was second best among active Division I coaches. No. 1 is his new league rival, Tom Osborne of Nebraska (.827), who heads the most powerful program among a number of tough Big Eight members entering the Big 12. Slocum knew his teams would be tested as never before but he welcomed it.

"The Big 12 will be a real challenge but I feel we'll be a good, strong member," he said. "We're anxious to make a turn through the new league. That will help us learn how we perform in different competition and learn more about our new conference rivals."

Bible once urged his players to rise to the challenge, even creating the tradition of the 12th Man to help them beat a heavily favored opponent in A&M's first postseason game, the 1922 Dixie Classic. Slocum, after dominating the final seven Southwest Conference seasons with an .856 winning percentage, believes his program is strong enough to play with the best in the new league for two reasons.

R.C. Slocum

One, the team has battled through tough times and still won a lot.

Two, A&M for years has recruited well, particularly in its talent-rich home state.

Slocum says proudly that the Aggies have proved they possess integrity as well as talent. They came through the

The "Wrecking Crew" was an integral part of R.C. Slocum's teams.

Leeland McElroy was in the running for the Heisman Trophy in 1995.

A program from the 1994 Cotton Bowl.

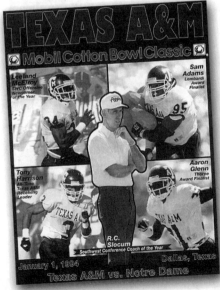

shock and embarrassment of being ruled ineligible for the SWC title and a bowl game in '94 because several players accepted money from a supporter for non-existent summer jobs. Losses to Texas Tech and Texas denied Slocum his fourth SWC title in '95 but the Aggies tuned up for Big 12 action with an impressive win over Michigan in the Alamo Bowl to finish final SWC season 9-3.

As he enters his 24th year as a member of the A&M football program, Slocum appreciates the stature the Aggies have achieved since he was promoted to head coach after Jackie Sherrill's hurried departure.

"The most enjoyable thing about these past seven years is our dramatic move upward in the eyes of people across the country," he said. "They believe we know how to run our program in compliance with NCAA rules. The problem a few years ago was external. The NCAA checked everything and found that everyone in our football program was following the rules. It was painful to be penalized for wrongdoing outside our program but it helped draw a line in the dirt. It sent a message to all of our alumni and friends that we're running a clean program.

"We've won a bunch of games but this is what I am proudest of. An honest program gives us stability. The bottom is not going to fall out on A&M football."

Consistently strong recruiting should help keep the Aggies in contention.

KYLE FIELD: WOODEN BLEACHERS TO CONCRETE COLOSSUS

A&M's legendary stadium began in the early 1900s as a covered grandstand purchased from the Bryan Fair Grounds flanked by two sets of wooden bleachers. Seating capacity: 500.

Since the Aggie athletic department had no money to buy the grandstand or lumber to build the bleachers, athletic council chairman Edwin Jackson Kyle gave his personal note to cover the costs. Today the triple-decked stadium bearing his name has grown to a permanent seating capacity of 70,210 and can be expanded to 78,000-plus with temporary seating. The stadium record of 78, 573 was set in 1987 when A&M beat Texas, 20-13, to win its third straight Southwest Conference title.

Home of the 12th Man, Kyle Field is famous for the constant roar of A&M students and fans which gives the Aggies one of the greatest home field advantages in college football. R.C. Slocum's Kyle Field record in seven seasons as head coach is 39-2-1.

A packed Kyle Field.

Quarterback Bucky Richardson.

Quarterback Bucky Richardson.

38. What international athletic honor did Darrow Hooper earn?

"I really believe in the product," said Slocum, who attended A&M games as a young boy and grew into an all-district tight end at Stark High School in Orange on the Gulf Coast of Southeast Texas. "I grew up in the state of Texas and coached 23 years in the Southwest Conference. There aren't many places in this state I haven't been. I know a lot of coaches and a lot of people."

Slocum also believes in low-key recruiting, even when he's competing with the Texas Longhorns for a top player.

"I tell the kids, 'OK, let's talk about you and your interests and your future. The bottom line is I want you to come to A&M because you want to come. Some people don't like it here. The University of Texas is a fine university, but it's in the city. We're in the country. You should visit both schools and decide for yourself.'"

So many good players have decided on A&M that Slocum has averaged almost 10 wins a season as head coach. His rosters have abounded with big-play athletes like Bucky Richardson, Patrick Bates, Marcus Buckley,

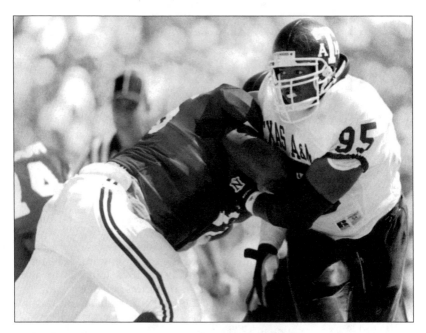

Leeland McElroy, Quentin Coryatt, Darren Lewis, Greg Hill, Kevin Smith, Aaron Glenn and Sam Adams. There should be more as the Aggies march into the Big 12.

The coach leading them knows his school and his state and he knows football. Somewhere D.X. must enjoy watching R.C. do his job.

All-American Sam Adams, a defensive lineman, was a finalist for the 1993 Lombardi Award.

The A&M–Texas Rivalry
Only One Like It

R.C. Slocum and sons Shawn and John Harvey left Austin early the morning after the Aggies' 34-10 victory over Texas in 1994, bound for their traditional postgame deer hunt. When they stopped at a barbecue stand in Llano, Texas, the A&M coach's reception from the diners told all about how people feel toward the 103-year-old rivalry between Texas A&M and the University of Texas.

"Half of them stood up and cheered," Slocum said, "and half of them just sat there."

Slocum, who grew up in Orange, Texas, always has admired the emotions this game has inspired since the schools first faced each other in 1894. It quickly became the Southwest Conference showcase event when the league began competition in 1915 and remained so until the teams last met as SWC members at College Station in 1995.

"Football is an important part of our culture in the state of Texas and the rivalry of these two big public schools epitomizes this," said Slocum, who has helped coach the Aggies in 23 of these games and is 5-2 as head coach. "From the offices of bank presidents in Dallas and Houston to the barber shops in Orange and Pecos, it's the most talked-about of games. I tell our players it's a special opportunity in their lives to be part of this."

TRACING TRADITION This rivalry has been the stage for national champions, legendary coaches and historic plays. It led to the famed A&M bonfire, which still burns each year, and to a barbecue of the first Bevo in Austin, where UT Athletic Director L. Theo Bellmont hoped the ornery orange and white longhorn would prove a better meal than he did a mascot.

Bellmont, the SWC founding father who reunited the two schools in the new

A program from the 1939 A&M-Texas game, in which the Aggies had a lot riding. A 20-0 victory allowed A&M to finish with an undefeated record, win its first SWC title since 1927 and play in the Sugar Bowl. The Aggies won the bowl and the national championship.

league after athletic relations had been suspended from 1912 through 1914, was a true diplomat when he issued invitations to the dinner in January 1920. He even included the notorious A&M branding party which had burned the 1915 Aggies' winning score of 13-0 on the steer's side, a brand his UT keepers quickly altered to read "Bevo," the name of a non-alcoholic near-beer.

The entree was nothing to cheer about, though. "It was pretty poor barbecue," said Alfred "Grip" Penn, a guard on the 1916, '17 and '19 Longhorns.

The game itself, fortunately, has been of much higher quality.

FROM OUTSIDE AND IN Retired Texas coach Darrell Royal has seen this rivalry from more than one vantage point.

"It was big when I got here," said Royal, the Oklahoma native who was 17-3 against the Aggies from 1957-76. "And I haven't seen anything overshadow it. Both schools have tremendous numbers of alumni

ALL FIRED UP FOR TEXAS

The entire Texas A&M student body helps to build the world's largest bonfire. Logs and lumber are gathered for weeks preceding the climactic game with Texas and a 10-story tower is built on the polo fields on the northeast corner of the campus. The Aggies traditionally pay tribute to the Longhorns by topping it with an outhouse, then get ready to fire it up.

The Aggie Bonfire, symbolizing a burning desire to beat Texas and an undying love for Texas A&M, glows across the Central Texas sky the night before A&M plays Texas in College Station and two nights before the ancient rivals play in Austin. The Corps of Cadets stands at attention while the Fightin' Texas Aggie Band plays "The Spirit of Aggieland" and burrheaded yell leaders whip the crowd into a frenzy.

For the last dozen seasons, the bonfire has ignited success against the Longhorns. A&M is 10-2 in those games.

An Aggie Bonfire.

Darrell Royal enjoyed the Aggie bonfire after he retired as the Longhorns' coach.

within the state who get very excited about this game. The loser has to take a beating for a year."

Royal, whose teams won national championships in '63, '69 and '70, knew the Longhorns always would be fired up to play the Aggies.

"It just happened naturally," he said. "You'd have to be blind not to see how special this game is."

So special that after Royal retired he joined an Austin friend and drove to A&M the night of the bonfire to watch the 10-story tower of logs go up in flames and listen to the band and yell leaders whip thousands of Aggies into a frenzy.

"I had heard about it for years, so I just stood back on the edge of the crowd and took it in," he said.

SHARING BIBLE D.X. Bible was the only coach who knew how deeply the emotions ran at both schools and he made history at each.

Bible built the Aggies into an early SWC power, producing perfect-record unscored-on teams his first two seasons as head coach — 8-0-0 in 1917 and 10-0-0 in 1919 — serving as an Army Air Corps World War I pursuit pilot in between. He remained at A&M through 1928, winning five SWC titles during a period when

A key to A&M's 1991 victory against Texas was this 73-yard punt return for a touchdown by cornerback Kevin Smith. Smith was later a No. 1 draft pick by the Dallas Cowboys.

Texas won only two. He always inspired his players personally as well as athletically, a quality so admired by his arch-rivals that the UT athletic council framed a resolution of regret when he accepted an attractive offer from Nebraska.

It commended Bible as "an exemplary sportsman both in victory and defeat" and noted that Bible deserved much credit for improved relations between the two schools during the previous decade.

While the Aggies won more SWC games during the Bible era, they didn't win more games in their biggest rivalry. A&M and Texas were 5-5-1 during those years but Bible left his mark in another way. The Aggies' 14-7 upset of heavily-favored Texas in the 1922 game at Clark Field in Austin was a tribute to Bible's masterful preparation.

A half-century later, Bible recalled that day when he was interviewed by Wilbur Evans in researching for the book *The Twelfth Man*, a history of Texas A&M football.

"I drew a line on the ground, taking the idea, of course, from the Alamo," Bible said. "I made a little talk and remember asking those to cross the line who were willing to go back in there and fight in such a way that the memory of the way you play will live, and that it will be a pleasant memory for all of us. Bless your heart —

D.X. Bible coached both A&M and UT.

The Aggies defeated the Longhorns, 31-14, in 1991. Here running back Greg Hill (1991-93) stretches for the end zone.

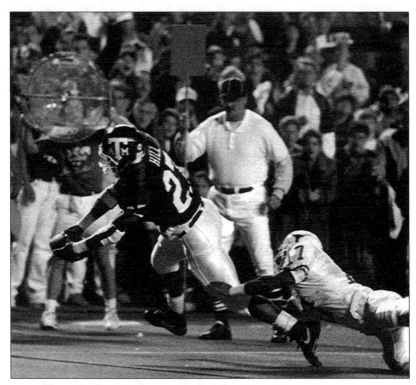

they went out there and played in such a manner that it will never be forgotten."

Bible proved an equally powerful motivator after moving back to Texas from Nebraska in 1937, accepting UT's astounding offer of a 10-year contract paying him $15,000 per year as head coach and athletic director. His 1940 Longhorns' 7-0 upset of the defending national champion Aggies at Memorial Stadium remains a classic in the storied rivalry.

This was a promising 6-3 junior team, but it had been pounded 20-0 by coach Homer Norton's powerful Aggies at Kyle Field in 1939. A&M rode a 19-0 streak into Austin but was derailed by a Texas touchdown in the first minute and an entire game of inspired defense.

Just before kickoff, Bible read the Longhorns the Edgar A. Guest poem, "It Can Be Done," and his players

FIVE MEMORABLE TEXAS-A&M GAMES

1915 — A&M 13, TEXAS 0

The Aggies celebrated resumption of competition against Texas after a three-year break in relations with an upset in the first SWC game between the schools. To make it sweeter yet, this also was the first game the two rivals played on Kyle Field. Rip Collins' remarkable punting and the Aggies' fierce defensive play highlighted their victory. Before the game, each Aggie received an inspirational letter from Uncle Charley Moran, the controversial A&M coach of the six previous seasons who apparently was forced out as a condition of Texas' resuming relations with A&M. Moran urged them to "beat those people from Austin."

1940 — TEXAS 7, A&M 0

The most inspired Texas performance in D.X. Bible's 10 years as UT head coach dealt the defending national champion Aggies their only loss in 27 games from 1938-41. A&M coach Homer Norton had a Rose Bowl bid in his

pocket when he took the Aggies to Austin for the game, but Texas ruined it by scoring with shocking speed in the first 57 seconds and then playing great defense. Tailback Pete Layden hit two passes to cover 64 of the 65 yards in the touchdown drive — the first to Jack Crain for 32 yards to the A&M 33-yard line, the second to Noble Doss, who made his historic twisting "Impossible Catch" before falling out of bounds at the 1-yard line and setting up Layden's scoring plunge.

1965 — TEXAS 21, A&M 17

One play made this game memorable. Early in the second quarter of a scoreless game, the Aggies had yet to make a first down when first-year coach Gene Stallings sprang "The Texas Special" on second-and-9 from their 9-yard line. Quarterback Harry Ledbetter bounced a lateral out to Jim Kaufmann on his far left and Kaufmann stomped his feet in disgust and clutched the ball as he took a couple of steps toward took the field believing it could.

"He had the ability to make you rise to the occasion," said Noble Doss, who certainly knew. Doss was the wingback who made the legendary "Impossible Catch" of Pete Layden's pass on the A&M 1-yard line to set up Layden's touchdown plunge and whose three interceptions snuffed out repeated comeback threats.

Bible went on to six more victories over A&M before retiring, giving him an 8-2 record against the school he once served so heroically. And that 1940 upset helped Texas remain unbeaten against the Aggies in Memorial Stadium until 1956, when another coaching legend, Bear Bryant, led A&M to a 34-21 win over a 1-9 Texas team.

Bear Bryant won only once in four attempts at beating Texas.

BRYANT'S TRIUMPH That win in 1956 was Bryant's only victory over Texas in four years as A&M coach before he

Ledbetter. The Texas secondary relaxed while receiver Dude McLean sped past and then watched in astonishment as Kaufmann sailed a long pass to McLean for an easy 91-yard touchdown. The inspired Aggies widened their lead to 17-0 by halftime, but the favored Longhorns scored once in the third quarter and punched out two touchdowns in the fourth to win.

1967 — A&M 10, TEXAS 7

This game served as a dramatic climax to the Aggies' turnaround, going from an 0-4 start to win six straight SWC games and earn the school's first Cotton Bowl bid in 26 years. Texas took a 7-3 lead on Bill Bradley's 2-yard dive early in the fourth quarter, but A&M quickly wiped it out when Edd Hargett and Bob Long teamed on an 80-yard touchdown pass the first play after kickoff. Texas' last threat died at the A&M 15-yard line when Buster Adami made a backward lunge to intercept Bradley's pass.

1990 — TEXAS 28, A&M 27

The Longhorns' last SWC victory over A&M in Austin came hard, and it was scary near the end. Tailback Darren Lewis led the Aggies' early dominance that saw them pound out a 14-0 lead while outgaining Texas in total yards, 153-8. Texas' offense and defense then took charge for a couple of quarters to lead the Longhorns to a 21-14 lead. But A&M tied it again, 21-21, early in the fourth quarter. Texas quarterback Peter Gardere capped another drive with an 11-yard touchdown run, but A&M marched again. Quarterback Bucky Richardson scored on a 32-yard bootleg and, with slightly less than four minutes left, the Aggies lined up to go for two points on the conversion play. Blitzing linebacker Brian Jones forced Richardson to pitch early and deep to Lewis, and cornerback Mark Berry stopped him at the 5. Texas finished 8-0 in the SWC, wrapping up its last trip to the Cotton Classic.

A&M's defense was the key in the Aggies' 34-13 victory in 1992. Defensive back Aaron Glenn, right, returned an interception 95 yards for a touchdown. Below, linebacker Jason Atkinson harasses UT quarterback Peter Gardere.

"went home" to Alabama after the 1957 season. But his 1956 seniors, survivors of Bryant's first thin, struggling 1-9 team in 1954, will always savor that win.

"We knew we were good, but we were afraid to get too excited until it was over," said Gene Stallings, a senior end who returned to his alma mater as head coach in 1965-71 and now coaches Alabama. "A&M has a history of messing up in Austin. But we had a great celebration in the locker room. I still have a picture in my house of the seniors with coach Bryant."

WHAT GOES AROUND... R.C. Slocum knows from personal experience why Gene Stallings cherishes that photo from the '56 victory over the Longhorns.

"I have an old friend in Orange, Homer Barksdale Hill Stark, whose father, Lutcher Stark, was a powerful UT regent in the '30s and a lifelong supporter of the Longhorns," he said. "But Homer loved the Aggies and went to A&M while his twin brother, Bill, went to Texas. I was lucky that Homer started taking me to the A&M-Texas game when I was just a youngster. I grew up absorbed in the excitement and emotion of the game. Now I feel humbled and honored to be part of it."

Half the diners in that barbecue stand in Llano are glad he is, too.

R.C. Slocum, wearing his Cotton Bowl hat, and the 1993 Aggies celebrate an 18-9 victory.

College Station
Aggieland Today

The women of Texas A&M love their school as strongly as the men of Texas A&M.

Brooke Leslie grew up on a ranch near the little Central Texas town of Glen Rose. Active in Future Farmers of America and 4-H programs in high school, she earned a full FFA scholarship to Texas A&M's College of Agricultural Administration. Delighted to receive a free education, she enrolled as a freshman in August 1990 with the goal of entering a top law school elsewhere upon graduation.

"I really knew nothing about the spirit and traditions of A&M when I arrived," she said. "As soon as I got there I just fell in love with the school and the people. A&M is like one big family. I sensed this my first day on campus when I saw friendly people hurrying everywhere. These were just 42,000 friends I hadn't met yet."

Brooke Leslie became the first female president of the Texas A&M Student Body in 1994-95.

Brooke seems to have met them all during her years at Aggieland. Four years later, she became the first female president of the student body in Texas A&M history, drawing 61 percent of the vote in the student government election for 1994-95.

The resulting media attention to her election at a school once famous as a male bastion stirred lots of reaction across the nation, but not on the A&M campus.

"We're in the '90s and A&M has been a large, diversified coed institution for more than 30 years," said Brooke, a statuesque young woman who entered her second year of law school at the University of Texas in the fall of 1996. At A&M, she was active in campus government from her freshman year and was selected to be Cotton Bowl Classic Queen for the thrilling Aggies-Notre Dame game on New Year's Day 1994. "I ran on the platform that I was the best candidate, with the most experience and the best ideas."

AGGIE QUIZ

39. What was Gene Stallings' position on Bear Bryant's Alabama staff before he returned to A&M as head coach in 1965?

Her career at A&M seems quite typical of Aggieland today, where a large, enthusiastic female enrollment is an asset in attracting heavily-recruited young players to a highly successful football program.

These Aggie football players can not envision the school without women.

"An all-male school?" mused quarterback Branndon Stewart. "I don't think I could handle that."

And A&M football games surely would not have become the tremendous experience they are today without female Aggies.

Said Leslie: "You hear a lot about the Spirit of Aggieland and the 12th Man but you never know what it is until you're standing there with 70,000 crazy fans, yelling, swinging, swaying. When you have 40,000 students yelling and singing the "Aggie War Hymn" in synch, it's an amazing experience."

Aggieland veterans like football coach R.C. Slocum and 1957 Heisman Trophy winner and All-American halfback John David Crow also love the chemistry and emotional electricity on the campus today.

"A thriving coed institution and a strong football program go hand in hand," said Slocum, who began his 24th year on the A&M staff as the Aggies began competition in the new Big 12 Conference in the fall of 1996. "If you don't have an attractive university, you can't recruit good players. Conversely, our football program is a great showcase for all of the excitement at A&M — the kids, the campus, Kyle Field, the spirit and tradition. This has interested a lot of outstanding young students in coming to school here."

Crow's A&M experience began in 1954 when he was Bear Bryant's first prized recruit. He shakes his head

AGGIE QUIZ

40. *What was the combined winning percentage for Emory Bellard, Tom Wilson and Jackie Sherill from 1972-88?*

Perhaps the most delightful Aggie tradition is observed each time A&M scores a touchdown or field goal. The Aggie gets to kiss his or her date. During some long-ago lean seasons, Aggies reportedly got to kiss their dates after every first down.

when he recalls the gray, grim look of a much smaller all-male school.

"No question this would be a struggling university if it hadn't changed back in the '60s and welcomed females into the student body," said Crow, formerly athletic director and now director of development for the athletic department. "General Rudder and the powers-that-be did it gradually the first few years but in the early '70s the boom began. Pretty soon half of our enrollment was female. But the beauty of all this is how none of our traditions were destroyed. They just expanded. The Corps of Cadets is much smaller today (approximately 2,000 members) but it remains a key part of A&M and there are female members, too."

This pleases two generations of the Crow family. Daughter Jeannie graduated from A&M and feels just as strongly about the school as her dad.

"She didn't want anything to change either," he said. "When you hear that band and watch it marching across the field, it's a wonderful thrill for Aggies of all ages. The more kids come here, the more they want it to remain the same. There's still a small-town atmosphere on the campus but Bryan-College Station is the heart of a trade area with 250,000 population. You also have the influences of Houston and Dallas, which aren't that distant in these days of modern transportation."

So A&M in the '90s is a delightful blend of old and

Coeds mingle at a campus cookout in 1996. That wasn't always the case when A&M was an all-male institution.

new. Like Brooke Leslie, plenty of other female Aggies will always love the school.

Karin Chavis is a native of tiny Red Oak, N.C., who "lived out in the woods" on the family farm as a young girl. She developed her love for jazz singing as she listened for countless hours to her mother's record collection of legends like Ella Fitzgerald, Billie Holliday, Sarah Vaughn, Carmen MacRae and Nancy Wilson. Her love for Texas A&M would come much later.

She entered the University of North Carolina in 1982 but suddenly found herself transferring to A&M in August of 1984. Karin was following her heart, having married a young Wake Forest graduate who had received a fellowship at A&M.

That love didn't last, ending in divorce five years later, but two special loves have endured. One is for her 11-year-old son, Steve. The other is for A&M.

"I thought I'd never be anything but a Tar Heel, but A&M grows on you," said Karin, who graduated in 1988 with a degree in industrial sociology and now is employee relations manager at A&M.

She is married to Dr. Craig Blakely, associate director of policy research at A&M and they have a son, Hunter Boone, born in January of '96. Karin has become a

Aggie enthusiasm breaks out at this cookout in 1996.

A former North Carolina Tar Heel, Karin Chavis is now a proud Aggie. Another of her loves is jazz singing.

successful jazz singer in her own right, blessed with a wide-ranging voice that is both lovely and lusty. She travels to Austin clubs a few nights each month and delights audiences with renditions from Ella Fitzgerald to Aretha Franklin. But she's always glad to return home. Now A&M represents everything dearest to her.

"You get tied in here," Karin said. "You're at a football game, singing the "Aggie War Hymn" and when you get to 'saw Varsity's horns off' you grab the person's waist on each side and begin swaying. You're kin — and that's kinda neat."

Dr. Sallie Sheppard, a College Station native who was among the first female students to enter A&M in the fall of '63, found it much the same in those first days of coeducation at Aggieland. Today she's a key administrator at A&M, the assistant provost for undergraduate programs and academic services and cherishes the enduring traditions.

"Aggie football always has been exciting," she said. "The 12th Man spirit was here when I entered A&M and it still is."

Karen Arrington was fresh out of Brazosport High School in 1973 when she entered A&M but she already was imbued with Aggie spirit, thanks to a campus visit in the spring of '72 on the weekend of the spring football game.

"I was so taken with the friendliness of A&M," Karen said. "No one passed you without saying hello. I couldn't wait to go to school there. Once the spirit of Aggieland touches your heart, it's with you forever."

Karen loved the A&M experience but she graduated

AGGIE QUIZ

41. What was the combined winning percentage for Jim Myers, Hank Foldberg and Gene Stalling from 1958-71?

with a degree in journalism a year early, with the Centennial Class of 1976, the first to be 51 percent female. "That was right after Watergate and there was mushrooming interest in journalism all over the country. I thought the sooner I graduated, the better my chances for a good newspaper job."

Her fast pace, and her ability, paid off. Karen worked a year on the *Abilene Reporter News* as a copy editor, then became the first female member of the *Dallas Morning News* sports staff. Two and a half years later she transferred to the travel department to become assistant travel editor and since January of 1981 has been travel editor. She and David Jordan, a native of Florida and graduate of DeVry Institute in Atlanta, married in May of 1982. David soon became as avid about Aggie football as his wife.

A 1972 spring football game helped lure Karen Jordan to Texas A&M.

"We belong to the 12th Man Foundation, have season tickets and go to all the Aggie home games and lot on the road," she said. "And now that we have Lauren (age 5), she goes to College Station with us. She gets in the middle of the pregame excitement around the campus, then stays in a day-care center during the game. But it won't be too much longer before she'll go to the games, too."

Look for Lauren Jordan to enter A&M in about 2009.

"Now we have plenty of Aggie mothers," Slocum said. "A second generation of female Aggies is coming in."

Kara Wilson, winner of the Aggie Spirit Award on Parents Weekend in April '96 as a sophomore, first visited Aggieland in August '92. She traveled 2,400 miles from her home in Fossil, Oregon (population 500) to spend three months in an oxygen therapy experiment at A&M's Beutel Health Center.

"That's when I started falling in love with Texas A&M," Kara said.

AGGIE QUIZ

42. World record-holder and Olympic shot put champion Randy Matson — an A&M alum — did not play football for the Aggies, but he was drafted. Which NFL team picked him?

Kara, bitten by a tick when she was six years old, has Lyme Disease and must always use a wheelchair. As soon as she arrived at A&M to participate in the experiment, she was befriended by Aggies from across the campus. Stephen Ruth, the student body president for 1992-93, took Kara to Midnight Yell Practice before a football game, and she was hooked.

"I was astounded by the bond between students, alumni and the football team," she said. "There was no doubt in my mind I was going to A&M when I finished high school. I didn't care that it was a long way from home. I'd go around the world to be an Aggie."

Kara entered A&M in August of '94 and soon was hustling around the campus in her motorized wheelchair, busy with classes and meeting new friends.

Kara became active on campus and served as

HUMPING IT

The 12th Man, the A&M student body, always stands throughout the game. But when it's time to yell, everyone bends forward with hands placed just above knees, properly aligning the back, mouth and throat for maximum volume. In Aggieland, this is known as "humping it."

During the game, Aggie yell leaders use hand signals to identify the next yell. Students on the first row in the stands pick up the signal and pass it up row by row until the entire student body knows what is coming up. The resulting roar never fails to awe non-Aggies.

An Aggieland tradition.

president of the Margaret Rudder Hall council, where she became close friends with the namesake, the widow of legendary Aggie Earl Rudder. "She's a little light in my life — a mother and a friend," Kara said.

"I've never known anyone with more spirit and love for this school than Kara," said Margaret Rudder, who might have known more Aggies than anyone in history. "Just being around her makes you feel better about life."

Kara has competed in barrel racing at rodeos since high school, riding on a special saddle which enables her to put her legs over the pommel and on the horse's neck. "And once a week the Cavalry lets me ride one of their

horses," she said. "It's really neat. That's my way of walking."

Kara, looking up from her wheelchair with an infectious smile, always will stand tall in the best tradition of Aggieland.

"For six years after I was bitten by that tick, my problem was misdiagnosed as rheumatoid arthritis," she said. "If they had caught it immediately I wouldn't have wound up in this wheelchair."

Then that smile broadened. "I have no regrets. Otherwise, I wouldn't be an Aggie."

Kara Wilson, shown here with Cadet Alex King and A&M mascot Reveille VI, has become good friends with Margaret Rudder, wife of the Aggies' greatest hero.

Aggies In The
Bowl Games

1922 DIXIE CLASSIC

Texas A&M 22, Centre College 14
Fair Park Stadium, Dallas, Jan. 2, 1922

A&M's first postseason game remains its most historic. In a moment of grand inspiration, Aggie Coach D.X. Bible created the tradition of the 12th Man and his battered, thin team proceeded to upset a heavily-favored opponent that had allowed only six points all season.

Fair Park Stadium, located on the site where the Cotton Bowl now stands, had no dressing rooms so both squads changed into their uniforms at their downtown hotels before riding to the State Fairgrounds in a fleet of taxis. Bible saw all of his players off from their hotel, then invited E. King Gill, a reserve end he had excused from football in early December to join the basketball team, to ride with him.

Bible asked Gill to sit in the press box and spot Aggie players for Waco sportswriter Jinx Tucker. "But be ready to play," Bible told Gill. "I may send for you."

The Aggie defense played a tremendous first half. The powerful visitors from Kentucky, coached by former Aggie Coach Charley Moran, were stopped twice on the A&M 1-foot line in the second quarter and the Aggies led, 2-0, thanks to a first-quarter safety when T.F. (Puny) Wilson tackled a Centre ball carrier in the Colonels' end zone. Injuries had hit Bible's starting lineup hard, however, and he sent his manager to the press box to fetch Gill.

On the sideline, Bible told Gill to go under the stands and put on an injured Aggie's uniform while the other man slipped into Gill's street clothes. Then he told Gill to stand beside him during the second half in case he needed to send him into the game.

Gill didn't play that day but the sight of this 12th Man ready to help his team and his school excited every Aggie in Fair Park Stadium that day. Since then every Aggie has stood throughout every A&M football game, symbolic of their support for their team.

The Aggies, 5-1-2 for the regular season, were considered as much as 40-point underdogs to Centre and their victory was the rage of college football. "They were imbued with the fighting spirit the Aggies have always shown," Bible said.

Moran accepted the upset gracefully.

"The Aggies displayed the old fighting spirit, and I am

free to state that I had rather be whipped by them than any other eleven," he said.

Texas A&M	2	0	14	6	— **22**
Centre	0	0	7	7	— **14**

A&M — Safety, Puny Wilson tackled Bartlett in end zone
Centre — Snoddy, 3 run (Roberts kick)
A&M — H.J. Evans, 15 pass from Puny Wilson (W.G. McMillan kick)
A&M — Puny Wilson, 5 run (W.G. McMillan kick)
A&M — Ted Winn, 45 interception return (kick failed)
Centre — Covington, 2 pass from McMillin (Roberts kick)
Attendance — 20,000

1940 SUGAR BOWL

#1 Texas A&M 14, #4 Tulane 13
Tulane Stadium, New Orleans, Jan. 1, 1940

All-American fullback John Kimbrough lived up to his nickname of Jarrin' Jawn as he powered the Aggies to a fourth-quarter comeback that secured their claim to the 1939 national championship.

Kimbrough battered the Tulane defense for 159 yards on 25 carries and scored both A&M touchdowns, and Homer Norton's team finished with an 11-0 record.

Herbie Smith blocked the extra-point kick after Tulane scored its second touchdown to go ahead, 13-7. That play left the Aggies with a chance to win with one

Edd Hargett, shown here against Texas, completed 10 of 20 passes for two touchdowns in the 1968 Cotton Bowl, in which A&M defeated Alabama, 20-16.

touchdown march and they cashed in.

The Aggies, fueled by Kimbrough's smashes at the middle of the Tulane defense, drove 69 yards for the touchdown to tie it, 13-13. Jim Thomason then kicked the extra point to seal the school's only national title.

Texas A&M	7	0	0	7	— **14**
Tulane	0	7	0	6	— **13**

A&M — John Kimbrough, 11 run (Jim Thomason kick)
Tulane — Kellogg 76 punt return (Thiabut kick)
Tulane — Butler 1 run (kick blocked by Herbie Smith)
A&M — John Kimbrough 24 run (Jim Thomason kick)
Attendance — 72,000

1941 COTTON BOWL

#6 Texas A&M 13, #12 Fordham 12
Cotton Bowl, Dallas, Jan. 1, 1941

This was a memorable day for a couple of Smiths and the largest crowd ever to see a football game in the Southwest — a sellout 45,507.

Before the opening kickoff the crowd stood and joined Kate Smith in singing her greatest hit, "God Bless America." Later, Aggie halfback Earl "Bama" Smith ignited his team with one spectacular pass catch.

He was the receiver when A&M Coach Homer Norton used his pet "hideout play" to perfection to take charge of the game in the third quarter. The Rams, who held a 6-0 halftime lead, didn't notice Bama Smith trotting to the sideline as his teammates broke their huddle and lined up.

Smith, standing just inside the field of play, was the 11th Aggie on the field and an eligible pass receiver. When the ball was snapped, Smith sped undetected far downfield and caught a 62-yard touchdown pass from quarterback Marion Pugh to pull the Aggies even at 6-6.

A&M moved ahead to stay when fullback John Kimbrough banged over from the 1-yard line to climax a long drive. Pugh, who missed his extra-point kick after the first touchdowns, converted this time to make the score 13-6.

A fierce rush by tackle Martin Ruby to deflect Fordham tackle Steve Hudsack's kick for the tying extra point after Fordham's fourth quarter touchdown saved the victory for the Aggies.

Hudsack, hoping to redeem himself for his errant kick after the Rams' first touchdown, kicked the ball straight and solid but Ruby's hands deflected the ball into a high arc. The ball came down on the crossbar of the goalposts and bounced back, no good.

The game launched a long stretch of A&M appearances in the Cotton Bowl Classic. It was the Aggies' first of nine appearances in the Dallas game over a stretch of 53 years.

```
Fordham        0    6    0    6   — 12
Texas A&M      0    0   13    0   — 13
```
Fordham — Filipowicz 2 run (kick failed)
A&M — Bama Smith 62 pass from Marion Pugh (kick failed)
A&M — John Kimbrough 1 run (Marion Pugh kick)
Fordham — Blumenstock 15 run (kick blocked by Martin Ruby)
Attendance — 45,507

1942 COTTON BOWL

#20 Alabama 29, #9 Texas A&M 21
Cotton Bowl, Dallas, Jan. 1, 1942

In one of the goofiest games in college bowl history, the Aggies made 13 first downs to Alabama's one and out-gained the Crimson Tide in total offense, 309-65, and lost.

Turnovers did in A&M.

The Aggies committed 12, losing the football seven times on pass interceptions and five more on fumbles. Alabama, forced to punt 16 times by a rugged Aggie defense, still managed to outscore a bumbling Aggie offense and went home a surprise winner.

This game was played just 24 days after America was drawn into World War II by the Japanese attack on Pearl Harbor and most of Homer Norton's players undoubtedly were preoccupied with thoughts of their military duty to their country. Texas A&M went on to send more commissioned officers to service in WW II than the United States Military Academy.

```
Alabama        0    7   13    9   — 29
Texas A&M      0    7    0   14   — 21
```
A&M — Harold Cowley 12 pass from Leo Daniels (Jake Webster kick)
Alabama — Craft 8 run (Hecht kick)
Alabama — Jimmy Nelson 72 punt return (Hecht kick)
Alabama — Jimmy Nelson 21 run (kick blocked)
Alabama — Hecht 31 FG
Alabama — Rast 10 interception return (kick failed)
A&M — Jake Webster 1 run (Webster kick)
A&M — James Sterling 35 pass from Derace Moser (Webster kick)
Attendance — 33,000

1944 ORANGE BOWL

Louisiana State 19, Texas A&M 14
Orange Bowl, Miami, Jan. 1, 1944

Homer Norton's 1943 "Kiddie Korps" was an eager gang of teenagers, freshmen and sophomores excited about playing a season of college football before they were called to wartime military duty. They surprised the nation with a 28-13 upset of LSU at Baton Rouge during a 7-2-1 regular season, but they couldn't duplicate that feat in the Orange Bowl.

Steve Van Buren, a future Hall of Fame halfback, was involved in all of LSU's scoring. He ran for 172 yards, scored two touchdowns, passed for another and kicked one extra point.

Aggie quarterback Babe Hallmark countered with two

touchdown passes but A&M's defense never stopped Van Buren.

Texas A&M	7	0	7	0	—14
LSU	12	0	7	0	—19

LSU — Steve Van Buren 11 run (kick failed)
A&M — Jesse Burditt 20 pass from Babe Hallmark (Stanley Turner kick)
LSU — Goode 21 pass from Steve Van Buren (kick failed)
LSU — Steve Van Buren 63 run (Van Buren kick)
A&M — Marion Settegast 25 pass from Babe Hallmark (Stanley Turner kick)
Attendance — 27,000

1950 PRESIDENTIAL CUP

Texas A&M 40, Georgia 20
Byrd Stadium, College Park, Md., Dec. 8, 1950

Fullback Bob Smith celebrated the Aggies' first post-season action in seven seasons with an awesome perform-ance, contributing 301 yards to A&M's runaway victory.

Smith opened the game with a 100-yard kickoff return for a touchdown and later sped 81 yards from scrimmage for another as A&M built a 33-0 halftime lead. Smith, who had rushed for 1,320 yards in the regular season, added 160 yards on 20 carries against the Bulldogs. In addition to that 100-yard kickoff return, he gained 121 yards on punt returns, 22 yards receiving and five yards passing.

In Harry Stiteler's final game as Aggie head coach, Billy Tidwell rushed for three more touchdowns and

Curtis Dickey, shown here avoiding Texas tacklers, racked up 276 yards rushing from his tailback position in the 1978 Hall of Fame Bowl. The Aggies beat Iowa State, 28-12, in that bowl.

Glenn Lippman one.

Georgia	0	0	7	13	— **20**
Texas A&M	20	14	6	0	— **40**

A&M —Bob Smith 100 kickoff return (Darrow Hooper kick)
A&M — Glenn Lippman 2 run (kick failed)
A&M — Bob Smith 81 run (Darrow Hooper kick)
Georgia — Morocco 30 run (Durand kick)
A&M — Billy Tidwell 6 run (Darrow Hooper kick)
A&M — Billy Tidwell 6 run (Darrow Hooper kick)
A&M — Billy Tidwell 36 run (kick failed)
Georgia — Morocco 65 punt return (Durand kick)
Georgia — Hargrove 1 run (kick failed)
Attendance — 12,245

1957 GATOR BOWL

#13 Tennessee 3, #9 Texas A&M 0
Gator Bowl, Jacksonville, Fla., Dec. 27, 1957

The Aggies, 8-0 and ranked No. 1 in mid-November, suffered their third straight narrow loss in Coach Bear Bryant's final game of his four-year A&M career.

The Aggies, who finished the regular season with a 7-6 loss to Rice and a 9-7 loss to Texas, managed little offense in this rugged defensive battle. Heisman Trophy halfback John David Crow tried valiantly to ignite the Aggie attack but both teams slugged it out between the 35-yard lines until late in the game, when the Vols inched close enough to kick a short field goal.

The crowd of 43,709 was a Gator Bowl record.

Tennessee	0	0	0	3	— **3**
Texas A&M	0	0	0	0	— **0**

Tennessee —Burklow 17 FG
Attendance — 43,709

1968 COTTON BOWL

Texas A&M 20, #8 Alabama 16
Cotton Bowl, Dallas, Jan. 1, 1968

The Aggies climaxed a terrific turnaround in sensational style as Gene Stallings, a former player under Bear Bryant, coached A&M to a thrilling upset of his old A&M coach.

Bryant appeared almost as happy about Stallings' success as the young Aggie coach. At the final gun, Bryant met Stallings at midfield with a grin and a big hug that lifted Stallings off the soggy field like he was a child.

Thus the Aggies finished the long road back from a deflating 0-4 start that began on national television with underdog SMU driving the length of the field with a whiz-bang passing attack in the final minute to win, 20-17, at College Station. But Stallings and his players kept the faith and pulled off a 7-0 stretch run climaxed by a much happier show on national television on New Year's Day.

Alabama	7	3	6	0	— **16**
Texas A&M	7	6	7	0	— **20**

Alabama — Ken Stabler 3 run (Davis kick)
A&M — Larry Stegent 13 pass from Edd Hargett (Charlie Riggs kick)

Alabama — Davis 36 FG
A&M — Tommy Maxwell 7 pass from Edd Hargett (kick failed)
A&M — Wendell Housley 20 run (Charlie Riggs kick)
Alabama — Ken Stabler 2 run (run failed)
Attendance — 73,800

1975 LIBERTY BOWL

Southern California 20, #6 Texas A&M 0
Liberty Bowl, Memphis, Tenn., Dec. 22, 1975

The Aggies, 10-0 princes after beating Texas on national television on Thanksgiving weekend, continued to look more like frogs in their third straight national showcase game.

Still listless after ending their regular season with a 31-6 loss at Arkansas in early December that cost them a possible national title, Emory Bellard's Aggies were easy pickings for a USC team rebounding from four straight losses. This was John McKay's final game as head coach before taking over the NFL Tampa Bay Buccaneers and the Trojans sent him off happy.

Southern Cal	3	17	0	0	**— 20**
Texas A&M	0	0	0	0	**— 0**

USC — Walker 45 FG
USC — Tatupu 1 run (Walker kick)
USC — Walker 40 FG
USC — Bell 76 pass from Evans (Walker kick)
Attendance — 52,129

1977 SUN BOWL

#10 Texas A&M 37, #20 Florida 14
Sun Bowl, El Paso, Tex., Jan. 2, 1977

The Aggies closed a 10-2 season with a bang, dominating the Gators in almost every phase of the game with kicker Tony Franklin and fullback George Woodard in starring roles.

Franklin, the barefoot Aggie with the powerful leg, highlighted his three field goals with an NCAA bowl-record 62-yarder as A&M breezed to a 16-0 halftime lead. Woodard, a thunderous 250-pounder, scored three touchdowns and rushed for 124 yards.

The Aggie defense also had a great impact, forcing five turnovers and flattening Florida with minus 12 yards total offense in the decisive second quarter.

Florida	0	0	7	7	**— 14**
Texas A&M	3	13	8	13	**— 37**

A&M — Tony Franklin 39 FG
A&M — David Walker 9 run (Tony Franklin kick)
A&M — Tony Franklin 62 FG
A&M — Tony Franklin 33 FG
A&M — George Woodard 1 run (Woodard run)
Florida — Chandler 29 run (Posey kick)
A&M — Woodard 4 run (Tony Franklin kick)
Florida — LeCount 1 run (Posey kick)
A&M — Woodard 15 pass from Walker (kick failed)
Attendance — 33,252

1977 BLUEBONNET BOWL

#20 Southern California 47, #17 Texas A&M 28
Astrodome, Houston, Tex., Dec. 31, 1977

The Aggies jumped to a quick 14-0 lead but then
were overwhelmed by a Trojan horse.

Rob Hertel was his name and passing was his game.
The USC quarterback threw four touchdown passes as
his team scored 34 unanswered points that forced A&M
to settle for an 8-4 season.

The Aggies punched in 14 fourth-quarter points to
make it look a little closer than it actually was. Fullback
George Woodard and quarterback Mike Mosley gave
great statistical performances, rushing for 185 and 184
yards, but they couldn't overcome five lost A&M
fumbles that helped switch the early momentum to USC.

Southern Cal	7	13	14	13	— **47**
Texas A&M	14	0	0	14	— **28**

A&M — George Woodard 3 run (Tony Franklin kick)
A&M — Mike Mosley 44 run (Tony Franklin kick)
USC — Sweeney 29 pass from Hertel (Jordan kick)
USC — White 25 pass from Hertel (Jordan kick)
USC — Jordan 22 FG
USC — Jordan 29 FG
USC — Sweeney 40 pass from Hertel (Burns pass from Hertel)
USC — Simmrin 14 pass from Hertel (kick failed)
A&M — George Woodard 1 run (Tony Franklin kick)
USC — Ford 94 run (run failed)
USC — Tatupu 8 run (Jordan kick)
A&M — Adger Armstrong 4 run (Tony Franklin kick)
Attendance — 52,842

1978 HALL OF FAME BOWL

Texas A&M 28, Iowa State 12
Legion Field, Birmingham, Ala., Dec. 20, 1978

Tom Wilson, interim head coach since Emory
Bellard's abrupt resignation in mid-season, closed on a
high note as Curtis Dickey raced for 276 yards on 34
carries. The Aggies finished 8-4 and were 4-2 under
Wilson, who was named permanent head coach and
given a new contract.

Dickey's 276 yards was the second highest single
game rushing total in A&M history, 21 behind Bob
Smith's 297 against SMU in 1950.

Texas A&M	0	14	0	14	— **28**
Iowa State	0	6	6	0	— **12**

ISU — Green 5 pass from Grant (kick failed)
A&M — David Brothers 1 run (Tony Franklin kick)
A&M — Gerald Carter 4 pass from Mike Mosley (Tony Franklin kick)
ISU — Green 28 run (pass failed)
A&M — Curtis Dickey 19 run (Tony Franklin kick)
A&M — Adger Armstrong 5 run (Tony Franklin kick)
Attendance — 41,150

1981 INDEPENDENCE BOWL

Texas A&M 33, Oklahoma State 16
Fair Park Stadium, Shreveport, La., Dec. 12, 1981

In what proved to be Tom Wilson's final game as head coach, quarterback Gary Kubiak and halfback Ernest Jackson led the Aggies' awesome offensive display that netted 448 yards. Meanwhile, A&M defenders limited the potent Cowboys attack to 257 yards.

Kubiak passed for 253 yards, hitting 15 of 20 that included touchdown throws of 50 and 38 yards to flanker Jimmie Williams. Jackson rushed for 123 yards.

The victory enabled the Aggies to finish 7-5, giving Wilson a 21-19 record in three and a half seasons.

Oklahoma State	7	3	0	6	— **16**
Texas A&M	3	17	6	7	— **33**

OSU — Anderson 1 run (Roach kick)
A&M — David Hardy 33 FG
OSU — Roach 42 FG
A&M — Jimmie Williams 50 pass from Gary Kubiak (David Hardy kick)
A&M — Jimmie Williams 38 pass from Gary Kubiak (David Hardy kick)
A&M — David Hardy 50 FG
A&M — David Hardy 18 FG
OSU — Orange 5 run (run failed)
A&M — Johnny Hector 4 run (David Hardy kick)
Attendance — 47,300

Rod Bernstine (29) looks for room to run during A&M's 36-16 victory against Auburn and Bo Jackson in the 1986 Cotton Bowl.

1986 COTTON BOWL

#11 Texas A&M 36, #16 Auburn 16
Cotton Bowl, Dallas, Jan. 1, 1986

The Aggies' fired-up defense stopped Heisman Trophy winner Bo Jackson on four tries at the A&M end

zone early in the fourth quarter to repulse Auburn's last shot at the lead. Then the versatile offense padded a 21-16 lead for a relatively easy victory.

It was A&M's first Cotton Bowl Classic appearance in 18 years and the second straight in which the Aggies beat a national power from the state of Alabama. In the 1968 game, A&M edged Alabama, 20-16.

Quarterback Kevin Murray set a Cotton Bowl Classic record by passing for 292 yards, but strong safety Domingo Bryant was voted the A&M's Outstanding Player with two pass interceptions, the second setting up the last Aggie touchdown.

| Auburn | 7 | 6 | 3 | 0 | — 16 |
| Texas A&M | 12 | 3 | 6 | 15 | — 36 |

Auburn — Bo Jackson 5 run (Johnson kick)
A&M — Harry Johnson 11 run (kick failed)
A&M — Keith Woodside 22 run (pass failed)
Auburn — Bo Jackson 73 pass from Washington (run failed)
A&M — Scott Slater 26 FG
A&M — Toney 21 run (pass failed)
Auburn — Johnson 26 FG
A&M — Keith Woodside 9 pass from Kevin Murray (Rod Bernstine run)
A&M — Anthony Toney 1 run (Scott Slater kick)
Attendance — 73,157

1987 COTTON BOWL

#13 Ohio State 28, #8 Texas A&M 12
Cotton Bowl, Dallas, Jan. 1, 1987

This was a nightmarish afternoon of turnovers for the Aggies. Quarterback Kevin Murray, in what would be his final game for A&M, threw five interceptions, two of which were returned for touchdowns.

Fullback Roger Vick was one of the few bright spots for A&M, rushing for 113 yards on 24 carries, including the only Aggie touchdown. Vick was voted Outstanding Player for A&M.

| Ohio State | 0 | 7 | 14 | 7 | — 28 |
| Texas A&M | 3 | 3 | 0 | 6 | — 12 |

A&M — Scott Slater 30 FG
OSU — Karsatos 3 run (Frantz kick)
A&M — Scott Slater 44 FG
OSU — Spielman 24 interception return (Frantz kick)
OSU — Workman 8 run (Frantz kick)
A&M — Roger Vick 2 run (pass failed)
OSU — Kee 49 interception return (Frantz kick)
Attendance — 74,188

1988 COTTON BOWL

#13 Texas A&M 35, #12 Notre Dame 10
Cotton Bowl, Dallas, Jan. 1, 1988

Notre Dame Heisman Trophy winner Tim Brown returned to his hometown and gave the Fighting Irish an early lead with a 17-yard touchdown catch, but the Aggies took charge in the second quarter and then dominated the second half.

Freshman quarterback Bucky Richardson was voted A&M's Outstanding Player, and he certainly was. Bucky rushed for 96 yards and scored twice as A&M's powerful running game rolled over Notre Dame.

Notre Dame	7	3	0	0	— 10
Texas A&M	3	15	7	10	— 35

ND — Tim Brown 17 pass from Andrysiak (Gradel kick)
A&M — Scott Slater 26 FG
ND — Gradel 36 FG
A&M — Tony Thompson 24 pass from Darren Lewis (Scott Slater kick)
A&M — Larry Horton 2 run (Wally Hartley run)
A&M — Bucky Richardson 1 run (Scott Slater kick)
A&M — Scott Slater 25 FG
A&M — Bucky Richardson 8 run (Scott Slater kick)
Attendance — 73,006

1989 JOHN HANCOCK BOWL

#23 Pittsburgh 31, #16 Texas A&M 28
Sun Bowl, El Paso, Tex., Dec. 30, 1989

In one of the best spectator bowl games ever, Pitt finally outlasted the Aggies when quarterback Alex Van Pelt connected with wide receiver Henry Tuten on a 44-yard touchdown pass with 2:19 left to play. The Aggies thus lost for the third time in the closing minutes under first-year Coach R.C. Slocum and finished with an 8-4 record.

Fullback Robert Wilson rushed for 145 yards on 16 carries to lead a 252-yard rushing performance by the Aggies.

Pittsburgh	7	10	7	7	— 31
Texas A&M	7	3	12	6	— 28

Pitt — Richards 12 run (Frazier kick)
A&M — Lance Pavlas 9 run (Layne Talbot kick)
Pitt — Frazier 24 FG
A&M — Layne Talbot 39 FG
Pitt — Redmond 8 pass from Van Pelt (Frazier kick)
Pitt — Van Pelt 1 run (Frazier kick)
A&M — Keith McAfee 31 run (run failed)
A&M — Keith McAgee 1 run (pass failed)
A&M — Randy Simmons 5 run (run failed)
Pitt — Tuten 44 pass from Van Pelt (Frazier kick)
Attendance — 44,887

1990 HOLIDAY BOWL

#19 Texas A&M 65, #9 Brigham Young 14
Jack Murphy Stadium, San Diego, Calif., Dec. 29, 1990

Quarterback Bucky Richardson, who missed the 1989 season with a knee injury, climaxed his comeback year with 322 yards in total offense (203 passing, 119 rushing). Bucky figured in four touchdowns — running for two, passing for a third and catching a pass for a fourth.

This was one of the brightest nights in A&M history and one of BYU's darkest. The Aggies outgained the vaunted Cougar attack, 680-185. BYU was limited to minus 12 yards rushing and Heisman Trophy quarterback Ty Detmer completed only 11 of 23 passes for 120 yards before leaving with a shoulder injury.

Texas A&M	14	23	7	21	— **65**
Brigham Young	7	0	7	0	— **14**

A&M — Robert Wilson 1 run (Layne Talbot kick)
BYU — C. Smith 8 pass from Detmer (Kauffman kick)
A&M — Darren Lewis 6 run (Layne Talbot kick)
A&M — Bucky Richardson 6 run (Layne Talbot kick)
A&M — Safety
A&M — Bucky Richardson 22 pass from Darren Lewis (Layne Talbot kick)
A&M — Shane Garrett 6 pass from Bucky Richardson (Layne Talbot kick)
BYU — B. Clark 1 pass from Evans (Kauffman kick)
A&M — Bucky Richardson 27 run (Layne Talbot kick)
A&M — Darren Lewis 3 run (Layne Talbot kick)
A&M — Cornelius Patterson 14 pass from Lance Pavlas (Layne Talbot kick)
A&M — Shane Krahl 9 pass from Lance Pavlas (Layne Talbot kick)
Attendance — 61,441

1992 COTTON BOWL

#5 Florida State 10, #9 Texas A&M 2
Cotton Bowl, Dallas, Jan. 1, 1992

A&M's lusty defense deserved a better fate.

Early in the game, halfback Greg Hill sprinted 39 yards toward the end zone but fumbled the ball through the end zone when he was hit on the Florida State 2-yard line. The Seminoles were awarded possession on the 1.

Two possessions later, an Aggie receiver dropped a

Aggie quarterback Gary Kubiak passed for 255 yards and three touchdowns to lead A&M to a 33-16 victory against Oklahoma State in the 1981 Independence Bowl.

sure touchdown pass in the end zone. In the second quarter, safety Chris Crooms returned an interception 42 yards for an apparent touchdown but he stepped out of bounds on the 26-yard line.

FSU managed only 280 yards against A&M's No. 1-ranked defense but the Aggie offense did worse, gaining only 180 yards.

Texas A&M	2	0	0	0	— 2
Florida State	7	0	0	3	— 10

A&M — Safety (Quentin Coryatt tackled Casey Weldon in the end zone)
FSU — Weldon 4 run (Thomas kick)
FSU — Thomas 37 FG
Attendance — 73,728

1993 COTTON BOWL

#5 Notre Dame 28, #3 Texas A&M 3
Cotton Bowl, Dallas, Jan. 1, 1993

Notre Dame quarterback Rick Mirer broke open a tough defensive first half when he hit Lake Dawson with a 40-yard touchdown pass 36 seconds before halftime. The Fighting Irish used that momentum to pull away to an easy victory in the second half.

The Irish offense outgained the Aggies, 439-165, but sophomore linebacker Jessie Cox played valiantly in defeat, making 17 tackles.

Texas A&M	0	0	0	3	— 3
Notre Dame	0	7	14	7	— 28

ND — Dawson 40 pass from Mirer (Hentrich kick)
ND— Bettis 26 pass from Mirer (Hentrich kick)
ND— Bettis 1 run (Hentrich kick)
A&M — Terry Venetoulias 41 FG
ND — Bettis 4 run (Hentrich kick)
Attendance — 71,615

1994 COTTON BOWL

#4 Notre Dame 24, #6 Texas A&M 21
Cotton Bowl, Dallas, Jan. 1, 1994

The rematch was a dandy. A&M led twice and it took a Notre Dame field goal with less than four minutes left to win it. In the closing seconds, the Aggies still came close to salvaging at least a tie.

Facing fourth-and-17 from the Aggie 41-yard line, Corey Pullig hit Tony Harrison for a 14-yard gain. Harrison, still on his feet, tried to lateral the ball to trailing Leeland McElroy but the pitch sailed high and Notre Dame recovered.

Notre Dame	7	0	14	3	— 24
Texas A&M	7	7	7	0	— 21

ND — McDougal 19 run (Pendergast kick)
A&M — Greg Hill 8 run (Terry Venetoulias kick)
A&M — Darren Smith 15 pass from Corey Pullig (Terry Venetoulias kick)
ND — Zellars 2 run (Pendergast kick)
A&M — Rodney Thomas 1 run (Terry Venetoulias kick)
ND — Edwards 2 run (Pendergast kick)

ND — Pendergast 31 FG
Attendance — 69,855

1995 ALAMO BOWL

#19 Texas A&M 22, #14 Michigan 20
Alamodome, San Antonio, Tex., Dec. 28, 1995

Aggie kicker Kyle Bryant redeemed himself for a mediocre year with a five field goal performance that enabled A&M to end its 9-3 season on a high note. The loss was a big letdown for 9-4 Michigan, which had knocked rival Ohio State out of the Cotton Bowl in the regular-season finale.

This was A&M's final game as a Southwest Conference member and this finish bolstered Aggie hopes for a strong debut in the new Big 12 Conference in 1996.

Michigan	7	3	3	7	— **20**
Texas A&M	10	3	3	6	— **22**

A&M — Eric Bernard 9 run (Kyle Bryant kick)
Michigan — Amani Toomer 41 pass from Brian Griese (Hamiton kick)
A&M — Kyle Bryant 27 FG
Michigan — Hamilton 28 FG
A&M — Kyle Bryant 49 FG
A&M — Kyle Bryant 47 FG
Michigan — Hamilton 26 FG
A&M — Kyle Bryant 31 FG
A&M — Kyle Bryant 37 FG
Michigan — Toomer 44 pass from Griese (Hamilton kick)
Attendance — 64,597

By the Numbers

The statistics, lists and records that appear in this chapter are taken from the Texas A&M media guide, which is produced by the Texas A&M Sports Information Office. The text was updated through the 1995 season.

SEASON-BY-SEASON

Year	Overall W-L-T	SWC W-L-T	SWC Finish	Bowl	Final Rank	Coach	Captain(s)
1894	1-1-0					F.D. Perkins	A.P. Watts
1895	Did not field team						
1896	2-0-1					A.M. Soule, H.W. South	F.D. Perkins
1897	1-2-0					C.W. Taylor	J.B. Stearns
1898	4-2-0					H.W. Williams	Hal Moseley
1899	4-2-0					W.A. Murray	Hal Moseley
1900	2-2-1					W.A. Murray	R.M. Brown
1901	1-4-0					W.A. Murray	C.F. Schulz
1902	7-0-2					J.E. Platt	T.W. Blake
1903	7-3-1					J.E. Platt	T.W. Blake
1904	4-2-0					J.E. Platt	R.B. Boettcher
1905	7-2-0					W.E. Bachman	G.T. Haltom
1906	6-1-0					W.E. Bachman	F.S. Puckett
1907	6-1-1					L.L. Larson	Joe Utay
1908	3-5-0					N.A. Merriam	C.A. DeWare
1909	7-0-1					C.B. Moran	L.A. Hamilton
1910	8-1-0					C.B. Moran	G.W. Barnes
1911	6-1-0					C.B. Moran	Caesar Hahn
1912	8-1-0					C.B. Moran	Tyree Bell
1913	3-4-2					C.B. Moran	W.B. Beasely
1914	6-1-1					C.B. Moran	Tyree Bell
1915	6-2-0	1-1-0	4th-T			E.H. Harlan	J.P. Garrity
1916	6-3-0	2-1-0	3rd-T			E.H. Harlan	J.W. Rollins
1917	8-0-0	2-0-0	1st			D.X. Bible	M.H. Ford
1918	6-1-0	1-1-0	3rd-T			D.V. Graves	S. Alexander
1919	10-0-0	4-0-0	1st			D.X. Bible	E.S. Wilson
1920	6-1-1	5-1-0	3rd			D.X. Bible	Jack Mahan
1921	6-1-2	3-0-2	1st	Dixie Classic		D.X. Bible	W.C. Weir
1922	5-4-0	2-2-0	3rd-T			D.X. Bible	T.F. Wilson
1923	5-3-1	0-3-1	8th			D.X. Bible	W.D. Johnson
1924	7-2-1	2-2-1	4th			D.X. Bible	T.L. Miller (Chas. Waugh, acting capt.)
1925	7-1-1	4-1-0	1st			D.X. Bible	Fay Wilson
1926	5-3-1	1-3-1	6th			D.X. Bible	L.G. Dieterich
1927	8-0-1	4-0-1	1st			D.X. Bible	Joel Hunt
1928	5-4-1	1-3-1	5th			D.X. Bible	Z.W. Bartlett
1929	5-4-0	2-3-0	6th			Matty Bell	T.W. Mills
1930	2-7-0	0-5-0	7th			Matty Bell	J.G. Floyd
1931	7-3-0	3-2-0	3rd			Matty Bell	G.D. Moulden
1932	4-4-2	1-2-2	4th			Matty Bell	J.W. Aston
1933	6-3-1	2-2-1	4th			Matty Bell	C.M. Cummings
1934	2-7-2	1-4-1	6th			Homer Norton	E.O. Fowler
1935	3-7-0	1-5-0	7th			Homer Norton	W.T. Wilkins, N.W. Willis
1936	8-3-1	3-2-1	3rd-T			Homer Norton	C.A.DeWare,Jr., L.L. Cummings
1937	5-2-2	2-2-2	5th			Homer Norton	Joe Routt, R.D. Vitek
1938	4-4-1	2-3-1	5th			Homer Norton	Dick Todd, Owen Rogers
1939	11-0-0	6-0-0	1st	Sugar	1st	Homer Norton	Joe Boyd, Herb Smith, Waleman Price
1940	9-1-0	5-1-0	1st-T	Cotton	6th	Homer Norton	J.N. Thomason, Tommy Vaughan
1941	9-2-0	5-1-0	1st	Cotton	9th	Homer Norton	Martin Ruby, Marshall Spivey
1942	4-5-1	2-3-1	5th			Homer Norton	Cullen Rogers, Elvis Simmons
1943	7-2-1	4-1-0	2nd	Orange		Homer Norton	Goble Bryant, Marion Flanagan
1944	7-4-0	2-3-0	4th-T			Homer Norton	Monte Moncrief, Damon Tassos
1945	6-4-0	3-3-0	3rd-T			Homer Norton	Monte Moncrief, R.L. Butchofsky
1946	4-6-0	3-3-0	4th			Homer Norton	Monte Moncrief, Willie Zapalac
1947	3-6-1	1-4-1	5th-T			Homer Norton	Bob Gary, Barney Welch
1948	0-9-1	0-5-1	7th			Harry Stiteler	Jim Cashion, J. Winkler, O.Stautzenberger

Year	Overall W-L-T	SWC W-L-T	SWC Finish	Bowl	Final Rank	Coach	Captain(s)
1949	1-8-1	0-5-1	7th			Harry Stiteler	Bobby Goff, Wray Whittaker
1950	7-4-0	3-3-0	3rd-T	Pres. Cup		Harry Stiteler	Max Greiner, Carl Molberg
1951	5-3-2	1-3-2	5th			Raymond George	Bob Smith, Hugh Meyer
1952	3-6-1	1-4-1	6th			Raymond George	Jack Little, Ray Graves
1953	4-5-1	1-5-0	6th-T			Raymond George	Durwood Scott
1954	1-9-0	0-6-0	7th			Paul "Bear" Bryant	Bennie Sinclair, Norbert Ohlendorf
1955	7-2-1	4-1-1	2nd		14th	Paul "Bear" Bryant	Billy Huddleston
1956	9-0-1	6-0-0	1st		5th	Paul "Bear" Bryant	Gene Stallings, Jack Pardee, Loyd Hale
1957	8-3-0	4-2-0	3rd	Gator	9th	Paul "Bear" Bryant	John David Crow, Charles Krueger
1958	4-6-0	2-4-0	5th-T			Jim Myers	John Tracey, Richard Gay, Ken Beck
1959	3-7-0	0-6-0	7th			Jim Myers	Charles Milstead, Gale Oliver
1960	1-6-3	0-4-3	7th			Jim Myers	Roy Northrup, Powell Berry
1961	4-5-1	3-4-0	4th			Jim Myers	Wayne Freiling, Wayland Simmons
1962	3-7-0	3-4-0	4th-T			Hank Foldberg	Jerry Hopkins, Sam Byer
1963	2-7-1	1-5-1	8th			Hank Foldberg	Ray Kubala, Ronnie Carpenter
1964	1-9-0	1-6-0	7th			Hank Foldberg	John Brotherton, Rodney Moore
1965	3-7-0	1-6-0	7th-T			Gene Stallings	Joe Wellborn, Jerry Nichols
1966	4-5-1	4-3-0	4th			Gene Stallings	Dan Westerfield, Ken Lamkin
1967	7-4-0	6-1-0	1st	Cotton		Gene Stallings	Grady Allen, Dan Schneider, Robert Cortez
1968	3-7-0	2-5-0	6th-T			Gene Stallings	Edd Hargett, Tom Buckman
1969	3-7-0	2-5-0	6th-T			Gene Stallings	Larry Stegent, Ross Brupbacher, Buster Adami
1970	2-9-0	0-7-0	8th			Gene Stallings	Dave Elmendorf, Jim Parker, Winston Beam, Jimmy Sheffield
1971	5-6-0	4-3-0	4th			Gene Stallings	David Hoot, Joe Mac King, Van Odom
1972	3-8-0	2-5-0	7th-T			Emory Bellard	Boice Best, Todd Christopher, Brad Dusek, Grady Hoermann
1973	5-6-0	3-4-0	6th			Emory Bellard	Mike Jay, Ricky Seeker, Ed Simonini, Larry Ellis
1974	8-3-0	5-2-0	2nd-T		15th	Emory Bellard	Warren Trahan, Ricky Seeker, Pat Thomas
1975	10-2-0	6-1-0	1st-T	Liberty	11th	Emory Bellard	Ed Simonini, Bubba Bean
1976	10-2-0	6-2-0	3rd	Sun	7th	Emory Bellard	Jimmy Dean, Robert Jackson, David Walker, Dennis Swilley, Craig Glendenning
1977	8-4-0	6-2-0	3rd	Bluebonnet		Emory Bellard	David Walker, Mike Williams, Kevin Monk, Mark Dennard
1978	8-4-0	4-4-0	5th	Hall of Fame	18th	Emory Bellard	Cody Risien, Tom Wilson, Russell Mikeska, Jacob Green, Eugene Sanders
1979	6-5-0	4-4-0	5th			Tom Wilson	Carl Grulich, Jacob Green, Ed Pustejovsky, Curtis Dickey
1980	4-7-0	3-5-0	6th			Tom Wilson	Mike Mosley, Zach Guthrie, John Dawson, Elroy Steen, Doug Carr
1981	7-5-0	4-4-0	5th	Independence		Tom Wilson	Mike Whitwell, David Bandy, Mike Little, Keith Baldwin, Dan Davis
1982	5-6-0	3-5-0	6th-T			Jackie Sherrill	Gary Kubiak, Jerry Bullitt, David Hardy
1983	5-5-1	4-3-1	3rd-T			Jackie Sherrill	Tommy Robison, Greg Berry, Kyle Stuard, Tom Bumgardner (12th Man)
1984	6-5-0	3-5-0	7th			Jackie Sherrill	Ray Childress, Matt Darwin, Ken Ford, Ike Liles, Tom Arthur (12th Man)
1985	10-2-0	7-1-0	1st	Cotton	6th	Jackie Sherrill	Domingo Bryant, Anthony Toney, Doug Williams, Dennis Mudd (12th Man)
1986	9-3-0	7-1-0	1st	Cotton	12th	Jackie Sherrill	Johnny Holland, Kevin Murray, Roger Vick, Rod Bernstine, Bobby Middleton (12th Man)
1987	10-2-0	6-1-0	1st	Cotton	9th	Jackie Sherrill	Craig Stump, Sammy O'Brient, Kip Corrington, Matt Wilson, Louis Cheek, Dean Berry (12th Man)
1988	7-5-0	6-1-0	2nd			Jackie Sherrill	Dana Batiste, Leon Cole, Jerry Fontenot, Rod Harris, Brian Edwards (12th Man)
1989	8-4-0	6-2-0	2nd-T	Hancock	20th	R.C. Slocum	Richmond Webb, Gary Jones, John Cooper, Bubba Hillje (12th Man)
1990	9-3-1	5-2-1	2nd-T	Holiday	13th	R.C. Slocum	Bucky Richardson, Chris Crooms, William Thomas, Keith Francis (12th Man)
1991	10-2-0	8-0-0	1st	Cotton	12th	R.C. Slocum	Bucky Richardson, Chris Crooms, Kevin Smith, Jay Elliott (12th Man)

Year	Overall W-L-T	SWC W-L-T	SWC Finish	Bowl	Final Rank	Coach	Captain(s)
1992	12-1-0	7-0-0	1st	Cotton	7th	R.C. Slocum	Doug Carter, Marcus Buckley, David Davis, Jay Elliott (12th Man)
1993	10-2-0	7-0-0	1st	Cotton	8th	R.C. Slocum	Rodney Thomas, Aaron Glenn, Billy Mitchell, Cole Reinarz (12th Man)
1994	10-0-1	6-0-1	Inel.		8th	R.C. Slocum	Rodney Thomas, Reggie Graham, Billy Mitchell, Kevin Caffey (12th Man)
1995	9-3-0	5-2-0	2nd-T	Alamo	15th	R.C. Slocum	Corey Pullig, Ray Mickens, Sean Terry, Thomas Little (12th Man)

COACHING RECORDS

Year	Coach	W	L	T	Pct.
1894	F.D. Perkins	1	1	0	.500
1896	A.M. Soule, H.W. South	2	0	1	1.000
1897	C.W. Taylor	1	2	0	.333
1898	H.W. Williams	4	2	0	.447
1899-1901	W.A. Murray	7	8	1	.469
1902-04	J.E. Platt	18	5	3	.750
1905-06	W.E. Bachman	13	3	0	.813
1907	L.L. Larson	6	1	1	.813
1908	N.A. Merriam	3	5	0	.375
1909-14	C.B. Moran	38	8	4	.800
1915-16	E.H. Harlan	12	5	0	.706
1918	D.V. Graves	1	1	0	.500
1917, 19-28	D.X. Bible	28	14	7	.643
1929-33	Matty Bell	8	14	3	.380
1934-47	Homer Norton	82	53	10	.600
1948-50	Harry Stiteler	8	21	2	.290
1951-53	Raymond George	12	14	4	.467
1954-57	Paul "Bear" Bryant	25	14	2	.634
1958-61	Jim Myers	12	24	4	.350
1962-64	Hank Foldberg	6	23	1	.217
1965-71	Gene Stallings	27	49	1	.357
1972-78	Emory Bellard	52	29	0	.642
1979-81	Tom Wilson	17	17	0	.500
1982-88	Jackie Sherrill	52	28	1	.648
1989-95	R.C. Slocum	68	10	2	.863

YEAR-BY-YEAR RESULTS

1894 — COACH F.D. PERKINS (1-1)

Aggies 14	Galveston HS (Ball) 6
Aggies 0	at Texas 38
Aggies Tot. Pts. 14	Opp. Tot. Pts. 44

1895

— No Team

1896 — COACH A.M. SOULE & H.W. SOUTH (2-0-1)

Aggies 0	Galveston HS (Ball) 0
Aggies 22	Austin College 4
Aggies 28	Houston HS 0
Aggies Tot. Pts. 50	Opp. Tot. Pts. 4

1897 — COACH C.W. TAYLOR (1-2)

Aggies 0	Houston HS 10
Aggies 6	TCU 30
Aggies 4	Austin College 0
Aggies Tot. Pts. 10	Opp. Tot. Pts. 40

1898 — COACH H.W. WILLIAMS (4-2)

Aggies 51	Houston HS 0
Aggies 0	at Texas 48
Aggies 0	Houston HS 6
Aggies 16	at TCU (W) 0
Aggies 22	Austin College 6
Aggies 28	Fort Worth U 0
Aggies Tot. Pts. 117	Opp. Tot. Pts. 60

1899 — COACH W.A. MURRAY (4-2)

Aggies 43	Houston HS 0
Aggies 0	Sewanee 10
Aggies 22	Tulane 0
Aggies 52	LSU 0
Aggies 33	Baylor 0
Aggies 0	at Texas (SA) 6
Aggies Tot. Pts. 150	Opp. Tot. Pts. 16

1900 — COACH W.A. MURRAY (2-2-1)

Aggies 6	Kan. City Medics 6
Aggies 0	at Texas (SA) 5
Aggies 0	at Texas 11
Aggies 11	Waxahachie Ath. Club 0
Aggies 44	Henry College 0
Aggies Tot. Pts. 61	Opp. Tot. Pts. 22

1901 — COACH W.A. MURRAY (1-4)

Aggies 6	Baylor 0
Aggies 6	Baylor 17
Aggies 0	at Texas (SA) 17
Aggies 0	at Texas 32
Aggies 0	Baylor 46
Aggies Tot. Pts. 12	Opp. Tot. Pts. 112

1902 — COACH J.E. PLATT (7-0-2)

Aggies 11	St. Edwards 0
Aggies 0	Trinity 0
Aggies 11	Baylor 6
Aggies 22	Baylor 0
Aggies 0	Texas (SA) 0
Aggies 17	Tulane 5
Aggies 22	at TCU (W) 0
Aggies 34	Trinity 0
Aggies 11	at Texas 0
Aggies Tot. Pts. 128	Opp. Tot. Pts. 11

1903 — COACH J.E. PLATT (7-3-1)

Aggies 16	Trinity 0
Aggies 11	at TCU (W) 0
Aggies 6	Arkansas 0
Aggies 0	Oklahoma 6
Aggies 0	Baylor 0
Aggies 18	Baylor 0
Aggies 16	TCU 0
Aggies 0	Trinity 18
Aggies 5	Baylor 0
Aggies 6	at Texas 29
Aggies 14	TCU 6
Aggies Tot. Pts. 92	Opp. Tot. Pts. 59

1904 — COACH J.E. PLATT (4-2)

Aggies 49	Deaf & Dumb Inst. 0
Aggies 5	Baylor 0
Aggies 29	TCU 0
Aggies 5	Sewanee 17
Aggies 6	at Texas 34
Aggies 10	Baylor 0
Aggies Tot. Pts. 104	Opp. Tot. Pts. 51

1905 — COACH W.E. BACHMAN (7-2)

Aggies 29	Houston 0
Aggies 20	TCU 0
Aggies 42	Baylor 0
Aggies 24	Trinity 0
Aggies 18	Austin College 11
Aggies 24	at TCU (W) 11
Aggies 6	Transylvania Ky. 29
Aggies 17	Baylor 5
Aggies 0	at Texas 27
Aggies Tot. Pts. 180	Opp. Tot. Pts. 83

1906 — COACH W.E. BACHMAN (6-1)

Aggies 42	TCU 0
Aggies 34	Daniel Baker 0
Aggies 22	at TCU (W) 0
Aggies 18	Tulane 0
Aggies 32	Haskell Institute 6
Aggies 22	LSU 12
Aggies 0	at Texas 24
Aggies Tot. Pts. 170	Opp. Tot. Pts. 42

1907 — COACH L.L. LARSON (6-1-1)

Aggies 34	Fort Worth Univ. 0
Aggies 0	Texas (D) 0
Aggies 11	LSU 5
Aggies 5	Haskell Institute 0
Aggies 32	TCU 5
Aggies 18	Tulane 6
Aggies 19	Oklahoma 0
Aggies 6	at Texas 11
Aggies Tot. Pts. 125	Opp. Tot. Pts. 27

1908 — COACH N.A. MERRIAM (3-5)

Aggies 6	Trinity 0
Aggies 5	Baylor 6
Aggies 0	LSU 26
Aggies 13	at TCU (W) 10
Aggies 8	Texas (H) 24
Aggies 0	Haskell Institute 23
Aggies 32	Southwestern 0
Aggies 12	at Texas 28
Aggies Tot. Pts. 76	Opp. Tot. Pts. 117

1909 — COACH C.B. MORAN (7-0-1)

Aggies 17	Austin College 0
Aggies 0	TCU 0
Aggies 15	Haskell Institute 0
Aggies 9	Baylor 6
Aggies 23	Texas (H) 0
Aggies 47	Trinity 0
Aggies 14	Oklahoma 8
Aggies 5	at Texas 0
Aggies Tot. Pts. 130	Opp. Tot. Pts. 14

1910 — COACH C.B. MORAN (8-1)

Aggies 48	Marshall School 0
Aggies 27	Austin College 5
Aggies 35	TCU 0
Aggies 33	Transylvania Ky. 0
Aggies 0	at Arkansas 5
Aggies 23	at TCU 6
Aggies 14	Texas (H) 8
Aggies 6	Southwestern 0
Aggies 17	Tulane 0
Aggies Tot. Pts. 203	Opp. Tot. Pts. 24

1911 — COACH C.B. MORAN (6-1)

Aggies 22	Southwestern 0
Aggies 33	Austin College 0
Aggies 16	Auburn 0
Aggies 17	Mississippi 0
Aggies 0	Texas (H) 6
Aggies 22	Baylor 11
Aggies 24	Dallas U. 0
Aggies Tot. Pts. 134	Opp. Tot. Pts. 17

1912 — COACH C.B. MORAN (8-1)

Aggies 50	Daniel Baker 0
Aggies 59	Trinity 0
Aggies 27	Arkansas (D) 0
Aggies 57	Austin College 0
Aggies 28	Oklahoma 6
Aggies 41	Miss. State 7
Aggies 41	Tulane 0
Aggies 10	Kansas State 13
Aggies 53	Baylor 0
Aggies Tot. Pts. 366	Opp. Tot. Pts. 26

1913 — COACH C.B. MORAN (3-4-2)

Aggies 7	Trinity 0
Aggies 6	Austin College 0
Aggies 19	Polytechnic College 6
Aggies 0	Miss. State 6
Aggies 0	Kansas State 12
Aggies 0	Oklahoma A&M 3
Aggies 0	Haskell Institute 28
Aggies 14	Baylor 14
Aggies 7	LSU 7
Aggies Tot. Pts. 53	Opp. Tot. Pts. 76

1914 — COACH C.B. MORAN (6-1-1)

Aggies 32	Austin College 0
Aggies 0	Trinity 0
Aggies 40	TCU 0
Aggies 0	Haskell Institute (FW) 10
Aggies 63	LSU (D) 9
Aggies 32	Rice 7
Aggies 24	Oklahoma A&M 0
Aggies 14	Mississippi (D) 7
Aggies Tot. Pts. 205	Opp. Tot. Pts. 33

1915 — COACH E.H. HARLAN (6-2)

Aggies 40	Austin College 0
Aggies 62	Trinity 0
Aggies 13	at TCU 10
Aggies 33	Mo. School of Mines 3
Aggies 21	Haskell Institute (D) ... 7
Aggies 0	at Rice 7
Aggies 13	Texas 0
Aggies 0	Miss. State 7
Aggies Tot. Pts. 182	Opp. Tot. Pts. 34

1916 — COACH E.H. HARLAN (6-3)

Aggies 6	Southwestern 0
Aggies 20	Dallas U. 6
Aggies 0	LSU (G) 13
Aggies 62	SMU 0
Aggies 13	Haskell Institute (D) 6
Aggies 0	at Rice 20
Aggies 3	at Baylor 0
Aggies 77	Mo. School of Mines 0
Aggies 7	at Texas 21
Aggies Tot. Pts. 188	Opp. Tot. Pts. 66

1917 — COACH D.X. BIBLE (8-0)

SWC Champions

Aggies 66	Austin College 0
Aggies 98	Dallas U. 0
Aggies 20	Southwestern 0
Aggies 27	LSU (B) 0
Aggies 35	Tulane 0
Aggies 7	at Baylor 0
Aggies 7	Texas 0
Aggies 10	at Rice 0
Aggies Tot. Pts. 270	Opp. Tot. Pts. 0

1918 — COACH D.V. GRAVES (6-1)

Aggies 6	Ream Field 0
Aggies 12	Camp Travis 6
Aggies 19	at Baylor 0
Aggies 7	Southwestern 0
Aggies 19	Camp Mabry 6
Aggies 0	at Texas 7
Aggies 60	Camp Travis 0
Aggies Tot. Pts. 123	Opp. Tot. Pts. 19

1919 — COACH D.X. BIBLE (10-0)

SWC Champions

Aggies 77	Sam Houston STC 0
Aggies 28	San Marcos STC 0
Aggies 16	at SMU 0
Aggies 12	Howard Payne 0
Aggies 42	Trinity 0
Aggies 28	Oklahoma A&M 0
Aggies 10	at Baylor 0
Aggies 48	TCU 0
Aggies 7	Southwestern 0
Aggies 7	Texas 0
Aggies Tot. Pts. 275	Opp. Tot. Pts. 0

1920 — COACH D.X. BIBLE (6-1-1)

SWC Champions

Aggies 110	Daniel Baker 0
Aggies 3	at SMU 0
Aggies 0	LSU 0
Aggies 47	Phillips U. 0
Aggies 35	at Oklahoma A&M 0
Aggies 24	at Baylor 0
Aggies 7	Rice 0
Aggies 3	at Texas 7
Aggies Tot. Pts. 229	Opp. Tot. Pts. 7

1921 — COACH D.X. BIBLE (6-1-2)

SWC Champions

Aggies 14	Howard Payne 7
Aggies 13	at SMU 0
Aggies 0	at LSU 6
Aggies 17	Arizona 13
Aggies 23	Oklahoma A&M 7
Aggies 14	at Baylor 3
Aggies 7	at Rice 7
Aggies 0	Texas 0

Dixie Classic

Aggies 22	Centre College 14
Aggies Tot. Pts. 110	Opp. Tot. Pts. 57

1922 — COACH D.X. BIBLE (5-4)

Aggies 7	Howard Payne 13
Aggies 10	Tulsa U. (D) 13
Aggies 33	Southwestern 0
Aggies 46	at LSU 0
Aggies 19	Ouichita College 6
Aggies 7	at Baylor 13
Aggies 6	at SMU 17
Aggies 24	Rice 0
Aggies 14	at Texas 7
Aggies Tot. Pts. 166	Opp. Tot. Pts. 69

1923 — COACH D.X. BIBLE (5-3-1)

Aggies 53	Sam Houston STC 0
Aggies 21	Howard Payne 0
Aggies 13	Southwestern 0
Aggies 14	Sewanee (D) 0
Aggies 28	at LSU 0
Aggies 0	SMU 10
Aggies 0	at Baylor 0
Aggies 6	at Rice 7
Aggies 0	Texas 6
Aggies Tot. Pts. 135	Opp. Tot. Pts. 23

1924 — COACH D.X. BIBLE (7-2-1)

Aggies 40	John Tarleton SC 0
Aggies 33	Trinity 0
Aggies 54	Southwestern 0
Aggies 7	Sewanee (D) 0
Aggies 40	Arkansas A&M 0
Aggies 7	at SMU 7
Aggies 7	at Baylor 15
Aggies 28	TCU 0
Aggies 13	Rice 6
Aggies 0	at Texas 7
Aggies Tot. Pts. 229	Opp. Tot. Pts. 35

1925 — COACH D.X. BIBLE (7-1-1)

SWC Champions

Aggies 20	Trinity 10
Aggies 23	Southwestern 6
Aggies 6	Sewanee (D) 6
Aggies 7	SMU 0
Aggies 77	Sam Houston STC 0
Aggies 13	at Baylor 0
Aggies 0	at TCU 3
Aggies 17	at Rice 0
Aggies 28	Texas 0
Aggies Tot. Pts. 191	Opp. Tot. Pts. 25

1926 — COACH D.X. BIBLE (5-3-1)

Aggies 26	Trinity 0
Aggies 35	Southwestern 0
Aggies 6	Sewanee (D) 3
Aggies 63	New Mexico 0
Aggies 7	at SMU 9
Aggies 9	at Baylor 20
Aggies 13	TCU 13
Aggies 20	Rice 0
Aggies 5	at Texas 14
Aggies Tot. Pts. 184	Opp. Tot. Pts. 59

1927 — COACH D.X. BIBLE (8-0-1)

SWC Champions

Aggies 45	Trinity 0
Aggies 31	Southwestern 0
Aggies 18	Sewanee (D) 0
Aggies 40	Arkansas 6
Aggies 0	at TCU 0
Aggies 47	Texas Tech 6
Aggies 39	at SMU 13
Aggies 14	at Rice 0
Aggies 28	Texas 7
Aggies Tot. Pts. 262	Opp. Tot. Pts. 32

1928 — COACH D.X. BIBLE (5-4-1)

Aggies 21	Trinity 0
Aggies 21	Southwestern 0
Aggies 69	Sewanee (D) 0
Aggies 0	Centenary 6
Aggies 0	TCU 6
Aggies 12	at Arkansas 27
Aggies 44	North Texas STC 0
Aggies 19	at SMU 19
Aggies 19	Rice 0
Aggies 0	at Texas 19
Aggies Tot. Pts. 205	Opp. Tot. Pts. 77

1929 — COACH MADISON BELL (5-4)

Aggies 54	Southwestern 7
Aggies 10	at Tulane 13
Aggies 19	Kansas State (D) 0
Aggies 7	at TCU 13
Aggies 13	Arkansas 14
Aggies 54	SF Austin STC 0
Aggies 7	SMU 12
Aggies 26	at Rice 6
Aggies 13	Texas 0
Aggies Tot. Pts. 203	Opp. Tot. Pts. 65

1930 — COACH MADISON BELL (2-7)

Aggies 43	Southwestern 0
Aggies 0	at Nebraska 13
Aggies 9	Tulane (D) 19
Aggies 0	at Arkansas (LR) 13
Aggies 0	TCU 3
Aggies 7	Centenary 6
Aggies 7	at SMU 13
Aggies 0	Rice 7
Aggies 0	at Texas 26
Aggies Tot. Pts. 66	Opp. Tot. Pts. 100

1931 — COACH MADISON BELL (7-3)

Aggies 33	Southwestern 0
Aggies 21	John Tarleton SC 0
Aggies 0	at Tulane 7
Aggies 29	Iowa U. (D) 0
Aggies 0	at TCU 6
Aggies 33	Baylor 7
Aggies 7	at Centenary 0
Aggies 0	SMU 8
Aggies 7	at Rice 0
Aggies 7	Texas 6
Aggies Tot. Pts. 137	Opp. Tot. Pts. 34

1932 — COACH MADISON BELL (4-4-2)

Aggies 7	Texas Tech (A) 0
Aggies 14	at Tulane 26
Aggies 26	Sam Houston STC 0
Aggies 14	Texas A&I 0
Aggies 0	TCU 17
Aggies 0	at Baylor 0
Aggies 0	at Centenary 7
Aggies 0	at SMU 0
Aggies 14	Rice 7
Aggies 0	at Texas 21
Aggies Tot. Pts. 75	Opp. Tot. Pts. 78

1933 — COACH MADISON BELL (6-3-1)

Aggies 38	Trinity 0
Aggies 13	at Tulane 6
Aggies 34	Sam Houston STC 14
Aggies 17	Texas A&I 0
Aggies 7	at TCU 13
Aggies 14	Baylor 7
Aggies 0	at Centenary 20
Aggies 0	SMU 19
Aggies 27	at Rice 0
Aggies 10	Texas 10
Aggies Tot. Pts. 160	Opp. Tot. Pts. 89

1934 — COACH H.H. NORTON (2-7-2)

Aggies 28	Sam Houston STC 0
Aggies 14	Texas A&I 14
Aggies 6	at Temple 40
Aggies 0	Centenary (B) 13
Aggies 0	TCU 13
Aggies 10	at Baylor 7
Aggies 7	Arkansas 7
Aggies 0	at SMU 28
Aggies 6	Rice 25
Aggies 0	at Texas 13
Aggies 13	Michigan State (SA) 26
Aggies Tot. Pts. 84	Opp. Tot. Pts. 186

1935 — COACH H.H. NORTON (3-7)

Aggies 37	SF Austin STC 6
Aggies 25	at Sam Houston STC 0
Aggies 0	Temple 14
Aggies 6	at Centenary 7
Aggies 14	at TCU 19
Aggies 6	Baylor 14
Aggies 7	at Arkansas (LR) 14
Aggies 10	at Rice 17
Aggies 20	Texas 6
Aggies 0	SMU 24
Aggies Tot. Pts. 125	Opp. Tot. Pts. 121

1936 — COACH H.H. NORTON (8-3-1)

Aggies 39	Sam Houston STC 6
Aggies 3	at Hardin-Simmons 0
Aggies 3	at Rice 0
Aggies 18	TCU 7
Aggies 0	at Baylor 0
Aggies 0	Arkansas 18
Aggies 22	at SMU 6
Aggies 38	at U. of San Francisco 14
Aggies 20	Utah 7
Aggies 0	at Centenary 3
Aggies 0	Texas 7
Aggies 13	Manhattan College 6
Aggies Tot. Pts. 156	Opp. Tot. Pts. 74

1937 — COACH H.H. NORTON (5-2-2)

Aggies 14	at Manhattan College 7
Aggies 14	Miss. State 0
Aggies 7	at TCU 7
Aggies 0	Baylor 13
Aggies 13	at Arkansas 26
Aggies 14	SMU 0
Aggies 6	at Rice 6
Aggies 7	Texas 0
Aggies 42	at U. of San Francisco 0
Aggies Tot. Pts. 117	Opp. Tot. Pts. 59

1938 — COACH H.H. NORTON (4-4-1)

Aggies 52	Texas A&I 0
Aggies 20	Tulsa 0
Aggies 0	Santa Clara 7
Aggies 6	TCU 34
Aggies 6	at Baylor 6
Aggies 13	Arkansas 7
Aggies 7	at SMU 10
Aggies 6	at Texas 7
Aggies 27	Rice 0
Aggies Tot. Pts. 137	Opp. Tot. Pts. 71

1939 — COACH H.H. NORTON (11-0)

National Champions

Aggies 32	at Oklahoma A&M 0
Aggies 14	Centenary 0
Aggies 7	at Santa Clara 3
Aggies 33	Vilanova 7
Aggies 20	at TCU 6
Aggies 20	Baylor 0
Aggies 27	at Arkansas 0
Aggies 6	SMU 2
Aggies 19	at Rice 0
Aggies 20	Texas 0

Sugar Bowl

Aggies 14	Tulane 13
Aggies Tot. Pts. 212	Opp. Tot. Pts. 31

1940 — COACH H.H. NORTON (9-1)

SWC Co-Champions

Aggies 26	Texas A&I 0
Aggies 41	Tulsa (SA) 6
Aggies 7	at UCLA 0
Aggies 21	TCU 7
Aggies 14	at Baylor 7
Aggies 17	Arkansas 0
Aggies 19	at SMU 7
Aggies 25	Rice 0
Aggies 0	at Texas 7

Cotton Bowl

Aggies 13	Fordham 12
Aggies Tot. Pts. 183	Opp. Tot. Pts. 46

1941 — COACH H.H. NORTON (9-2)

SWC Champions

Aggies 54	Sam Houston STC 0
Aggies 41	Texas A&I (SA) 0
Aggies 49	at New York U. 7
Aggies 14	at TCU 0
Aggies 48	Baylor 0
Aggies 7	at Arkansas (LR) 0
Aggies 21	SMU 10
Aggies 19	at Rice 6
Aggies 0	Texas 23
Aggies 7	Wash. State (T) 0

Cotton Bowl

Aggies 21	Alabama 29
Aggies Tot. Pts. 281	Opp. Tot. Pts. 75

1942 — COACH H.H. NORTON (4-5-1)

Aggies 7	at LSU 16
Aggies 19	Texas Tech 0
Aggies 7	at Corpus Christi NAS... 18
Aggies 2	TCU 7
Aggies 0	at Baylor 6
Aggies 41	Arkansas 0
Aggies 27	at SMU 20
Aggies 0	at Rice 0
Aggies 6	at Texas 12
Aggies 21	Wash. State 0
Aggies Tot. Pts. 130	Opp. Tot. Pts. 79

1943 — COACH H.H. NORTON (7-2-1)

Aggies 48	Bryan AFB 6
Aggies 13	at Texas Tech 0
Aggies 28	at LSU 13
Aggies 13	at TCU 0
Aggies 0	North Texas AC 0
Aggies 13	at Arkansas 0
Aggies 22	SMU 0
Aggies 20	at Rice 0
Aggies 13	Texas 27

Orange Bowl

Aggies 14	LSU 19
Aggies Tot. Pts. 184	Opp. Tot. Pts. 65

1944 — COACH H.H. NORTON (7-4)

Aggies 39	Bryan AFB 0
Aggies 27	Texas Tech (SA) 14
Aggies 14	at Oklahoma 21
Aggies 7	TCU 13
Aggies 7	at LSU 0
Aggies 61	North Texas AC 0
Aggies 6	Arkansas 7
Aggies 39	at SMU 6
Aggies 19	at Rice 6
Aggies 0	at Texas 6
Aggies 70	at Miami U. 14
Aggies Tot. Pts. 289	Opp. Tot. Pts. 87

1945 — COACH H.H. NORTON (6-4)

Aggies 54	Ellington Field 0
Aggies 16	at Texas Tech 6
Aggies 19	Oklahoma 14
Aggies 12	LSU 31
Aggies 12	at TCU 13
Aggies 19	Baylor 13
Aggies 34	at Arkansas 0
Aggies 3	SMU 0
Aggies 0	at Rice 6
Aggies 10	Texas 20
Aggies Tot. Pts. 179	Opp. Tot. Pts. 103

1946 — COACH H.H. NORTON (4-6)

Aggies 47	North Texas State 0
Aggies 0	Texas Tech (SA) 6
Aggies 7	at Oklahoma 10
Aggies 9	at LSU 33
Aggies 14	TCU 0
Aggies 17	at Baylor 0
Aggies 0	Arkansas 7
Aggies 14	at SMU 0
Aggies 10	Rice 27
Aggies 7	at Texas 24
Aggies Tot. Pts. 125	Opp. Tot. Pts. 107

1947 — COACH H.H. NORTON (3-6-1)

Aggies 48	Southwestern 0
Aggies 29	Texas Tech (SA) 7
Aggies 14	at Oklahoma 26
Aggies 13	at LSU 19
Aggies 0	at TCU 26
Aggies 24	Baylor 0
Aggies 21	at Arkansas 21
Aggies 0	SMU 13
Aggies 7	at Rice 41
Aggies 13	Texas 32
Aggies Tot. Pts. 169	Opp. Tot. Pts. 185

1948 — COACH H. STITELER (0-9-1)

Aggies 14	at Villanova 34
Aggies 14	Texas Tech (SA) 20
Aggies 14	at Oklahoma U. 42
Aggies 13	at LSU 14
Aggies 14	TCU 27
Aggies 14	at Baylor 20
Aggies 6	Arkansas 28
Aggies 14	at SMU 20
Aggies 6	Rice 28
Aggies 14	at Texas 14
Aggies Tot. Pts. 123	Opp. Tot. Pts. 247

1949 — COACH H. STITELER (1-8-1)

Aggies 0	Villanova 35
Aggies 26	Texas Tech (SA) 7
Aggies 13	at Oklahoma 33
Aggies 0	at LSU 34
Aggies 6	at TCU 28
Aggies 0	Baylor 21
Aggies 6	at Arkansas 27
Aggies 27	SMU 27
Aggies 0	at Rice 13
Aggies 14	Texas 42
Aggies Tot. Pts. 92	Opp. Tot. Pts. 267

1950 — COACH H. STITELER (7-4)

Aggies 48	Nevada (SA) 18
Aggies 34	at Texas Tech (SA) 13
Aggies 28	at Oklahoma U. 34
Aggies 52	Virginia Mil. Ins. 0
Aggies 42	TCU 23
Aggies 20	at Baylor 27
Aggies 42	Arkansas 13
Aggies 25	at SMU 20
Aggies 13	Rice 21
Aggies 0	at Texas 17

Presidential Cup

Aggies 40	Georgia 20
Aggies Tot. Pts. 344	Opp. Tot. Pts. 206

1951 — COACH R. GEORGE (5-3-2)

Aggies 21	at UCLA 14
Aggies 20	Texas Tech (D) 7
Aggies 14	Oklahoma U. 7
Aggies 53	at Trinity 14
Aggies 14	at TCU 20
Aggies 21	Baylor 21
Aggies 21	at Arkansas 33
Aggies 14	SMU 14
Aggies 13	at Rice 28
Aggies 22	Texas 21
Aggies Tot. Pts. 213	Opp. Tot. Pts. 179

1952 — COACH R. GEORGE (3-6-1)

Aggies 21	at Houston 13
Aggies 14	Oklahoma A&M (D) 7
Aggies 7	Kentucky 10
Aggies 6	at Mich. State 48
Aggies 7	TCU 7
Aggies 20	at Baylor 21
Aggies 31	Arkansas 12
Aggies 13	at SMU 21
Aggies 6	Rice 16
Aggies 12	at Texas 32
Aggies Tot. Pts. 137	Opp. Tot. Pts. 187

1953 — COACH R. GEORGE (4-5-1)

Aggies 7	at Kentucky 6
Aggies 14	Houston 14
Aggies 14	Georgia (D) 12
Aggies 27	at Texas Tech 14
Aggies 20	at TCU 7
Aggies 13	Baylor 14
Aggies 14	at Arkansas (LR) 41
Aggies 0	SMU 23
Aggies 7	at Rice 34
Aggies 12	Texas 21
Aggies Tot. Pts. 128	Opp. Tot. Pts. 186

1954 — COACH PAUL BRYANT (1-9)

Aggies 9	Texas Tech 41
Aggies 6	Oklahoma A&M (D) 14
Aggies 6	at Georgia 0
Aggies 7	at Houston 10
Aggies 20	TCU 21
Aggies 7	at Baylor 20
Aggies 7	Arkansas 14
Aggies 3	at SMU 6
Aggies 19	Rice 29
Aggies 13	at Texas 22
Aggies Tot. Pts. 97	Opp. Tot. Pts. 177

1955 — COACH PAUL BRYANT (7-2-1)

Aggies 0	at UCLA 21
Aggies 28	LSU (D) 0
Aggies 21	Houston 3
Aggies 27	at Nebraska 0
Aggies 19	at TCU 16
Aggies 19	Baylor 7
Aggies 7	at Arkansas 7
Aggies 13	SMU 2
Aggies 20	at Rice 12
Aggies 6	Texas 21
Aggies Tot. Pts. 160	Opp. Tot. Pts. 89

1956 — COACH PAUL BRYANT (9-0-1)

SWC Champions

Aggies 19	Villanova 0
Aggies 9	at LSU 6
Aggies 40	Texas Tech (D) 7
Aggies 14	at Houston 14
Aggies 7	TCU 6
Aggies 19	at Baylor 13
Aggies 27	Arkansas 0
Aggies 33	at SMU 7
Aggies 21	Rice 7
Aggies 34	at Texas 21
Aggies Tot. Pts. 223	Opp. Tot. Pts. 81

1957 — COACH PAUL BRYANT (8-3)

Aggies 21	Maryland (D) 13
Aggies 21	at Texas Tech 0
Aggies 28	Missouri 0
Aggies 28	Houston 6
Aggies 7	at TCU 0
Aggies 14	Baylor 0
Aggies 7	at Arkansas 6
Aggies 19	SMU 6
Aggies 6	at Rice 7
Aggies 7	Texas 9

Gator Bowl

Aggies 0	Tennessee 3
Aggies Tot. Pts. 158	Opp. Tot. Pts. 50

1958 — COACH JIM MYERS (4-6)

Aggies 14	Texas Tech (D) 15
Aggies 7	at Houston 39
Aggies 12	Missouri 0
Aggies 14	at Maryland 10
Aggies 8	TCU 24
Aggies 33	at Baylor 27
Aggies 8	Arkansas 21
Aggies 0	at SMU 33
Aggies 28	at Rice 21
Aggies 0	at Texas 27
Aggies Tot. Pts. 124	Opp. Tot. Pts. 217

1959 — COACH JIM MYERS (3-7)

Aggies 14	Texas Tech (D) 20
Aggies 9	at Michigan State 7
Aggies 7	at Miss. Southern 3
Aggies 28	Houston 6
Aggies 6	at TCU 39
Aggies 0	Baylor 13
Aggies 7	at Arkansas 12
Aggies 11	SMU 14
Aggies 2	at Rice 7
Aggies 17	Texas 20
Aggies Tot. Pts. 101	Opp. Tot. Pts. 141

1960 — COACH JIM MYERS (1-6-3)

Aggies 0	at LSU 9
Aggies 14	Texas Tech 14
Aggies 14	at Trinity 0
Aggies 0	at Houston 17
Aggies 14	TCU 14
Aggies 0	at Baylor 14
Aggies 3	Arkansas 7
Aggies 0	at SMU 0
Aggies 14	at Rice 21
Aggies 14	at Texas 21
Aggies Tot. Pts. 73	Opp. Tot. Pts. 117

1961 — COACH JIM MYERS (4-5-1)

Aggies 7	Houston 7
Aggies 7	at LSU 16
Aggies 38	at Texas Tech 7
Aggies 55	at Trinity 0
Aggies 14	at TCU 15
Aggies 23	Baylor 0
Aggies 8	at Arkansas 15
Aggies 25	SMU 12
Aggies 7	at Rice 21
Aggies 0	Texas 25
Aggies Tot. Pts. 184	Opp. Tot. Pts. 118

1962 — COACH H. FOLDBERG (3-7)

Aggies 0	at LSU 21
Aggies 3	at Houston 6
Aggies 7	Texas Tech 3
Aggies 6	at Florida 42
Aggies 14	TCU 20
Aggies 6	at Baylor 3
Aggies 7	Arkansas 17
Aggies 12	at SMU 7
Aggies 3	at Rice 23
Aggies 3	at Texas 13
Aggies Tot. Pts. 61	Opp. Tot. Pts. 155

1963 — COACH H. FOLDBERG (2-7-1)

Aggies 6	at LSU 14
Aggies 0	at Ohio State 17
Aggies 0	at Texas Tech 10
Aggies 23	Houston 13
Aggies 14	at TCU 14
Aggies 7	Baylor 34
Aggies 7	at Arkansas (LR) 21
Aggies 7	SMU 9
Aggies 13	at Rice 6
Aggies 13	Texas 15
Aggies Tot. Pts. 90	Opp. Tot. Pts. 153

1964 — COACH H. FOLDBERG (1-9)

Aggies 6	at LSU 9
Aggies 0	at Houston 10
Aggies 12	at Texas Tech 16
Aggies 7	at Southern Cal. 31
Aggies 9	TCU 14
Aggies 16	at Baylor 20
Aggies 0	Arkansas 17
Aggies 23	at SMU 0
Aggies 8	at Rice 19
Aggies 7	at Texas 26
Aggies Tot. Pts. 88	Opp. Tot. Pts. 162

1965 — COACH G. STALLINGS (3-7)

Aggies 0	at LSU 10
Aggies 14	at Georgia Tech 10
Aggies 16	at Texas Tech 20
Aggies 10	Houston 7
Aggies 9	at TCU 17
Aggies 0	Baylor 31
Aggies 0	at Arkansas (LR) 31
Aggies 0	SMU 10
Aggies 14	at Rice 13
Aggies 17	Texas 21
Aggies Tot. Pts. 80	Opp. Tot. Pts. 170

1966 — COACH G. STALLINGS (4-5-1)

Aggies 3	at Georgia Tech 38
Aggies 13	at Tulane 21
Aggies 35	Texas Tech 14
Aggies 7	at LSU 7
Aggies 35	TCU 7
Aggies 17	at Baylor 13
Aggies 0	Arkansas 34
Aggies 14	at SMU 21
Aggies 7	at Rice 6
Aggies 14	at Texas 22
Aggies Tot. Pts. 145	Opp. Tot. Pts. 183

1967 — COACH G. STALLINGS (7-4)

SWC Champions

Aggies 17	SMU 20
Aggies 20	Purdue (D) 24
Aggies 6	at LSU 17
Aggies 18	Florida State 19
Aggies 28	at Texas Tech 24
Aggies 20	at TCU 0
Aggies 21	Baylor 3
Aggies 33	Arkansas 21
Aggies 18	at Rice 3
Aggies 10	Texas 7

Cotton Bowl

Aggies 20	Alabama 16
Aggies Tot. Pts. 211	Opp. Tot. Pts. 154

1968 — COACH G. STALLINGS (3-7)

Aggies 12	at LSU 13
Aggies 35	at Tulane 3
Aggies 14	at Florida State 20
Aggies 16	Texas Tech 21
Aggies 27	TCU 7
Aggies 9	at Baylor 10
Aggies 22	Arkansas 25
Aggies 23	at SMU 36
Aggies 24	Rice 14
Aggies 14	at Texas 35
Aggies Tot. Pts. 196	Opp. Tot. Pts. 184

1969 — COACH G. STALLINGS (3-7)

Aggies 6	at LSU 35
Aggies 0	at Nebraska 14
Aggies 20	at Army 13
Aggies 9	at Texas Tech 13
Aggies 6	at TCU 16
Aggies 24	Baylor 0
Aggies 13	at Arkansas 35
Aggies 20	SMU 10
Aggies 6	at Rice 7
Aggies 12	Texas 49
Aggies Tot. Pts. 116	Opp. Tot. Pts. 192

1970 — COACH G. STALLINGS (2-9)

Aggies 41	Wichita State 14
Aggies 20	at LSU 18
Aggies 13	at Ohio State 56
Aggies 10	at Michigan 14
Aggies 7	Texas Tech 21
Aggies 15	TCU 31
Aggies 24	at Baylor 29
Aggies 6	Arkansas 45
Aggies 3	at SMU 6
Aggies 17	Rice 18
Aggies 14	at Texas 52
Aggies Tot. Pts. 170	Opp. Tot. Pts. 304

1971 — COACH G. STALLINGS (5-6)

Aggies 41	Wichita State 7
Aggies 0	at LSU 37
Aggies 7	at Nebraska 34
Aggies 0	Cincinnati 17
Aggies 7	at Texas Tech 28
Aggies 3	at TCU 14
Aggies 10	Baylor 9
Aggies 17	at Arkansas (LR) 9
Aggies 27	SMU 10
Aggies 18	at Rice 13
Aggies 14	Texas 34
Aggies Tot. Pts. 144	Opp. Tot. Pts. 212

1972 — COACH E. BELLARD (3-8)

Aggies 36	at Wichita State 13
Aggies 7	at Nebraska 37
Aggies 17	at LSU 42
Aggies 14	Army 24
Aggies 14	Texas Tech 17
Aggies 10	TCU 13
Aggies 13	at Baylor 15
Aggies 10	Arkansas 7
Aggies 27	at SMU 17
Aggies 14	Rice 20
Aggies 3	at Texas 38
Aggies Tot. Pts. 165	Opp. Tot. Pts. 243

1973 — COACH E. BELLARD (5-6)

Aggies 48	Wichita State 0
Aggies 23	at LSU 28
Aggies 24	Boston College 32
Aggies 30	at Clemson 15
Aggies 16	at Texas Tech 28
Aggies 35	at TCU 16
Aggies 28	Baylor 22
Aggies 10	at Arkansas 14
Aggies 45	SMU 10
Aggies 20	at Rice 24
Aggies 13	Texas 42
Aggies Tot. Pts. 292	Opp. Tot. Pts. 231

1974 — COACH E. BELLARD (8-3)

Aggies 24	Clemson 0
Aggies 21	at LSU 14
Aggies 28	at Washington 15
Aggies 10	at Kansas 28
Aggies 28	Texas Tech 7
Aggies 17	TCU 0
Aggies 20	at Baylor 0
Aggies 20	Arkansas 10
Aggies 14	at SMU 18
Aggies 37	Rice 7
Aggies 3	at Texas 32
Aggies Tot. Pts. 222	Opp. Tot. Pts. 131

1975 — COACH E. BELLARD (10-2)

SWC Tri-Champions

Aggies 7	Mississippi 0
Aggies 39	at LSU 8
Aggies 43	Illinois 13
Aggies 10	at Kansas State 0
Aggies 38	at Texas Tech 9
Aggies 14	at TCU 6
Aggies 19	Baylor 10
Aggies 36	SMU 3
Aggies 33	at Rice 14
Aggies 20	Texas 10
Aggies 6	at Arkansas (LR) 31

Liberty Bowl

Aggies 0	So. Cal 20

Aggies Tot. Pts. 265 Opp. Tot. Pts. 124

1976 — COACH E. BELLARD (10-2)

Aggies 19	Virginia Tech 0
Aggies 34	Kansas State 14
Aggies 10	at Houston 21
Aggies 14	at Illinois 7
Aggies 16	Texas Tech 27
Aggies 24	Baylor 0
Aggies 57	Rice 34
Aggies 36	at SMU 0
Aggies 31	at Arkansas (LR) 10
Aggies 59	TCU 10
Aggies 27	at Texas 3

Sun Bowl

Aggies 37	Florida 14

Aggies Tot. Pts. 364 Opp. Tot. Pts. 140

1977 — COACH E. BELLARD (8-4)

Aggies 28	Kansas 14
Aggies 27	at Virginia Tech 6
Aggies 33	at Texas Tech 17
Aggies 3	at Michigan 41
Aggies 38	at Baylor 31
Aggies 28	at Rice 14
Aggies 38	SMU 21
Aggies 20	Arkansas 26
Aggies 52	at TCU 23
Aggies 28	Texas 57
Aggies 27	Houston 7

Bluebonnet Bowl

Aggies 28	USC 47

Aggies Tot. Pts. 350 Opp. Tot. Pts. 304

1978 — COACHES BELLARD & WILSON (8-4)

Coach E. Bellard (4-2)

Aggies 37	at Kansas 10
Aggies 37	at Boston College 2
Aggies 58	Memphis State 0
Aggies 38	Texas Tech 9
Aggies 0	at Houston 33
Aggies 6	Baylor 24

Coach Tom Wilson (4-2)

Aggies 38	Rice 21
Aggies 20	at SMU 17
Aggies 7	at Arkansas (LR) 26
Aggies 15	TCU 7
Aggies 7	at Texas 22

Hall of Fame Bowl

Aggies 28	Iowa St 12

Aggies Tot. Pts. 291 Opp. Tot. Pts. 183

1979 — COACH TOM WILSON (6-5)

Aggies 17	Brigham Young (H) 18
Aggies 7	at Baylor 17
Aggies 27	at Penn State 14
Aggies 17	at Memphis State 7
Aggies 20	at Texas Tech 21
Aggies 14	Houston 17
Aggies 41	at Rice 15
Aggies 47	SMU 14
Aggies 10	Arkansas 22
Aggies 30	at TCU 7
Aggies 13	Texas 7

Aggies Tot. Pts. 243 Opp. Tot. Pts. 159

1980 — COACH TOM WILSON (4-7)

Aggies 23	at Mississippi 20
Aggies 0	at Georgia 42
Aggies 9	Penn State 25
Aggies 41	Texas Tech 21
Aggies 13	at Houston 17
Aggies 7	Baylor 46
Aggies 6	Rice 10
Aggies 0	at SMU 27
Aggies 24	at Arkansas 27
Aggies 13	TCU 10
Aggies 24	at Texas 14

Aggies Tot. Pts. 160 Opp. Tot. Pts. 259

1981 — COACH TOM WILSON (7-5)

Aggies 29	at California-Berkeley 28
Aggies 12	at Boston College 13
Aggies 43	Louisiana Tech 7
Aggies 24	at Texas Tech 23
Aggies 7	Houston 6
Aggies 17	at Baylor 19
Aggies 51	at Rice 26
Aggies 7	SMU 27
Aggies 7	Arkansas 10
Aggies 37	TCU 7
Aggies 13	Texas 21

Independence Bowl

Aggies 33	Oklahoma State 16

Aggies Tot. Pts. 280 Opp. Tot. Pts. 203

1982 — COACH J. SHERRILL (5-6)

Aggies 16	Boston College 38
Aggies 61	UT-Arlington 22
Aggies 38	Louisiana Tech 27
Aggies 15	Texas Tech 24
Aggies 20	at Houston 24
Aggies 28	Baylor 23
Aggies 49	Rice 7
Aggies 9	at SMU 47
Aggies 0	at Arkansas (LR) 35
Aggies 34	TCU 14
Aggies 16	at Texas 53

Aggies Tot. Pts. 286 Opp. Tot. Pts. 314

1983 — COACH J. SHERRILL (5-5-1)

Aggies 17	California 19
Aggies 38	Arkansas State 17
Aggies 15	Oklahoma State 34
Aggies 0	at Texas Tech 3
Aggies 30	Houston 7
Aggies 13	at Baylor 13
Aggies 29	at Rice 10
Aggies 7	SMU 10
Aggies 36	Arkansas 23
Aggies 20	at TCU 10
Aggies 13	Texas 45

Aggies Tot. Pts. 218 Opp. Tot. Pts. 174

1984 — COACH J. SHERRILL (6-5)

Aggies 20	Texas-El Paso 17
Aggies 38	Iowa State 17
Aggies 22	Arkansas State 21
Aggies 12	Texas Tech 30
Aggies 7	at Houston 9
Aggies 16	Baylor 20
Aggies 38	Rice 14
Aggies 20	at SMU 28
Aggies 0	at Arkansas 28
Aggies 35	TCU 21
Aggies 37	at Texas 12
Aggies Tot. Pts. 245	Opp. Tot. Pts. 217

1985 — COACH J. SHERRILL (10-2)

SWC Champions

Aggies 10	at Alabama (B) 23
Aggies 31	Northeast Louisiana 17
Aggies 45	Tulsa 10
Aggies 8	at Texas Tech 27
Aggies 43	Houston 16
Aggies 15	at Baylor 20
Aggies 43	at Rice 28
Aggies 19	SMU 17
Aggies 10	Arkansas 6
Aggies 53	at TCU 6
Aggies 42	Texas 10

Cotton Bowl

Aggies 36	Auburn 16
Aggies Tot. Pts. 375	Opp. Tot. Pts. 196

1986 — COACH J. SHERRILL (9-3)

SWC Champions

Aggies 17	at LSU 35
Aggies 48	North Texas State 28
Aggies 16	So. Mississippi 7
Aggies 45	Texas Tech 8
Aggies 19	at Houston 7
Aggies 31	Baylor 30
Aggies 45	Rice 10
Aggies 39	at SMU 35
Aggies 10	at Arkansas 14
Aggies 74	TCU 10
Aggies 16	at Texas 3

Cotton Bowl

Aggies 12	Ohio State 28
Aggies Tot. Pts. 372	Opp. Tot. Pts. 215

1987 — COACH J. SHERRILL (10-2)

SWC Champions

Aggies 3	LSU 17
Aggies 29	Washington 12
Aggies 27	at So. Mississippi (J) 14
Aggies 21	at Texas Tech 27
Aggies 22	Houston 17
Aggies 34	at Baylor 10
Aggies 34	at Rice 21
Aggies 32	Louisiana Tech 3
Aggies 14	Arkansas 0
Aggies 42	at TCU 24
Aggies 20	Texas 13

Cotton Bowl

Aggies 35	Notre Dame 10
Aggies Tot. Pts. 313	Opp. Tot. Pts. 168

1988 — COACH J. SHERRILL (7-5)

Aggies 14	Nebraska (E) 23
Aggies 0	at LSU 27
Aggies 15	at Oklahoma State 52
Aggies 50	Texas Tech 15
Aggies 30	at Houston 16
Aggies 28	Baylor 14
Aggies 24	Rice 10
Aggies 56	Louisiana Tech 17
Aggies 20	at Arkansas 25
Aggies 18	TCU 0
Aggies 28	at Texas 24
Aggies 10	Alabama 30
Aggies Tot. Pts. 293	Opp. Tot. Pts. 253

1989 — COACH R.C. SLOCUM (8-4)

Aggies 28	LSU 16
Aggies 6	at Washington 19
Aggies 44	at TCU 7
Aggies 31	Southern Mississippi 14
Aggies 24	at Texas Tech 27
Aggies 17	Houston 13
Aggies 14	at Baylor 11
Aggies 45	at Rice 7
Aggies 63	SMU 14
Aggies 22	Arkansas 23
Aggies 21	Texas 10

John Hancock Bowl

Aggies 28	Pittsburgh 31
Aggies Tot. Pts. 343	Opp. Tot. Pts. 192

1990 — COACH R.C. SLOCUM (9-3-1)

Aggies 28	at Hawaii 13
Aggies 63	Southwestern La. 14
Aggies 40	North Texas 8
Aggies 8	at LSU 17
Aggies 28	Texas Tech 24
Aggies 31	at Houston 36
Aggies 20	Baylor 20
Aggies 41	Rice 15
Aggies 38	at SMU 17
Aggies 20	at Arkansas 16
Aggies 56	TCU 10
Aggies 27	at Texas 28

Holiday Bowl

Aggies 65	Brigham Young 14
Aggies Tot. Pts. 465	Opp. Tot. Pts. 232

1991 — COACH R.C. SLOCUM (10-2)

SWC Champions

Aggies 45	LSU 7
Aggies 34	at Tulsa 35
Aggies 34	Southwestern La. 7
Aggies 37	at Texas Tech 14
Aggies 34	at Baylor 12
Aggies 27	Houston 18
Aggies 38	at Rice 21
Aggies 44	at TCU 7
Aggies 13	Arkansas 3
Aggies 65	SMU 6
Aggies 31	Texas 14

Cotton Bowl

Aggies 2	Florida State 10
Aggies Tot. Pts. 404	Opp. Tot. Pts. 154

1992 — COACH R.C. SLOCUM (12-1)

SWC Champions

Aggies 10	Stanford (A) 7
Aggies 31	at LSU 22
Aggies 19	Tulsa 9
Aggies 26	at Missouri 13
Aggies 19	Texas Tech 17
Aggies 35	Rice 9
Aggies 19	Baylor 13
Aggies 41	at SMU (CB) 7
Aggies 40	Louisville 18
Aggies 38	at Houston 30
Aggies 37	TCU 10
Aggies 34	at Texas 13

Cotton Bowl

Aggies 3	Notre Dame 28
Aggies Tot. Pts. 352	Opp. Tot. Pts. 196

1993 — COACH R.C. SLOCUM (10-2)

SWC Champions

Aggies 24	LSU 0
Aggies 14	at Oklahoma 44
Aggies 73	Missouri 0
Aggies 31	at Texas Tech 6
Aggies 34	Houston 10
Aggies 34	at Baylor 17
Aggies 38	at Rice 10
Aggies 37	SMU 13
Aggies 42	Louisville 7
Aggies 59	at TCU 3
Aggies 18	Texas 9

Cotton Bowl

Aggies 21	Notre Dame 24
Aggies Tot. Pts. 425	Opp. Tot. Pts. 143

1994 — COACH R.C. SLOCUM (10-0-1)

Aggies 18	at LSU 13
Aggies 36	Oklahoma 14
Aggies 41	Southern Mississippi 17
Aggies 23	Texas Tech 17
Aggies 38	at Houston 7
Aggies 41	Baylor 21
Aggies 7	Rice 0
Aggies 21	at SMU (SA) 21
Aggies 34	at Texas 10
Aggies 26	at Louisville 10
Aggies 34	TCU 17
Aggies Tot. Pts. 319	Opp. Tot. Pts. 147

1995 — COACH R.C. SLOCUM (9-3)

Aggies 33	LSU	17
Aggies 52	Tulsa	9
Aggies 21	at Colorado	29
Aggies 7	at Texas Tech	14
Aggies 20	SMU	17
Aggies 24	at Baylor	9
Aggies 31	Houston	7
Aggies 17	at Rice	10
Aggies 56	Middle Tenn. State 14
Aggies 38	at TCU	6
Aggies 6	Texas	16

Alamo Bowl

Aggies 22	Michigan	20
Aggies Tot. Pts. 327	Opp. Tot. Pts. 168

TEAM OFFENSIVE RECORDS

TOTAL OFFENSE — MOST YARDS, GAME

Yds	Plays	Opponent, Year
774	76	SW Louisiana, 1990
705	103	TCU, 1986
702	84	Tulsa, 1985
687	91	TCU, 1977
670	84	SMU, 1990
622	92	Rice, 1976
615	87	Memphis State, 1978
602	83	Rice, 1987
594	90	TCU, 1991
592	74	Tulsa, 1995
587	71	TCU, 1976

Most Yards, Season: 5,653, 1990
Most Average Yards Per Game: 471.1, 1990
Most Average Yards Per Play, Game: 10.2 vs. SW Louisiana, 1990
Fewest Total Yards, Game: 12 vs. TCU, 1930

TOTAL OFFENSE — MOST PLAYS, GAME

Plays	Yds	Opponent, Year
103	705	TCU, 1986
98	442	Houston, 1988
94	469	Louisiana Tech, 1982
94	522	Texas Tech, 1986
92	622	Rice, 1976
92	539	NE Louisiana, 1985

Fewest Plays, Game: 29 vs. SMU, 1945
Most Plays, Season: 895 (514 run/381 pass), 1986; 897 (653 run/244 pass), 1988 (12-game season)

TOTAL OFFENSE — MOST FIRST DOWNS, GAME

No.	Opponent, Year
38	TCU, 1986
33	SW Louisiana, 1990
33	TCU, 1991
32	Tulsa, 1985
32	SMU, 1990

Fewest First Downs, Game: 0 vs. TCU, 1930
Most First Downs, Season: 291, 1990

RUSHING — MOST YARDS/GAME

Yds	Att	Opponent, Year
606	85	TCU, 1977
555	70	SMU, 1990
526	79	Rice, 1976
526	59	SW Louisiana, 1990
523	79	Memphis State, 1978
518	61	TCU, 1976
434	61	Clemson, 1974
432	66	SMU, 1973
417	73	LSU, 1974
409	63	LSU, 1991

Most Yards, Season: 3,829, 1990
Fewest Yards, Season: 731, 1965
Most Average Yards Per Game: 319.1, 1990
Most Average Yards Per Play, Game: 8.9 vs. SW Louisiana, 1990
Most Average Yards Per Carry, Season: 5.8, 1990

RUSHING — MOST ATTEMPTS, GAME

Att.	Yards	Opponent, Year
85	606	TCU, 1977
79	378	Rice, 1975
79	526	Rice, 1976
79	523	Memphis State, 1978
78	349	SMU, 1976

Most Attempts, Season: 709, 1977
Fewest Attempts, Game: 15 vs. SMU, 1947

RUSHING — MOST FIRST DOWNS, GAME

No.	Opponent, Year
28	SMU, 1990
25	TCU, 1977
24	Rice, 1976
24	Rice, 1978
23	Texas Tech, 1988

Most First Downs, Season: 196, 1990
Fewest First Downs, Game: 0 vs. TCU, 1930

RUSHING — MOST TOUCHDOWNS, GAME

TD's	Opponent, Year
11	Miami (Fla.), 1944
7	TCU, 1976
7	Memphis State, 1978
7	TCU, 1986
7	Missouri, 1993

PASSING — MOST YARDS, GAME

Yards	Opponent, Year
376	SMU, 1968
356	Tulsa, 1985
355	Arkansas, 1968
328	Rice, 1968
321	TCU, 1991
321	Rice, 1982
314	LSU, 1970
313	TCU, 1966
308	Baylor, 1986
306	TCU, 1986

Most Yards, Season: 2,691, 1986
Fewest Yards, Season: 336, 1960
Fewest Yards, Game: 0 vs. Texas Tech, 1954
Most Average Yards Per Game: 244.6, 1986

PASSING — MOST COMPLETIONS, GAME

No.	Yards	Opponent, Year
33	298	TCU, 1982
32	376	SMU, 1968
29	355	Arkansas, 1968
25	252	Texas Tech, 1982
25	321	Rice, 1982
25	280	Rice, 1983
25	218	LSU, 1986
25	308	Baylor, 1986
25	306	TCU, 1986
25	277	Texas, 1986

Most Completions, Season: 230, 1986
Fewest Completions, Season: 30, 1960

PASSING — MOST ATTEMPTS, GAME

Att.	Yards	Opponent, Year
58	376	SMU, 1968
55	319	Arkansas, 1968
49	278	Baylor, 1968
48	280	Rice, 1983
46	246	Texas Tech, 1995
45	221	Texas, 1968
45	249	Oklahoma State, 1988

Most Attempts, Season: 400, 1982
Fewest Attempts, Season: 70, 1956
Fewest Attempts, Game: 0 vs. SMU, 1974

PASSING — MOST INTERCEPTIONS THROWN, GAME

No.	Opponent, Year
7	Texas, 1943
7	Rice, 1953
5	LSU, 1948
5	Texas, 1968
5	LSU, 1986
5	Ohio State, 1986
5	Oklahoma, 1993

Most Passes Had Intercepted, Season: 30, 1941
Fewest Passes Had Intercepted, Season: 4, 1956; 5, 1992
Most Passes Thrown Without an Interception: 176, 1968

PASSING — MOST FIRST DOWNS, GAME

22	SMU, 1968
17	Arkansas, 1958
17	Baylor, 1968
17	Arkansas, 1968
16	Rice, 1968

Most First Downs, Season: 145, 1986

OTHER PASS RECORDS

Most Touchdowns, Game: 6 vs. Rice, 1981; 6 vs. Rice, 1982
Most Touchdowns, Season: 21, 1982
Best Completion Percentage, Game (10 att.): 90.5% vs. Arkansas, 1981 (19-of-21)
Best Completion Percentage, Season: 60.4%, 1986

SCORING — POINTS, GAME

Pts	Opponent, Year
110	Daniel Baker, 1920
98	Dallas University, 1917
77	Sam Houston STC, 1919
77	Missouri School of Mines, 1916
74	TCU, 1986
73	Missouri, 1993
70	Miami (Fla.), 1944
69	Sewanee, 1928
66	Austin College, 1917
65	SMU, 1991
65	Brigham Young, 1990

Most Points, Season: 425, 1993

SCORING — TOUCHDOWNS, GAME

(since 1944 only)

No.	Opponent, Year
11	Miami (Fla.), 1944
10	TCU, 1986
10	Missouri, 1993
9	SMU, 1991
9	Brigham Young, 1990
9	SW Louisiana, 1990
9	SMU, 1989

Most Touchdowns, Season: 52, 1993; 52, 1991
Most Field Goals, Game: 6 vs. Arkansas State, 1983
Most Field Goals, Season: 21, 1986
Most Extra Points, Game: 10 vs. Missouri, 1993
Most Extra Points, Season: 52, 1990
Consecutive Extra Points: 72, 1992-93

PUNT RETURNS

Most Returns, Game: 13 vs. LSU, 1975
Most Returns, Season: 69, 1943
Most Yards, Game: 319 vs. NATC, Arlington, 1943
Most Yards, Season: 933, 1941
Best Return Average, Season: 17.9, 1993
Most Touchdowns, Game: 1, many times
Most Touchdowns, Season: 4, 1987

KICKOFF RETURNS

Most Returns, Game: 8 vs. Ohio State, 1970; 8 vs. LSU, 1971
Most Yards, Game: 226 vs. Boston College, 1973
Best Return Average, Season: 31.2, 1993

PUNTING

Most Punts, Game: 17 vs. SMU, 1945
Fewest Punts, Game: 0 vs. SW Louisiana, 1990; 0 vs. Rice, 1990
Most Punts, Season: 92, 1946
Best Average, Game: 53.6 vs. Houston, 1977 (5 punts)
Best Average, Season: 43.6, 1965

FUMBLES

Most Fumbles, Game: 10 vs. Ellington Field, 1945; 10 vs. Texas, 1954
Most Fumbles Lost, Game: 9 vs. Ellington Field, 1945
Most Fumbles, Season: 50, 1973
Most Fumbles Lost, Season: 31, 1974

PENALTIES

Most Penalties, Game: 16 vs. Texas Tech, 1986; 16 vs. TCU, 1990
Most Penalties, Season: 108, 1995
Most Yards Penalized, Game: 167 vs. Texas Tech, 1949 (14 penalties)

Most Yards Penalized, Season: 895, 1991
Fewest Penalties, Game: 0, many times (last vs. Texas Tech, 1992)
Fewest Penalties, Season: 27, 1937
Fewest Yards Penalized, Season: 200, 1948 (31 penalties)
Most First Downs: 4 vs. Texas, 1989; 4 vs. Houston, 1990, 4 vs. Colorado, 1995

MISCELLANEOUS

Most Consecutive Games Won: 20, 1938-40
Most Consecutive SWC Games Won: 26, 1991-95
Most Consecutive Games Unbeaten, Including Ties: 20, 1938-40 (all wins)
Most Consecutive SWC Games Unbeaten, Including Ties: 29, 1991-95
Most Consecutive Home Games Unbeaten, Including Ties: 35, 1989-95
Most Consecutive Home Games Won: 31, 1990-95
Unbeaten SWC Seasons: 8—1917, 1919, 1921, 1927, 1939, 1956, 1991, 1992, 1993, 1994
Untied, Unbeaten Seasons: 3—1917, 1919, 1939
Unbeaten Seasons (with ties): 2—1927, 1956, 1994
National Championship Teams: 1—1939
SWC Titles Won or Shared: 17
Consecutive Shutouts: 19, 1918-1920 (SWC record)
Bowl Appearances: 22 (12-10)
Worst Defeat: 48-0 vs. Texas, 1898 (non-conference)
Worst Defeat, SWC: 52-14 vs. Texas, 1970

TEAM DEFENSIVE RECORDS

RUSHING

Fewest Rushes Allowed, Game: 14, Houston, 1992
Fewest Rushes Allowed, Season: 272, 1939
Fewest Yards Allowed, Game: -58, TCU, 1974
Fewest Yards Allowed, Season: 399, 1940 (9 games) (SWC record)
Lowest Average Allowed Per Rush, Season: 1.3, 1940
Lowest Average Allowed Per Game: 41.5, 1939

PASSING

Fewest Completions Allowed, Game: 0, Ellington Field, 1945; Oklahoma A&M, 1954; Arkansas, 1956; Texas, 1973; SMU, 1974; Arkansas, 1991
Fewest Completions Allowed, Season: 33, 1943 (138 att.) (SWC record)
Fewest Yards Allowed, Game: 0, same six opponents as above
Fewest Yards Allowed, Season: 348, 1939 (SWC record)
Fewest TD Passes Allowed, Season: 0, 1957 (SWC record)
Lowest Completion Percentage Allowed: 23.9, 1943 (33 of 138)
Lowest Average Allowed Per Game: 34.8, 1939
Most Interceptions, Per Game: 7 vs. Utah, 1936

QUARTERBACK SACKS

Most Sacks, Season: 56, 1991
Most Sack Yardage, Season: 388, 1991
Most Average Sacks Per Game: 5.1, 1991

TOTAL DEFENSE

Fewest Plays Allowed, Game: 38 vs. Ellington Field, 1945
Fewest Plays Allowed, Season: 447, 1939 (SWC record)
Fewest Average Yards Allowed, Play: 1.71, 1939 (447-763) (NCAA record)

Fewest Yards Allowed, Game: -19 vs. Ellington Field, 1945
Fewest Yards Allowed, Season: 763, 1939
Lowest Average Allowed, Season: 76.3, 1939
Fewest First Downs Allowed, Game: 0 vs. Ellington Field, 1945
Fewest First Downs Allowed, Season: 54, 1939 (SWC record)

PUNTING

Most Punts Forced, Game: 17 by Texas Tech, 1943 (SWC record)
Most Punts Forced, Season: 114, 1939
Lowest Average Punt, Game: (min. five) 22.1, TCU, 1944 (9 for 199)
Lowest Average Punt, Season: 34.4, 1949
Most Punts Blocked, Season: 5, 1941
Lowest Punt Return Average Allowed, Season: 1.3, 1973
Fewest Punt Returns Allowed, Season: 11, 1978 (52 punts)
Fewest Punt Return Yards Allowed, Season: 57, 1978 (11 returns)

PUNT RETURNS

Lowest Average Return Allowed, Season: 1.3, 1973

KICKOFF RETURNS

Lowest Average Return Allowed, Season: 13.9, 1955; 13.1, 1983 (12th Man Kickoff Team)

SCORING

Fewest Points Allowed, Season: 0, 1917 (eight games); 0, 1919 (10 games) (SWC record)

FUMBLES

Most Fumbles Recovered, Game: 7 vs. Baylor, 1982
Most Fumbles Recovered, Season: 29, 1952 (SWC record)

INDIVIDUAL OFFENSIVE RECORDS

(Data incomplete before 1950 — Asterisk indicates SWC record)

RUSHING — 1000-YARD CLUB

(Career Rushing Yards)

Player	Yards	Years
Darren Lewis	*5012*	1987-90
Curtis Dickey	3703	1976-79
Greg Hill	3262	1991-93
Rodney Thomas	3014	1991-94
George Woodard	2911	1975-79
Bubba Bean	2846	1972-75
Johnny Hector	2587	1979-82
Roger Vick	2471	1983-86
Leeland McElroy	2432	1993-95
Bob Smith	2415	1949-51
Bucky Richardson	2095	1987-91
Skip Walker	1878	1972-75
Robert Wilson	1739	1988-90
Larry Stegent	1736	1967-69
Keith Woodside	1720	1984-87
Dick Todd	1556	1936-38
Earnest Jackson	1539	1979-82
Glenn Lippman	1506	1949-51
John David Crow	1465	1955-57
Thomas Sanders	1379	1980-84
John Kimbrough	1357	1938-40
David Brothers	1269	1976-79
Anthony Toney	1238	1982-85
Mike Mosley	1206	1977-80
Roddy Osborne	1188	1955-57
Bucky Sams	1118	1973-75
Jack Pardee	1017	1954-57
Wendell Housley	1009	1966-68

RUSHING — LONGEST RUN

Player	Yards	Opp./Year
Bubba Bean	94	T. Tech/'75
Keith Woodside	90	Texas/'87
Darrell Smith	90	TCU/'76
Vic "Choc" Kelley	85	Oklahoma/'07
P.C. Colgin	85	†SHTC/'25
Rodney Thomas	84	Baylor/'92
Darren Lewis	84	Houston/'89
Bucky Richardson	82	So. Miss./'87
Leeland McElroy	81	Houston/'93
Bob Smith	81	Georgia/'50
Darren Lewis	80	TCU/'87
Bob Smith	80	T. Tech/'49
Rodney Thomas	80	LSU/'93
Earnest Jackson	80	TCU/'81
Curtis Dickey	80	TCU/'77
David Beal	80	Kansas/'78
Glenn Lippman	80	Nevada/'50

†Sam Houston Teachers College

RUSHING — GAME YARDS

Player	Yards	Opp./Year
Bob Smith	297	SMU/'50
Darren Lewis	232	T. Tech/'90
Curtis Dickey	230	TCU/'78
Leeland McElroy	229	LSU/'95
Earnest Jackson	219	TCU/'81
Bob Smith	215	T. Tech/'49
Greg Hill	212	LSU/'91
Darren Lewis	212	Texas/'88
Bubba Bean	204	Clemson/'73
Rodney Thomas	201	LSU/'93
Darren Lewis	201	Houston/'88
Darren Lewis	201	Rice/'89
Darren Lewis	194	TCU/'87
Darren Lewis	192	Arkansas/'88
Johnny Hector	191	TCU/'80

RUSHING — SEASON YARDS

Player	Year	Yards
Darren Lewis	1988	1692
Darren Lewis	1990	1691
Greg Hill	1992	1339
Bob Smith	1950	1302
Greg Hill	1991	1216
George Woodard	1976	1153
Curtis Dickey	1978	1146
Leeland McElroy	1995	1122
George Woodard	1977	1107
Rodney Thomas	1993	996
Curtis Dickey	1977	978
Darren Lewis	1989	961
Roger Vick	1986	960
Bubba Bean	1975	944
Bubba Bean	1974	938

RUSHES — GAME

Player	Att.	Opp./Year
Roger Vick	41	Texas/'86
Mark Green	41	SMU/'71
Darren Lewis	40	Houston/'88
George Woodard	39	Michigan/'77
George Woodard	39	Kansas St./'76
Darren Lewis	38	Texas/'88
Johnny Hector	37	TCU/'80
Roger Vick	37	T. Tech/'85
Leeland McElroy	35	LSU/'95
Darren Lewis	34	Arkansas/'88
Darren Lewis	34	La. Tech/'88
Curtis Dickey	34	TCU/'78
George Woodard	34	SMU/'76
Darren Lewis	34	T. Tech/'90
Darren Lewis	34	Baylor/'90

RUSHES — SEASON

Player	Att.	Year
Darren Lewis	306	1988
Darren Lewis	291	1990
Greg Hill	267	1992
Leeland McElroy	246	1995
George Woodard	245	1977
Greg Hill	240	1991
George Woodard	239	1976
Roger Vick	220	1986
Anthony Toney	208	1985
Curtis Dickey	205	1978
Rodney Thomas	199	1994
Bob Smith	199	1950
Larry Stegent	197	1969

RUSHES — CAREER

Player	Att.	Years
Darren Lewis	909	1987-90
Curtis Dickey	697	1976-79
Greg Hill	631	1991-93
George Woodard	625	1975-77; '79
Rodney Thomas	604	1991-94
Roger Vick	598	1983-86
Johnny Hector	550	1979-82
Bubba Bean	482	1972-75
Larry Stegent	463	1967-69
Leeland McElroy	448	1993-95
Bob Smith	439	1949-51
Skip Walker	371	1972-75

TOUCHDOWNS — SEASON

Player	Year	TD
Joel Hunt	1927	19
Darren Lewis	1990	18
George Woodard	1976	17
Greg Hill	1992	15
Jelly Woodman	1926	14
Bob Smith	1950	14
George Woodard	1977	13
Rodney Thomas	1992	13
Rodney Thomas	1993	13
Leeland McElroy	1995	13
Rodney Thomas	1994	12
Anthony Toney	1985	12
Greg Hill	1991	12
Bob Goode	1945	11
Darren Lewis	1989	11
John Kimbrough	1939	10
John David Crow	1956	10
Robert Wilson	1988	10
Roger Vick	1986	10
Bucky Richardson	1991	10

TOUCHDOWNS — CAREER

Player	Years	TD
Darren Lewis	1987-90	44
Rodney Thomas	1991-94	41
George Woodard	1975-77	35
Curtis Dickey	1976-79	34
Greg Hill	1991-93	33
Joel Hunt	1925-27	30
Bucky Richardson	1987-91	30
Leeland McElroy	1993-95	29
Skip Walker	1972-75	25
Bob Smith	1949-51	23
Roger Vick	1983-86	23
Johnny Hector	1979-82	20
John David Crow	1955-57	19
Bob Long	1966-68	19
Bubba Bean	1972-75	19

RUSHING YARDAGE RECORDS BY CLASS

Class	Player	Yards	Year
Freshman	Greg Hill	1216	1991
Sophomore	Darren Lewis	1692	1988
Junior	Bob Smith	1302	1950
Senior	Darren Lewis	1691	1990

FRESHMAN RUSHING

Player	Yards	Year
Greg Hill	1216	1991
Curtis Dickey	726	1976
Darren Lewis	668	1987
Leeland McElroy	613	1993
George Woodard	604	1975
Robert Wilson	425	1988
Roger Vick	425	1983

OTHER RUSHING RECORDS

Most Touchdowns, Game: Jelly Woodman, 7 vs. New Mexico, 1926

Best Average Per Carry, Season: Bucky Richardson, 6.9, 1990

Best Average Per Carry, Career: Bubba Bean, 5.9, 1972-75

Season 100-Yard Games: Darren Lewis, 10 (1988)

Career 100-Yard Games: Darren Lewis, 27 (1987-90)

Season 200-Yard Games: Darren Lewis, 2 (1988); Darren Lewis, 2 (1990)

Career 200-Yard Games: Darren Lewis, 5 (1987-90) (SWC Record)

Consecutive 100-Yard Games: Darren Lewis, 10 (Last 10 Games of 1988)

Season Yards Per Game: Bob Smith, 144.7, 1950

Career Yards Per Game: Darren Lewis, 113.9, 1987-90

100-YARD RUSHING GAMES (204)

(Since 1949 — Asterisk indicates Bowl Games)

Player	Opponent	Att-Yds
1995 (6 times)		
Leeland McElroy	Texas	29-145
Leeland McElroy	MTSU	17-118
Leeland McElroy	Rice	28-168
D'Andre Hardeman	SMU	26-130
Leeland McElroy	Tulsa	23-116
Leeland McElroy	LSU	35-229
1994 (6 times)		
Rodney Thomas	SMU	18-134
Rodney Thomas	Rice	21-136
Rodney Thomas	Baylor	14-108
Leeland McElroy	Baylor	22-105
Rodney Thomas	Texas Tech	22-124
Leeland McElroy	LSU	11-132
1993 (9 times)		
Greg Hill	Texas	23-125
Greg Hill	TCU	10-125
Greg Hill	SMU	21-129
Greg Hill	Houston	20-128
Rodney Thomas	Texas Tech	23-108
Rodney Thomas	Missouri	17-107
Leeland McElroy	Missouri	17-136
Rodney Thomas	Oklahoma	22-106
Rodney Thomas	LSU	25-201
1992 (10 times)		
Greg Hill	Texas	23-100
Greg Hill	TCU	25-187
Greg Hill	Louisville	26-142
Greg Hill	SMU	24-138
Greg Hill	Baylor	19-119
Rodney Thomas	Baylor	9-116
Greg Hill	Texas Tech	32-141
Rodney Thomas	Texas Tech	24-179
Greg Hill	Missouri	20-104
Greg Hill	Tulsa	26-125
1991 (7 times)		
Greg Hill	TCU	19-115
Greg Hill	Rice	18-109
Bucky Richardson	Rice	18-128
Greg Hill	Houston	25-160
Greg Hill	Texas Tech	24-137
Greg Hill	Tulsa	25-125
Greg Hill	LSU	30-212
1990 (18 times)		
Darren Lewis*	Brigham Young	25-104
Bucky Richardson*	Brigham Young	12-119
Darren Lewis	Texas	25-150
Bucky Richardson	Texas	16-109
Darren Lewis	TCU	23-113
Robert Wilson	Arkansas	18-115
Darren Lewis	SMU	31-207
Bucky Richardson	SMU	13-180
Darren Lewis	Rice	25-176
Darren Lewis	Baylor	34-179
Darren Lewis	Houston	21-124
Robert Wilson	Houston	15-111
Darren Lewis	Texas Tech	34-232
Darren Lewis	North Texas	26-132
Randy Simmons	SW Louisiana	11-141
Darren Lewis	SW Louisiana	16-141
Robert Wilson	SW Louisiana	8-116
Darren Lewis	Hawaii	24-117

Player	Opponent	Att-Yds	Player	Opponent	Att-Yds
1989 (7 times)			**1978 (11 times)**		
Robert Wilson*	Pittsburgh	16-145	Curtis Dickey*	Iowa State	34-276
Darren Lewis	SMU	18-126	Curtis Dickey	TCU	34-230
Darren Lewis	Rice	28-201	Curtis Dickey	Arkansas	28-104
Darren Lewis	Houston	12-120	Curtis Dickey	SMU	33-143
Robert Wilson	Houston	22-115	David Brothers	Rice	25-163
Darren Lewis	S. Mississippi	21-126	Raymond Belcher	Baylor	24-119
Robert Wilson	LSU	15-121	Curtis Dickey	Texas Tech	20-168
1988 (10 times)			Mike Mosley	Texas Tech	14-120
Darren Lewis	Alabama	24-128	Curtis Dickey	Memphis State	11-167
Darren Lewis	Texas	38-212	Curtis Dickey	Boston College	18-138
Darren Lewis	TCU	28-105	Curtis Dickey	Kansas	25-128
Darren Lewis	Arkansas	34-192	**1977 (14 times)**		
Darren Lewis	La. Tech	34-160	George Woodard*	Southern Calif.	27-185
Darren Lewis	Rice	18-170	Mike Mosley*	Southern Calif.	20-180
Darren Lewis	Baylor	28-138	Mike Mosley	Houston	12-109
Darren Lewis	Houston	40-201	Curtis Dickey	TCU	20-178
Darren Lewis	Texas Tech	27-177	George Woodard	TCU	20-163
Darren Lewis	Oklahoma State	25-168	George Woodard	Arkansas	28-116
1987 (7 times)			Curtis Dickey	Arkansas	20-101
Keith Woodside	Texas	12-135	David Walker	SMU	27-182
Darren Lewis	TCU	16-194	Curtis Dickey	Rice	15-106
Bucky Richardson	Rice	8-137	David Brothers	Baylor	9-103
Keith Woodside	Rice	17-122	George Woodard	Michigan	39-153
Darren Lewis	Baylor	25-103	Curtis Dickey	Virginia Tech	17-144
Darren Lewis	S. Mississippi	6-103	George Woodard	Kansas	20-150
Bucky Richardson	S. Mississippi	5-102	Curtis Dickey	Kansas	14-139
1986 (10 times)			**1976 (9 times)**		
Roger Vick*	Ohio State	24-113	George Woodard*	Florida	25 -124
Roger Vick	Texas	41-167	George Woodard	Texas	29 -109
Melvin Collins	TCU	20-110	Darrell Smith	TCU	4-147
Roger Vick	TCU	17-104	George Woodard	TCU	10-102
Roger Vick	Arkansas	28-117	George Woodard	SMU	34-155
Roger Vick	SMU	26-118	George Woodard	Rice	29-188
Roger Vick	Rice	16-115	Curtis Dickey	Texas Tech	18 -127
Roger Vick	Houston	25-104	George Woodard	Kansas State	39 -177
Roger Vick	Texas Tech	26-104	George Woodard	Virginia Tech	20-111
Keith Woodside	North Texas	10-107	**1975 (6 times)**		
1985 (6 times)			George Woodard	Rice	32-167
Anthony Toney	SMU	21-117	George Woodard	SMU	23-106
Keith Woodside	SMU	12-104	George Woodard	Baylor	24-101
Anthony Toney	Rice	25-116	Bubba Bean	Texas Tech	9-180
Roger Vick	Texas Tech	37-135	Bubba Bean	Illinois	12-158
Roger Vick	Tulsa	21-134	George Woodard	LSU	6-106
Anthony Toney	N.E. Louisiana	22-106	**1974 (8 times)**		
1984 (2 times)			Bubba Bean	Rice	10-138
Thomas Sanders	TCU	21-107	Jerry Honore	Arkansas	19-131
Thomas Sanders	Houston	23-112	Skip Walker	Texas Tech	21-138
1983 (1 times)			Skip Walker	LSU	16-130
Roger Vick	TCU	18-110	Bubba Bean	LSU	14-127
1982 (0 times)			Bucky Sams	LSU	24-107
1981 (5 times)			Bubba Bean	Clemson	18-182
Earnest Jackson*	Oklahoma State	22-123	Bucky Sams	Clemson	15-122
Earnest Jackson	TCU	19-219	**1973 (5 times)**		
Johnny Hector	Texas Tech	16-143	Skip Walker	SMU	13-184
Johnny Hector	California	16-125	Bubba Bean	SMU	13-100
Earnest Jackson	California	18-125	Skip Walker	TCU	11-122
1980 (5 times)			Bubba Bean	Clemson	22-204
Johnny Hector	TCU	37-191	Alvin Bowers	Wichita State	14-126
Johnny Hector	Arkansas	18-136	**1972 (3 times)**		
Johnny Hector	SMU	20-126	Brad Dusek	TCU	19-104
Johnny Hector	Rice	26-121	Brad Dusek	Texas Tech	21-112
Mike Mosley	Mississippi	16-116	Mark Green	Wichita State	25-165
1979 (4 times)			**1971 (2 times)**		
Curtis Dickey	Rice	21-127	Mark Green	Texas	25-106
Curtis Dickey	Memphis State	31-137	Mark Green	SMU	41-150
Curtis Dickey	Penn State	31-184	**1970 (1 times)**		
Curtis Dickey	Brigham Young	28-148	Doug Neill	Michigan	17-101

Player	Opponent	Att-Yds
1969 (4 times)		
Steve Burks	SMU	4-102
Larry Stegent	Arkansas	23-124
Larry Stegent	Texas Tech	29-117
Larry Stegent	Army	34-114
1968 (4 times)		
Larry Stegent	Rice	21-100
Dave Elmendorf	Florida State	17-129
Larry Stegent	Florida State	21-139
Larry Stegent	Tulane	12-111
1967 (1 times)		
Larry Stegent	Baylor	29-138
1966 (1 times)		
Wendell Housley	Baylor	33-127
1960-65 (0 times)		
1959 (1 times)		
Jesse McGuire	Texas Tech	15-149
1958 (0 times)		
1957 (2 times)		
John David Crow	Arkansas	21-116
Roddy Osborne	Houston	13-115
1956 (0 times)		
1955 (1 times)		
John David Crow	LSU	13-130
1954 (1 times)		
Elwood Kettler	Houston	16-113
1952-53 (0 times)		
1951 (4 times)		
Glenn Lippman	Texas	19-173
Glenn Lippman	Arkansas	10-105
Billy Tidwell	Baylor	10-139
Glenn Lippman	Texas Tech	18-156
1950 (11 times)		
Bob Smith*	Georgia	20-158
Bob Smith	Rice	27-101
Bob Smith	SMU	29-297
Bob Smith	Arkansas	16-133
Bob Smith	Baylor	6-101
Bob Smith	TCU	38-146
Billy Tidwell	Oklahoma	14-114
Bob Smith	Oklahoma	19-111
Bob Smith	Texas Tech	27-147
Glenn Lippman	Nevada	8-124
Billy Tidwell	Nevada	6-103
1949 (2 times)		
Bob Smith	SMU	31-214
Bob Smith	Texas Tech	23-175
Pre-1949 (Partial List)		
Dick Todd	TDU '36	17-170
Dick Todd	Manhattan '36	17-187
H.M. Pitney	Utah '36	22-104
Jacob Shockley	Utah '36	11-127
Choc Kelley	Oklahoma '07	??-125

200-YARD RUSHING GAMES (13)

Player	Opponent, Year	Att-Yds
Leeland McElroy	LSU, 1995	35-229
Rodney Thomas	LSU, 1993	25-201
Greg Hill	LSU, 1991	30-212
Darren Lewis	SMU, 1990	31-207
Darren Lewis	Texas Tech, 1990	34-232
Darren Lewis	Rice, 1989	28-201
Darren Lewis	Texas, 1988	38-212
Darren Lewis	Houston, 1988	40-201
Earnest Jackson	TCU, 1981	19-219
Curtis Dickey	Iowa State, 1978	34-276
Curtis Dickey	TCU, 1978	34-230
Bubba Bean	Clemson, 1973	22-204
Bob Smith	SMU, 1950	29-297

PASSING — LONGEST PASS PLAY

Players	Yds	Opp., Year	Receiver
Gary Kubiak	92	La. Tech, 1981	Don Jones
Jim Kaufmann	91	Texas, 1965	Dude McLean
Edd Hargett	84	TCU, 1968	Barney Harris
Chris Osgood	84	SMU, 1989	Shane Garrett
David Shipman	84	SMU, 1975	Skip Walker
Jacob Shockley	83	USF, 1936	Waylon Manning
Edd Hargett	80	Texas, 1967	Bob Long

PASSING YARDS — SINGLE GAME

Player	Yards	Opp./Year
Edd Hargett	376	SMU/68
Bucky Richardson	321	TCU/91
Edd Hargett	309	TCU/66
Kevin Murray	309	Tulsa/85
Kevin Murray	308	Baylor/86
Gary Kubiak	306	Rice/82

PASSING YARDS — SEASON

Player	Year	Yards
Kevin Murray	1986	2463
Edd Hargett	1968	2321
Corey Pullig	1995	2105
Corey Pullig	1994	2056
Kevin Murray	1985	1965
Gary Kubiak	1982	1948
Gary Kubiak	1981	1808
Corey Pullig	1993	1732
Lance Pavlas	1989	1681
Lex James	1970	1662
Kevin Murray	1983	1544

PASSING YARDS — CAREER

Player	Years	Yards
Corey Pullig	1992-95	6846
Kevin Murray	1983-86	6506
Edd Hargett	1966-68	5379
Gary Kubiak	1979-82	4078
Lance Pavlas	1987-90	3185
Bucky Richardson	1987-91	3039
Mike Mosley	1977-80	2545
David Walker	1973-77	2517
Lex James	1970-72	2297
Craig Stump	1984-87	2182
Charles Milstead	1957-59	2072
Ray Graves	1951-52	1610

PASS COMPLETIONS — SINGLE GAME

Player	Comp.	Opp./Year
Edd Hargett	32	SMU/68
Gary Kubiak	32	TCU/82
Gary Kubiak	25	Texas Tech/82
Kevin Murray	25	Baylor/86
Kevin Murray	25	Texas/86
Kevin Murray	25	Rice/83

TOUCHDOWN PASSES — SINGLE GAME

Player	TDs	Opp./Year
Gary Kubiak	6	Rice/81
Gary Kubiak	5	Rice/82
Kevin Murray	4	Tulsa/85
Kevin Murray	4	Arkansas/83
Jeff Granger	4	Tulsa/91

PASS COMPLETIONS — SEASON

Player	Comp.	Year
Kevin Murray	212	1987
Gary Kubiak	181	1982
Edd Hargett	169	1968
Corey Pullig	165	1995
Corey Pullig	161	1994
Kevin Murray	147	1985
Corey Pullig	144	1993
Lance Pavlas	134	1989
Kevin Murray	132	1983
Edd Hargett	132	1966
Gary Kubiak	111	1981
Lex James	111	1970

PASS COMPLETIONS — CAREER

Player	Comp.	Years
Corey Pullig	560	1992-95
Kevin Murray	534	1983-86
Edd Hargett	400	1966-68
Gary Kubiak	315	1979-82
Lance Pavlas	248	1987-90
Mike Mosley	204	1977-80
Bucky Richardson	196	1987-91
David Walker	177	1973-77
Craig Stump	174	1984-87
Charles Milstead	164	1957-59
Lex James	162	1970-72

PASS ATTEMPTS — SINGLE GAME

Player	Att.	Opp./Year
Edd Hargett	58	SMU/68
Edd Hargett	55	Arkansas/68
Kevin Murray	48	Rice/83
Gary Kubiak	46	TCU/82
Edd Hargett	44	Arkansas/66
Gary Kubiak	41	La. Tech/82
Gary Kubiak	40	Texas Tech/82
Kevin Murray	40	Baylor/86

PASS ATTEMPTS — SEASON

Player	Att.	Year
Kevin Murray	349	1986
Edd Hargett	348	1968
Gary Kubiak	324	1982
Corey Pullig	307	1995
Corey Pullig	269	1994
Edd Hargett	265	1966
Kevin Murray	251	1985
Kevin Murray	249	1983
Corey Pullig	243	1993
Lance Pavlas	227	1989
Lex James	225	1970
Gary Kubiak	209	1981

PASS ATTEMPTS — CAREER

Player	Att.	Year
Corey Pullig	992	1992-95
Kevin Murray	926	1983-86
Edd Hargett	821	1966-68
Gary Kubiak	594	1979-82
Lance Pavlas	439	1987-90
Bucky Richardson	405	1987-91
David Walker	374	1973-77
Mike Mosley	368	1977-80
Craig Stump	363	1984-87
Lex James	346	1970-72
Charles Milstead	319	1957-59
Ray Graves	262	1951-52

TOUCHDOWN PASSES — SEASON

Player	TDs	Year
Gary Kubiak	19	1982
Corey Pullig	17	1993
Kevin Murray	17	1986
Edd Hargett	16	1968
Corey Pullig	14	1995
Kevin Murray	14	1983
Corey Pullig	13	1994
Kevin Murray	13	1985
Gary Kubiak	11	1981
Lance Pavlas	10	1989
Edd Hargett	10	1966
Craig Stump	10	1984

TOUCHDOWN PASSES — CAREER

Player	TDs	Years
Kevin Murray	48	1983-86
Corey Pullig	47	1992-95
Edd Hargett	40	1966-68
Gary Kubiak	31	1979-82
Lance Pavlas	20	1987-90
David Walker	14	1973-77
Craig Stump	14	1984-87
Bucky Richardson	14	1987-91

COMPLETION PERCENTAGE — SEASON

(min. 100 attempts)

Player	Comp.-Att.	Pct.	Year
Kevin Murray	212-349	.607	1986
Corey Pullig	161-269	.599	1994
Corey Pullig	144-243	.593	1993
Lance Pavlas	134-227	.590	1989
Kevin Murray	147-251	.586	1985
Mike Mosley	82-142	.578	1979
Ray Graves	93-164	.567	1952
Gary Kubiak	181-324	.559	1982

COMPLETION PERCENTAGE — CAREER

(min. 200 attempts)

Player	Comp.-Att.	Pct.	Year
Kevin Murray	534-926	.577	1983-86
Corey Pullig	560-992	.565	1992-95
Lance Pavlas	248-439	.565	1987-90
Mike Mosley	204-368	.554	1977-80
Gary Kubiak	314-595	.527	1979-82
Ray Graves	141-271	.520	1950-52

PASSING YARDAGE RECORDS BY CLASS

Class	Player	Yards	Year
Freshman	Kevin Murray	1544	1983
Sophomore	Kevin Murray	1965	1985
Junior	Kevin Murray	2463	1986
Senior	Edd Hargett	2321	1968

OTHER PASSING RECORDS

Most Passes Had Intercepted, Game: Jim Cashion, 5, vs. LSU (1948); Edd Hargett, 5, vs. Texas (1968)

Most Passes Had Intercepted, Season: Derace Moser, 19, 1941; Edd Hargett, 19, 1966

Most Passes Had Intercepted, Career: Edd Hargett, 40 (1966-68)

Consecutive Completions: Lance Pavlas, 11, vs. Texas Tech, 1989; Corey Pullig, 11, vs. Tulsa, 1995

RECEIVING — GAME

Player	Rec.	Opp./Year
Ken McLean	13	Texas/'65
Barney Harris	13	SMU/'68
Keith Woodside	12	Arkansas/'86
Rod Harris	9	Okla. St./'88
Don Ellis	8	Arkansas/'52
Rod Bernstine	8	So. Miss./'86
Keith Woodside	8	Houston/'86
Rod Bernstine	8	TCU/'86
Keith Woodside	8	Texas/'86
Jeff Nelson	8	Tulsa/'85
Johnny Hector	8	Houston/82
Gary Oliver	8	Arkansas/'90
Greg Schorp	8	Louisville/'92

RECEIVING — SEASON

Player	Rec.	Year
Rod Bernstine	65	1986
Ken McLean	60	1965
Keith Woodside	52	1986
Jeff Nelson	51	1985
Barney Harris	49	1968
Albert Connell	41	1995
Shea Walker	40	1986
Rich Siler	40	1983
Gerald Carter	39	1979
Rod Harris	37	1988
John Tracey	37	1958
Mike Jones	36	1989
Percy Waddle	36	1989

RECEIVING — CAREER

Player	Rec.	Years
Keith Woodside	110	1983-87
Rod Bernstine	105	1983-86
Shea Walker	98	1983-86
Jeff Nelson	92	1982-85
Barney Harris	91	1967-69
Tony Harrison	89	1990-93
Rod Harris	87	1985-88
Richard Osborne	86	1972-75
Bob Long	79	1966-68
Ryan Mathews	76	1991-94
Jimmy Teal	74	1982-84

RECEPTION RECORDS BY CLASS

Class	Player	No.	Year
Freshman	Rod Bernstine	24	1983
Sophomore	Rich Siler	40	1983
Junior	Keith Woodside	57	1986
Senior	Rod Bernstine	65	1986

RECEIVING YARDS — SINGLE GAME

Player	Yds	Opp./Year
Ken McLean	250	Texas/'65
Hugh McElroy	180	LSU/'70
Jimmy Teal	173	SMU/'84
Barney Harris	162	SMU/'68

RECEIVING YARDS — SEASON

Player	Yds	Year
Ken McLean	835	1965
Barney Harris	745	1968
Mike Whitwell	731	1981
Rod Bernstine	710	1986
Albert Connell	653	1995
Jeff Nelson	651	1985
Jimmy Teal	631	1984
Mike Whitwell	603	1980
Keith Woodside	603	1986
Percy Waddle	600	1989
Rod Harris	592	1988
Tony Harrison	577	1991
Shea Walker	565	1986
Bob Long	541	1967
Gerald Carter	528	1979
Bob Long	507	1968

RECEIVING YARDS — CAREER

Player	Yds	Years
Tony Harrison	1576	1990-93
Shea Walker	1411	1983-86
Rod Harris	1395	1985-88
Mike Whitwell	1372	1978-81
Barney Harris	1298	1967-69
Bob Long	1298	1966-68
Jimmy Teal	1258	1982-84
Brian Mitchell	1232	1991-94
Richard Osborne	1181	1972-75
Ryan Mathews	1174	1991-94

RECEIVING TOUCHDOWNS — SINGLE GAME

Player	TDs	Opp./Year
Don Ellis	3	Arkansas/'52
Don Jones	3	Rice/'82

RECEIVING TOUCHDOWNS — SEASON

Player	TDs	Year
Bob Long	8	1968
Bob Long	8	1967
Albert Connell	7	1995
Jimmy Teal	6	1984
Don Jones	6	1981
Ross Brupbacher	6	1969
Andy Hillhouse	6	1950
Tony Harrison	6	1991
Rod Bernstine	5	1986
Keith Woodside	5	1986
Don Jones	5	1982
Homer May	5	1970
Percy Waddle	5	1989

RECEIVING TOUCHDOWNS — CAREER

Player	TDs	Years
Bob Long	19	1966-68
Tony Harrison	14	1990-93
Don Jones	11	1980-83
Jeff Nelson	11	1982-85
Jimmy Teal	9	1982-84
Rod Bernstine	8	1983-86
Shea Walker	8	1983-86
Homer May	8	1970-72
Rod Harris	7	1985-87
Brian Mitchell	7	1991-94
Albert Connell	7	1995-present

OTHER RECEIVING RECORDS

Most Yards Per Catch, Season: Brian Mitchell, 27.3 (19 rec. for 519), 1991

Most Yards Per Catch, Career: Brian Mitchell, 18.1, 1991-94

FIELD GOALS — LONGEST

Player	Yards	Opp/Year
Tony Franklin	65	Baylor/'76
Tony Franklin	64	Baylor/'76
Tony Franklin	62	Florida/'77
Kyle Bryant	61	USM/'94
Tony Franklin	59	Rice/'75
Layne Talbot	59	Baylor/'90
Alan Smith	59	Arkansas St./'83
David Hardy	57	UTA/'82
Tony Franklin	57	Texas/'76
Randy Haddox	57	Arkansas/'74
Alan Smith	57	Arkansas St./'83

FIELD GOALS — GAME

Player	No.	Opp/Year
Alan Smith	6	Arkansas St./'83
Tony Franklin	5	Rice/'76
David Hardy	4	UTA/'82
Scott Slater	4	Houston/'86
Scott Slater	4	TCU/'87

FIELD GOALS — SEASON

Player	Year	FG-Att.	Pct.
Scott Slater	1986	21-27	.778
Alan Smith	1983	18-26	.692
Tony Franklin	1976	17-26	.654
Kyle Bryant	1994	17-25	.680
David Hardy	1982	16-22	.727
Terry Venetoulias	1992	16-23	.696
Tony Franklin	1977	16-28	.571
Eric Franklin	1985	15-27	.556
Scott Slater	1987	15-22	.682
Terry Venetoulias	1991	13-18	.722
David Hardy	1981	13-19	.684
Terry Venetoulias	1993	13-19	.684
Alan Smith	1984	12-20	.600
Tony Franklin	1975	12-28	.429

FIELD GOALS — CAREER

Player	Years	FG-Att.	Pct.
Tony Franklin	1975-78	56-101	.554
David Hardy	1979-82	43-63	.683
Terry Venetoulias	1990-93	42-60	.700
Scott Slater	1986-88	42-61	.689
Alan Smith	1980-84	32-51	.627
Kyle Bryant	1994-	26-44	.591
Layne Talbot	1987-90	21-32	.656
Eric Franklin	1984-86	20-32	.625
Pat McDermott	1970-72	20-38	.526
Randy Haddox	1973-74	19-40	.475

FIELD GOALS — SEASON PERCENTAGE

(min. 12 FGM)

Player	Year	FG-ATT	Pct.
Scott Slater	1986	21-27	.778
David Hardy	1982	16-22	.727
Terry Venetoulias	1991	13-18	.722
Terry Venetoulias	1992	16-23	.696
Alan Smith	1983	18-26	.692

FIELD GOALS — CAREER PERCENTAGE

(min. 20 FGM)

Player	Year	FG-ATT	Pct.
Terry Venetoulias	1990-93	42-60	.700
Scott Slater	1985-88	42-61	.689
David Hardy	1879-82	43-63	.683
Layne Talbot	1987-90	21-32	.656
Alan Smith	1980-84	32-51	.627

OTHER FIELD GOAL RECORDS

Best Season Percentage, Under 40 Yards: Scott Slater, 1.000 (16-16), 1986

Best Career Percentage, Under 40 Yards: Terry Venetoulias, .882 (30-34), 1990-93

Best Season Percentage, Over 40 Yards: Alan Smith, .667 (12-18), 1983

Best Career Percentage, Over 40 Yards: Scott Slater, .591 (13-22), 1985-88

Most Field Goals, Game: 6, Alan Smith vs. Arkansas State, 1983

Most Field Goals Over 40 Yards, Game: 5, Alan Smith vs. Arkansas State, 1983

Most Field Goals Over 60 Yards, Game: 2, Tony Franklin vs. Baylor, 1976

Most Field Goals Attempted Over 60 Yards, Season: Tony Franklin, 1976

Most Field Goals Made Over 60 Yards, Season: 2, Tony Franklin, 1976

Most Field Goals Attempted Over 60 Yards, Career: 11, Tony Franklin, 1976-79

Most Field Goals Made Over 60 Yards, Career: 2, Tony Franklin, 1976-79

Most Field Goals Attempted Over 50 Yards, Career: 38, Tony Franklin, 1976-79

Most Field Goals Made Over 50 Yards, Career: 16, Tony Franklin, 1976-79

EXTRA POINTS — GAME

Player	No.	Opp/Year
Terry Venetoulias	10	Missouri/'93
Scott Slater	9	TCU/'86
Layne Talbot	9	SMU/'89
Layne Talbot	9	USL/'90
Terry Venetoulias	9	SMU/'91
Tony Franklin	8	TCU/'76
Kyle Bryant	7	Tulsa/'95
Tony Franklin	7	TCU/'77
David Hardy	7	Rice/'82
David Hardy	7	UTA/'82

EXTRA POINTS — SEASON

Player	Year	PAT-Att.
Terry Venetoulias	1993	51-51
Layne Talbot	1990	50-51
Terry Venetoulias	1991	49-50
Terry Venetoulias	1992	39-43
Layne Talbot	1989	38-38
Tony Franklin	1977	38-38
Scott Slater	1986	37-38
Darrow Hooper	1950	34-45
David Hardy	1982	32-32
Randy Haddox	1973	32-35

EXTRA POINTS — CAREER

Player	Years	PAT-Att.
Terry Venetoulias	1990-93	139-144
Tony Franklin	1975-78	123-132
Scott Slater	1986-88	96-99
David Hardy	1979-82	90-99
Layne Talbot	1987-90	88-89
Darrow Hooper	1950-52	62-83
Kyle Bryant	1994-	60-64
Randy Haddox	1973-74	59-63

SEASON–KICKER ONLY

Player	Year	PAT	FG	TP
Scott Slater	1986	37	21	100
Terry Venetoulias	1993	51	13	90
Terry Venetoulias	1991	49	13	88
Terry Venetoulias	1990	39	16	87
Tony Franklin	1977	38	16	86

CAREER–KICKER ONLY

Player	Year	PAT	FG	TP
Tony Franklin	1976-79	123	56	291
Terry Venetoulias	1990-93	139	42	265
Scott Slater	1985-88	96	42	222
David Hardy	1979-82	90	43	219
Layne Talbot	1987-90	88	21	151

SCORING — GAME

Player	Year	TD	Pts	Opponent
Jelly Woodman	1926	7	44	N. Mex./26
Preston Smith	1945	4	25	Ell. Fld/45
Leeland McElroy	1995	4	24	Tulsa/95

SCORING — SEASON

Player	Years	TD	PAT	FG	TP
Joel Hunt	1927	19	n/a	n/a	128
Darren Lewis	1990	19	0	0	114
George Woodard	1976	17	0	0	102
Greg Hill	1992	17	0	0	102
Scott Slater	1986	0	37	21	100
Leeland McElroy	1995	16	0	0	96
Rodney Thomas	1994	16	0	0	96
Terry Venetoulias	1993	0	51	13	90
Terry Venetoulias	1991	0	49	13	88
Terry Venetoulias	1992	0	39	16	87
Tony Franklin	1977	0	38	16	86
Leeland McElroy	1993	14	0	0	84
Bob Smith	1950	14	0	0	84
Jelly Woodman	1926	14	0	0	84

SCORING — CAREER

Player	Years	TD	PAT	FG	TP
Tony Franklin	1975-78	0	123	56	291
Rodney Thomas	1991-94	45	0	0	270
Darren Lewis	1987-90	45	0	0	270
Terry Venetoulias	1990-93	0	139	42	265
Joel Hunt	1925-27	30	29	5	224
Scott Slater	1985-88	0	96	42	222
David Hardy	1979-82	0	90	43	219
Leeland McElroy	1993-95	36	0	0	216
George Woodard	1975-77	35	0	0	210

TOTAL OFFENSE — SINGLE GAME

Player	Run/Pass/Total	Opp./Year
Edd Hargett	42/376/418	SMU/68
Bucky Richardson	120/231/359	Rice/91
Bucky Richardson	27/321/348	TCU/91
Gary Kubiak	7/306/313	Rice/82
Edd Hargett	-3/309/306	TCU/66
Kevin Murray	-7/309/302	Tulsa/85
Bob Smith	297/ 0/297	SMU/50

TOTAL OFFENSE — SEASON

Player	Run/Pass/Total	Year
Kevin Murray	-115/2463/2348	1986
Edd Hargett	9/2321/2330	1968
Corey Pullig	50/2105/2155	1995
Corey Pullig	-64/2056/1992	1994
Gary Kubiak	178/1808/1986	1981
Bucky Richardson	448/1492/1940	1991
Kevin Murray	-72/1965/1892	1985
Gary Kubiak	-63/1948/1885	1982
Darren Lewis	1691/ 57/1748	1990
Corey Pullig	-27/1732/1705	1993
Darren Lewis	1692/0/1692	1988
Lance Pavlas	-2/1681/1679	1989

TOTAL OFFENSE — CAREER

Player	Run/Pass/Total	Years
Corey Pullig	41/6846/6887	1992-95
Kevin Murray	-51/6506/6455	1983-86
Edd Hargett	32/5379/5411	1966-68
Darren Lewis	5012/ 150/5162	1987-90
Bucky Richardson	2095/3039/5134	1987-91
Gary Kubiak	188/4078/4266	1979-82
Mike Mosley	1396/2545/3941	1977-80
Curtis Dickey	3703/ 0/3703	1976-79
David Walker	912/2517/3429	1973-77
Greg Hill	3262/ 0/3262	1991-93
Lance Pavlas	-97/3212/3115	1987-90

OTHER TOTAL OFFENSE RECORDS

Most Total Plays, Game: Edd Hargett, 70 (12 rush, 58 pass, 418 total yards) vs. SMU (1968)

Most Total Plays, Season: Edd Hargett, 433 (1968)

Most Total Plays, Career: Kevin Murray, 1121 (1983-86)

Average Yards Per Play, Season: Bucky Richardson, 7.5, 1991

Average Yards Per Play, Career: Bucky Richardson, 6.6, 1987-91

ALL-PURPOSE YARDS — SEASON

Player	Year	Run	Rec	KR	PR	Total
Darren Lewis	1990	1691	48	0	0	1739
Leeland McElroy	1995	1122	379	208	0	1709
Darren Lewis	1988	1692	13	0	0	1705
Bob Smith	1950	1302	116	174	0	1592
Leeland McElroy	1993	613	224	590	0	1427
Larry Stegent	1967	568	365	292	20	1245
Rod Harris	1988	-2	592	388	235	1213
Dick Todd	1937	518	98	104	426	1146
Dick Todd	1938	507	42	179	403	1131
Don Ellis	1952	377	274	413	62	1126
Dick Todd	1936	529	53	215	318	1115

ALL-PURPOSE YARDS — CAREER

Player	Years	Run	Rec	KR	PR	Total
Darren Lewis	1987-90	5012	126	0	0	5138
Curtis Dickey	1976-79	3703	496	487	0	4706
Leeland McElroy	1993-95	2442	645	1099	10	4196
Larry Stegent	1967-69	1736	739	714	591	3780
Rod Harris	1985-88	60	1395	1209	971	3635
Dick Todd	1936-38	1556	193	488	1147	3384
Bob Smith	1949-51	2415	261	483	0	3159

LONGEST PUNT RETURNS

Player	Yards	Opp/Year
Bob Goode	98	Ellington Field/45
Charlie Royalty	93	Villanova/48
Carl Roaches	84	Rice/72
Aaron Glenn	76	Missouri/93
Preston Smith	74	Arkansas/45
Kevin Smith	73	Texas/91
Marion Flanagan	72	Oklahoma/46
Dick Todd	72	SMU/37
Kevin Smith	71	Rice/91
Carl Roaches	71	SMU/73
Barney Welch	71	Texas/42
Yale Lary	69	SMU/50

PUNT RETURN YARDS — SINGLE GAME

Player	Rt-	Yds	Opp/Year
Aaron Glenn	3-	131	Missouri/93
Rod Harris	8-	123	La. Tech/87
Billy Mitchell	8-	116	Houston/94
Rod Harris	7-	108	Arkansas/87
Billy Cannon	4-	110	Arkansas State/83
Ray Mickens	4-	99	Houston/95
Bob Goode	1-	98	Ellington Field/45
Carl Roaches	3-	96	SMU/73

PUNT RETURN YARDS — SEASON

Player	Rt-Yds	Avg.	Year
Marion Flanagan	49-475	9.7	1943
Rod Harris	37-391	10.6	1987
Yale Lary	24-388	16.2	1951
Rod Harris	42-345	8.2	1986
Aaron Glenn	17-339	19.9	1993
Jimmie Hawkins	39-331	8.5	1985
Dick Todd	31-318	10.3	1936
David Scott	46-318	6.9	1979
Derrick Frazier	29-301	10.4	1992
Jimmie Hawkins	33-298	9.0	1984
Carl Roaches	38-287	7.5	1972
Ray Mickens	24-281	11.7	1995

PUNT RETURN YARDS — CAREER

Player	Years	Rt-Yds	Avg.
Rod Harris	1985-88	116-971	8.4
Carl Roaches	1972-75	115-924	8.0
Jimmie Hawkins	1982-85	87-750	8.6
Billy Cannon	1980-83	86-649	7.6
Yale Lary	1949-51	33-597	18.1
David Scott	1979-80	79-439	9.3
Ray Mickens	1992-95	29-348	12.0
Dave Elmendorf	1968-70	37-345	4.4
Shane Garrett	1988-90	45-344	7.6
George Hargett	1961-63	37-341	9.2
Aaron Glenn	1992-93	17-339	19.9

PUNT RETURN YARDAGE RECORDS BY CLASS

Class	Player	Yards	Year
Freshman	Carl Roaches	287	1972
Sophomore	Marion Flanagan	475	1943
Junior	Rod Harris	391	1987
Senior	Yale Lary	388	1951

OTHER PUNT RETURN RECORDS

Single Game Returns: Carl Roaches, 10 (58 yards) vs. LSU, 1975 (SWC record)
Season Returns: Marion Flanagan, 49, 1943
Career Returns: Rod Harris, 116, 1985-88
Highest Career Average: Yale Lary, 18.1 (33 ret. for 597 yards), 1949-51
Season Returns for Touchdowns: Carl Roaches, 2, 1972; Rod Harris, 2, 1987; Aaron Glenn, 2, 1993
Career Returns for Touchdowns: Kevin Smith, 3, 1988-91

LONGEST KICKOFF RETURNS

Player	Yards	Opp/Year
Carl Roaches	100	Boston College/'73
Dan McIlhany	100	Texas Tech/'62
Bob Smith	100	Georgia/'50
Leeland McElroy	100	Texas/'93
Leeland McElroy	100	USM/'94
Joel Hunt	97	Arkansas/'27
Carl Roaches	97	LSU/'72
Billy Mitchell	95	Houston/'92
Hugh McElroy	94	Nebraska/'71
Leeland McElroy	93	Rice/'93
Larry Horton	92	LSU/'89
Bob Goode	90	Oklahoma/'48

KICKOFF RETURN YARDS — SINGLE GAME

Player	Yds	Opp/Year
Carl Roaches	193	Boston College/'73
Leeland McElroy	181	Rice/'93
Jack Pardee	139	Texas/'56
Billy Mitchell	133	Houston/'92

KICKOFF RETURN YARDS — SEASON

Player	Year	Rt-Yds	Avg.
Leeland McElroy	1993	15-590	39.3
Dave Elmendorf	1970	23-457	19.4
Hugh McElroy	1971	17-439	25.8
Carl Roaches	1973	15-426	28.4
Carl Roaches	1972	18-426	23.7
Larry Horton	1989	17-420	24.7
Don Ellis	1952	17-413	24.2
Bob Goode	1948	16-407	25.4
Rod Harris	1988	22-388	17.6
Billy Mitchell	1992	11-336	30.5
Rod Harris	1987	15-329	21.9

KICKOFF RETURN YARDS — CAREER

Player	Years	Rt-Yds	Avg.
Rod Harris	1985-88	59-1209	20.5
Leeland McElroy	1993-95	30-1099	36.6
Carl Roaches	1972-75	43-1087	25.3
Larry Stegent	1967-69	39-814	20.9
Dave Elmendorf	1968-70	35-689	19.7
Don Ellis	1952-53	26-566	21.8

KICKOFF RETURN YARDAGE RECORDS BY CLASS

Class	Player	Yards	Year
Freshman	Leeland McElroy	590	1993
Sophomore	Carl Roaches	426	1973
Junior	Larry Horton	420	1989
Senior	Dave Elmendorf	457	1970

OTHER KICKOFF RETURN RECORDS

Most Returns, Game: Carl Roaches, 6 vs. Texas, 1972
Most Returns, Season: Dave Elmendorf, 23, 1970
Most Returns, Career: Rod Harris, 59, 1985-88
Highest Return Average, Season: Leeland McElroy, 39.3, 1993
Highest Return Average, Career: Leeland McElroy, 36.6, 1993-95
Season Returns for Touchdowns: Leeland McElroy, 3, 1993
Career Returns for Touchdowns: Leeland McElroy, 4, 1993-95

LONGEST PUNTS

Player	Yards	Opp/Year
Bobby Goff	86	Texas Tech/'44
Wilbert Randow	85	Texas/'33
Kyle Stuard	81	La. Tech/'81
Todd Tschantz	80	Rice/'85
Sean Terry	76	Colorado/'95
David Davis	75	Tulsa/'92
Stan Hollmig	74	LSU/'47
Derace Moser	74	TCU/'41
Mitch Robertson	74	Rice/'71
Phil Scoggin	74	Texas/'65
Steve O'Neal	73	Baylor/'66
Phil Scoggin	73	SMU/'64

PUNTING — SEASON AVERAGE

(min. two punts per game)

Player	No-Yds	Avg.	Year
David Davis	70-3067	43.8	1992
Phil Scoggin	88-3833	43.6	1965
David Appleby	57-2466	43.3	1977
Sean Terry	60-2598	43.3	1995
Todd Tschantz	33-1406	42.6	1985
Sean Wilson	45-1906	42.4	1990
Steve O'Neal	67-2836	42.3	1966
Steve O'Neal	81-3402	42.0	1967
Mark Stanley	59-2479	42.0	1974
Kyle Stuard	67-2806	41.9	1983

PUNTING — CAREER AVERAGE

(min. 100 punts)

Player	Years	No-Yds	Avg.
Todd Tschantz	1984-86	106-4498	42.4
Phil Scoggin	1964-65	161-6739	41.9
Steve O'Neal	1966-68	212-8854	41.8
Kyle Stuard	1980-83	205-8472	41.3
Sean Wilson	1987-90	185-7577	41.0
David Davis	1991-92	122-4983	40.8
David Appleby	1976-79	226-9222	40.8
Sean Terry	1992-95	120-4868	40.6

PUNTING — SEASON NET AVERAGE

(min. 2 punts per game)

Player	Net	Avg	Year
Sean Terry	40.1	43.3	1995
Kyle Stuard	40.0	41.9	1983
Todd Tschantz	39.8	42.6	1985
David Davis	39.3	43.8	1992
Todd Tschantz	39.3	41.3	1984
Sean Wilson	38.9	41.7	1989

PUNTING — CAREER NET AVERAGE

(min. 100 punts)

Player	Net	Avg	Years
Todd Tschantz	39.9	42.4	1984-86
David Davis	38.2	41.8	1991-92
Kyle Stuard	37.9	41.3	1980-83
Steve O'Neal	37.6	41.8	1966-68
Sean Terry	37.4	40.6	1992-95
Sean Wilson	36.9	41.0	1987-90

OTHER PUNTING RECORDS

Most Punts, Single Game: Bob Goode, 17 vs. SMU, 1945

Most Punts, Season: Phil Scoggin, 88, 1965 (SWC record)

Most Punts, Career: David Appleby, 226, 1976-79

Most Yards, Season: Phil Scoggin, 3833, 1965

Most Yards, Career: David Appleby, 9222, 1976-79

Single Game Average: (min. 5 punts) 53.6 (five for 278 yards) David Appleby vs. Houston, 1977

INDIVIDUAL DEFFENSIVE RECORDS

INTERCEPTIONS — SINGLE GAME

Player	Int.	Opp/Year
Joe Boring	4	Arkansas/'52

INTERCEPTIONS — SEASON

Player	Year	Int
Bill Sibley	1941	10
Kevin Smith	1989	9
Lester Hayes	1976	8
Joe Boring	1952	8
Bill Hobbs	1967	7
Kevin Smith	1990	7
Lester Hayes	1975	6
Pat Thomas	1974	6
Dave Elmendorf	1970	6
Lee Hitt	1971	6
David Hoot	1970	6
Aaron Glenn	1992	6

INTERCEPTIONS — CAREER

Player	Years	Int
Kevin Smith	1988-91	20
Lester Hayes	1973-76	14
Pat Thomas	1972-75	13
John Kimbrough	1938-40	12
Dave Elmendorf	1968-70	12
Kip Corrington	1983-87	11
Bill Hobbs	1966-68	11
Joe Boring	1952-53	11
Domingo Bryant	1982-85	9
Aaron Glenn	1992-93	9
Ray Mickens	1992-95	9
John David Crow	1955-57	8
James Flowers	1983-86	8
Derrick Frazier	1989-92	8
Jeff Fuller	1980-83	8

LONGEST INTERCEPTION RETURNS

Player	Yards	Opp/Year
Bill Hobbs	100	TCU/67
Cullen Rogers	99	Arkansas/'42
Aaron Glenn	95	Texas/'92
Bill Conatser	92	TCU/'39
J.V. Sikes	92	Texas/'25
Derace Moser	90	New York U./'41
Ramsey Bradberry	89	SMU/'89
Ross Brupbacher	80	Tulane/'68
Kevin Smith	78	Rice/'90
Lester Hayes	77	Baylor/'75

INTERCEPTION RECORDS BY CLASS

Class	Player	No.	Year
Freshman	Several players with two		
Sophomore	Kevin Smith	9	1989
Junior	Bill Sibley	10	1941
Senior	Lester Hayes	8	1976

OTHER PASS INTERCEPTION RECORDS

Most Yards Interception Returns, Game: Bill Hobbs, 132 vs. TCU, 1967

Most Yards Interception Returns, Season: Ross Brupbacher, 167, 1967

Most Yards Interception Returns, Career: Kevin Smith, 289, 1988-91

Most Returns for Touchdowns, Season: Kevin Smith, 2, 1990

Most Returns for Touchdowns, Career: Kevin Smith, 3, 1988-91

TACKLES — SEASON

Player	Tackles	Year
Doug Carr	157	1978
Johnny Holland	155	1984
Larry Kelm	152	1986
Grady Hoermann	151	1971
Johnny Holland	150	1985

TACKLES — CAREER

Player	Years	Tackles
Johnny Holland	1983-86	455
Mike Little	1978-81	448
Ed Simonini	1972-75	425
Ray Childress	1981-84	360
Doug Carr	1977-80	359

TACKLES — GAME

Player	Tackles	Opp./Year
Larry Horton	24	Baylor/'90
Larry Kelm	24	SMU/'85
Johnny Holland	22	Alabama/'85
Jacob Green	22	Baylor/'79
Johnny Holland	20	S. Miss./'86
Jay Muller	19	Arkansas/'85
Larry Kelm	19	S. Miss./'86
Reggie Graham	19	Tx. Tech/'94

ANNUAL TACKLE LEADERS

Year	Player (Pos.)	No.
1995	Dat Nguyen, lb	94
1994	Reggie Graham, lb	101
1993	Sam Adams, de	78
1992	Patrick Bates, lb	95
1991	Jason Atkinson, lb	95
1990	Larry Horton, ss	117
1989	Larry Horton, ss	102
1988	Dana Batiste, lb	110
1987	John Roper, lb	104
1986	Johnny Holland, lb	147
1985	Larry Kelm, lb	152
1984	Johnny Holland, lb	155
1983	Ray Childress, de	117
1982	Jeff Fuller, db	90
	Bobby Strogen, lb	90
1981	Bobby Strogen,lb	133
1980	Mike Little, lb	116
1979	Doug Carr, lb	136
1978	Doug Carr, lb	157
1977	Carl Grulich, ss	132
1976	Robert Jackson, lb	143
1975	Ed Simonini, lb	101
1974	Ed Simonini, lb	98
1973	Ed Simonini, lb	130
1972	Grady Hoermann,lb	130
1971	Grady Hoermann, lb	151

TOTAL TACKLE RECORDS BY CLASS

Class	Player	No.	Year
Freshman	Ed Simonini	98	1972
Sophomore	Doug Carr	157	1978
Junior	Grady Hoermann	151	1971
Senior	Larry Kelm	152	1986

QUARTERBACK SACKS — GAME

Player	Sacks	Opponent/Year
Alex Morris	5	Houston/'87
Jacob Green	4	Baylor/'79
Ray Childress	4	Arkansas/'83
John Roper	4	Arkansas/'87
John Roper	4	Louisiana Tech/'87

QUARTERBACK SACKS — SEASON

Player	Sacks	Year
Jacob Green	20	1979
Ray Childress	15	1983
John Roper	15	1987
John Roper	15	1988
Aaron Wallace	14.5	1988
Jacob Green	13	1978
William Thomas	13	1990
Marcus Buckley	13	1991
Keith Mitchell	13	1995
Marcus Buckley	12	1992

QUARTERBACK SACKS — CAREER

Player	Sacks	Year
Aaron Wallace	42	1986-89
Jacob Green	37	1977-79
John Roper	36	1985-88
Marcus Buckley	29	1990-92
Ray Childress	25	1981-84
William Thomas	21.5	1987-90
Sam Adams	20.5	1991-93
Alex Morris	20	1985-88
Keith Mitchell	19.5	1993-

CAREER PASSES BROKEN UP

Player	PBUs	Years
Derrick Frazier	36	1989-92
Aaron Glenn	33	1992-93
Kevin Smith	32	1988-92
Ray Mickens	28	1992-95
Kip Corrington	27	1984-87
Chet Brooks	26	1984-87

SEASON PASSES BROKEN UP

Player	PBUs	Year
Aaron Glenn	20	1992
James Flowers	13	1986
Derrick Frazier	13	1991
Aaron Glenn	13	1993
Ray Mickens	13	1993
Chet Brooks	11	1986

OTHER DEFENSIVE RECORDS

Career Fumbles Caused: 12, Jacob Green (1977-78)

Season Fumbles Caused: 6, Jacob Green (1978); Aaron Wallace (1987)

Career Fumbles Recovered: 10, Marcus Buckley (1990-92)

Season Fumbles Recovered: 5, Lester Hayes (1975); Domingo Bryant (1985)

Career Quarterback Pressures: 48, Aaron Wallace (1986-89)

Season Quarterback Pressures: 30, William Thomas (1990)

*Career Tackles for Losses: 32, John Roper (1985-88)

*Season Tackles for Losses: 14, Edward Jasper (1995)

*-sacks not included

ANNUAL STATISTICAL LEADERS

RUSHING

Year	Player	Att-Yds	Avg.
1995	Leeland McElroy	246-1122	4.6
1994	Rodney Thomas	199- 868	4.4
1993	Rodney Thomas	191- 996	5.2
1992	Greg Hill	267-1339	5.0
1991	Greg Hill	240-1216	5.8
1990	Darren Lewis	291-1691	5.8
1989	Darren Lewis	185- 961	5.2
1988	Darren Lewis	306-1692*	5.5
1987	Darren Lewis	127- 668	5.3
1986	Roger Vick	220- 960*	4.4
1985	Anthony Toney	208- 845	4.4
1984	Thomas Sanders	167- 738	4.4
1983	Roger Vick	91- 425	4.7
1982	Johnny Hector	140- 554	3.9
1981	Earnest Jackson	153- 887	5.8
1980	Johnny Hector	173- 928	5.4
1979	Curtis Dickey	172- 894	5.0
1978	Curtis Dickey	205-1146	5.6
1977	George Woodard	245-1107	4.5
1976	George Woodard	239-1153	4.8
1975	Bubba Bean	144- 944	6.6
1974	Bubba Bean	158- 938	5.9
1973	Bubba Bean	112- 711	6.3
1972	Brad Dusek	124- 549	4.4
1971	Mark Green	181- 593	3.3
1970	Doug Neill	107- 426	4.0
1969	Larry Stegent	197- 676	3.4
1968	Larry Stegent	105- 527	4.7
1967	Larry Stegent	161- 568	3.5
1966	Wendell Housley	155- 548	3.5
1965	Bill Sallee	84- 272	3.1
1964	Lloyd Curington	99- 287	2.9
1963	Budgie Ford	62- 234	3.8
1962	Jim Linnstaedter	36- 167	4.6
1961	Lee Roy Caffey	85- 371	4.4
1960	Sam Byer	105- 381	3.6
1959	Gordon LeBoeuf	113- 351	3.0
1958	Luther Hall	70- 238	3.3
1957	John David Crow	129- 562	4.4
1956	Roddy Osborne	141- 568	4.0
1955	Jack Pardee	83- 452	5.4
1954	Elwood Kettler	149- 446	3.0
1953	Connie Magouirk	52- 283	5.4
1952	Don Ellis	156- 377	2.4
1951	Glenn Lippman	118- 801*	6.8
1950	Bob Smith	199-1302	6.5
1949	Bob Smith	145- 694	4.7

PASSING

Year	Player	Comp-Att.	Yards
1995	Corey Pullig	165-307	2105
1994	Corey Pullig	161-269	2056
1993	Corey Pullig	144-243	1732
1992	Corey Pullig	63-126	953
1991	Bucky Richardson	79-156	1492
1990	Lance Pavlas	56- 89	871
1989	Lance Pavlas	134-227	1681
1988	Chris Osgood	54-112	656
1987	Craig Stump	41- 98	524
1986	Kevin Murray	212-349	2463*
1985	Kevin Murray	147-251	1965*
1984	Craig Stump	94-189	1135
1983	Kevin Murray	132-249	1544
1982	Gary Kubiak	181-324	1948*
1981	Gary Kubiak	111-209	1808
1980	David Beal	45- 94	671

1979	Mike Mosley	82-142	938
1978	Mike Mosley	80-139	1157
1977	David Walker	49-107	750
1976	David Walker	51- 90	675
1975	David Shipman	24- 60	422
1974	David Walker	46-102	666
1973	Mike Jay	36- 86	682
1972	Don Dean	57-113	820
1971	Joe Mac King	36- 87	559
1970	Lex James	111-225	1662
1969	Rocky Self	87-199	1136
1968	Edd Hargett	169-348	2321
1967	Edd Hargett	99-208	1526
1966	Edd Hargett	132-265	1532
1965	Harry Ledbetter	83-182	940
1964	Dan McIlhany	47-111	598
1963	Charles LaGrange	28- 73	393
1962	Jim Keller	30- 80	343
1961	John Erickson	34- 73	468
1960	Daryle Keeling	18- 50	204
1959	Charles Milstead	62-117	752
1958	Charles Milstead	88-167	1135
1957	Charles Milstead	14- 35	185
1956	Roddy Osborne	14- 23	258
1955	James Wright	24- 67	368
1954	Elwood Kettler	36- 72	471
1953	Don Ellis	76-171	960
1952	Ray Graves	93-164	989*
1951	Ray Graves	45- 98	621
1950	Dick Gardemal	39- 66	559
1949	Don Nicholas	28- 58	311

RECEIVING

Year	Player	No-Yds	TD
1995	Albert Connell, se	41-653	7
1994	Ryan Mathews, se	29-395	2
1993	Toby Harrison, se	31-481	4
1992	Greg Schorp, te	24-280	1
1991	Tony Harrison, se	31-577	6
1990	Gary Oliver, fl	28-455	3
1989	Percy Waddle, se	36-600	5
1988	Rod Harris, se	37-592	1
1987	Keith Woodside, rb	25-237	0
1986	Rod Bernstine, te	65-710*	5
1985	Jeff Nelson, se	51-651*	4
1984	Jimmy Teal, se	35-631	6
1983	Rich Siler, te	40-465	4
1982	Don Jones, se	32-461	5
1981	Mike Whitwell, se	27-731	3
1980	Mike Whitwell, se	30-603	2
1979	Gerald Carter, se	39-528	2
1978	Russell Mikeska, te	29-429	0
1977	Curtis Dickey, rb	17-231	1
1976	Gary Haack, te	21-265	2
1975	Richard Osborne, te	13-191	2
1974	Richard Osborne, te	13-145	0
1973	Richard Osborne, te	29-405	1
1972	Richard Osborne, te	31-440	1
1971	Robert Murski, te	17-212	0
1970	Homer May, te	26-479	5
1969	Barney Harris, se	34-191	0
1968	Barney Harris, se	49-745	3
1967	Bob Long, te	24-541	8
1966	Tommy Maxwell, se	27-445	4
1965	Ken McLean, se	60-835*	2
1964	Billy Uzzell, se	22-246	1
1963	George Hargett, rb	12-162	1
1962	George Hargett, rb	14-194	0
1961	Travis Reagan, rb	10-201	1

1960	Randy Sims, rb	5- 66	1
1959	Russell Hill, se	19-341	1
1958	John Tracey, se	37-466*	2
1957	John Tracey, se	8-103	1
1956	John David Crow, rb	7-125	3
1955	Bobby Marks, se	7- 94	0
1954	Bennie Sinclair, se	22-293	2
1953	Bennie Sinclair, se	19-287	2
1952	Don Ellis, rb	33-273*	3
1951	Billy Tidwell, rb	13-256	2
1950	Andy Hillhouse, se	24-398	7
1949	Wray Whittaker, se	26-291	1

TOTAL OFFENSE

Year	Player	Plays-Yards	Avg.
1995	Corey Pullig	344-2155	6.3
1994	Corey Pullig	308-1992	6.5
1993	Corey Pullig	276-1705	6.2
1992	Greg Hill	269-1339	5.0
1991	Bucky Richardson	259-1940	7.5
1990	Darren Lewis	294-1748	5.9
1989	Lance Pavlas	291-1679	5.8
1988	Darren Lewis	309-1692	5.5
1987	Darren Lewis	128- 705	5.5
1986	Kevin Murray	393-2348	6.0
1985	Kevin Murray	295-1892	6.4
1984	Craig Stump	269-1280	4.8
1983	Kevin Murray	333-1643*	4.9
1982	Gary Kubiak	369-1885*	5.1
1981	Gary Kubiak	328-1986*	6.1
1980	Johnny Hector	173- 928	5.4
1979	Mike Mosley	217-1443	6.7
1978	Mike Mosley	220-1405	6.4
1977	David Walker	177-1144	6.5
1976	George Woodard	239-1153	4.8
1975	Bubba Bean	144- 944	6.6
1974	Bubba Bean	158- 938	5.9
1973	Mike Jay	88- 901	10.2
1972	Don Dean	132- 879	6.7
1971	Joe Mac King	85- 625	7.4
1970	Lex James	228-1473	6.5
1969	Rocky Self	214-1460	6.8
1968	Edd Hargett	433-2330	5.4
1967	Edd Hargett	214-1532	7.2
1966	Edd Hargett	203-1549	7.6
1965	Harry Ledbetter	314- 930	3.0
1964	Eddie McKaughan	109- 603	5.5
1963	Charles LaGrange	53- 328	6.2
	Jim Keller	80- 328	4.1
1962	Jim Keller	75- 456	6.1
1961	John Erickson	83- 489	5.9
1960	Sam Byer	105- 381	3.6
1959	Charles Milstead	175- 829	4.7
1958	Charles Milstead	279-1332*	4.8
1957	Roddy Osborne	149- 662	4.4
1956	Roddy Osborne	155- 826	5.3
1955	Jack Pardee	83- 452	5.5
1954	Elwood Kettler	221- 917	4.1
1953	Don Ellis	193-1028	5.3
1952	Ray Graves	247-1245	5.0
1951	Glenn Lippman	118- 801	6.8
1950	Bob Smith	199-1302	6.5
1949	Bob Smith	145- 694	4.8

SCORING

Year	Player	Pts.
1995	Leeland McElroy, rb	96
1994	Rodney Thomas, rb	96
1993	Terry Venetoulias, k	90
1992	Greg Hill, rb	102
1991	Terry Venetoulias, k	88
1990	Darren Lewis, rb	114
1989	Layne Talbot, k	71
1988	Robert Wilson, rb	60
1987	Scott Slater, k	70
1986	Scott Slater, k	100*
1985	Anthony Toney, rb	74
	Eric Franklin, k	74
1984	Alan Smith, k	51
1983	Alan Smith, k	72
1982	David Hardy, k	80
1981	David Hardy, k	65
1980	Johnny Hector, rb	30
1979	Curtis Dickey, rb	54
1978	Tony Franklin, k	61
1977	Tony Franklin, k	86
1976	George Woodard, rb	102*
1975	Tony Franklin, k	63
1974	Skip Walker, rb	54
1973	Randy Haddox, k	62
1972	Pat McDermott, k	33
1971	Mark Green, rb	42
1970	Pat McDermott, k	34
1969	Ross Brupbacher, te	36
1968	Bob Long, te	48
1967	Bob Long, te	48
1966	Tommy Maxwell, se	26
1965	Glynn Lindsey, k	20
1964	Glynn Lindsey, k	12
	Bubber Collins, rb	12
1963	Jerry Rogers, rb	18
	Travis Reagan, rb	18
	Bobby Lee, k	18
1962	Mike Clark, se	25
1961	Travis Reagan, rb	38
1960	Sam Byer, rb	18
1959	Randy Sims, rb	31
1958	Charles Milstead, qb	36
1957	Roddy Osborne, se	48
1956	John David Crow, rb	60*
1955	Loyd Taylor, rb	31
1954	Elwood Kettler, qb	54
1953	Don Ellis, qb	37
1952	Connie Magouirk, rb	30
1951	Darrow Hooper, k	32
1950	Bob Smith, rb	84*
1949	Bob Smith, rb	48

PUNTING

Year	Player	No.-Yards	Avg.
1995	Sean Terry	60-2598	43.3
1994	Sean Terry	58-2214	38.2
1993	James Bennett	53-2033	38.4
1992	David Davis	70-3067	43.8
1991	David Davis	52-2035	39.1
1990	Sean Wilson	45-1906	42.4
1989	Sean Wilson	36-1500	41.7
1988	Sean Wilson	62-2472	39.9
1987	Sean Wilson	42-1699	40.5
1986	Craig Stump	35-1296	37.0
1985	Todd Tschantz	33-1406	42.6
1984	Todd Tschantz	61-2517	41.3
1983	Kyle Stuard	67-2806	41.9
1982	Kyle Stuard	60-2430	40.5
1981	Randy Sawyer	63-2445	38.8
1980	Kyle Stuard	76-3097	40.8
1979	David Appleby	71-2935	41.3
1978	David Appleby	48-1835	38.2
1977	David Appleby	57-2466	43.3
1976	David Appleby	50-1986	39.7
1975	Mark Stanley	62-2383	38.4
1974	Mark Stanley	59-2479	42.0
1973	Mark Stanley	45-1718	38.2
1972	Robert Murski	69-2620	37.9

1971	Mitch Robertson	84-3100	37.0
1970	Jimmy Sheffield	66-2650	40.2
1969	Jimmy Sheffield	69-2749	39.8
1968	Steve O'Neal	64-2616	40.9
1967	Steve O'Neal	81-3402	42.0*
1966	Steve O'Neal	67-2836	42.3
1965	Phil Scoggin	88-3833	43.6*
1964	Phil Scoggin	73-2906	39.8
1963	Jim Keller	66-2738	41.5
1962	Jim Keller	42-1591	37.9
1961	Babe Craig	57-2215	38.9*
1960	Babe Craig	42-1701	40.5*
1959	Charles Milstead	39-1394	35.7
1958	Charles Milstead	29-1058	36.5
1957	Roddy Osborne	30-1095	36.5
1956	Roddy Osborne	28- 882	31.5
1955	Ed Dudley	15- 602	40.1
1954	Gene Henderson	14- 528	37.5
1953	Joe Boring	22- 835	38.0
1952	Roy Dollar	45-1682	37.3
1951	Yale Lary	33-1256	38.1
1950	Yale Lary	57-2183	38.3
1949	Yale Lary	71-2846	40.00

KICKOFF RETURNS

Year	Player	RT-YDS	AVG
1995	Leeland McElroy	9-208	23.1
1994	Leeland McElroy	6-301	50.2
1993	Leeland McElroy	15-590	39.3*
1992	Billy Mitchell	11-336	30.5
1991	Randy Simmons	10-181	18.1
1990	Randy Simmons	10-245	24.5
1989	Larry Horton	17-420	24.7
1988	Rod Harris	22-388	17.6
1987	Rod Harris	15-329	21.9
1986	Rod Harris	17-319	18.8
1985	Rod Harris	5-173	34.6
1984	Jeff Nelson	16-299	18.7
1983	Tony Slaton	4- 74	18.5
1982	Tony Slaton	17-291	17.1
1981	Billy Cannon	8-172	21.5
1980	Billy Cannon	14-291	20.8
1979	Earnest Jackson	10-213	21.3
1978	Temple Aday	8-188	23.5
1977	Curtis Dickey	15-302	20.1
1976	Darrell Smith	10-184	18.4
1975	Skip Walker	6-167	27.8
1974	Carl Roaches	5- 90	18.0
1973	Carl Roaches	15-426	28.4
1972	Carl Roaches	18-426	23.7
1971	Hugh McElroy	17-439	25.8*
1970	Dave Elmendorf	23-457	19.9
1969	Dave Elmendorf	12-232	19.3
1968	Larry Stegent	13-255	19.6
1967	Larry Stegent	16-292	18.3
1966	Wendell Housley	11-255	23.2
1965	Lloyd Curington	7-169	24.1
1964	Eddie McKaughan	8-144	18.0
1963	George Hargett	8-182	22.8
1962	George Hargett	7-158	22.6
1961	James Murphy	7-167	23.9
1960	James Murphy	10-219	21.9
1959	Bob Sanders	4-128	32.0
1958	Arthur Sims	9-210	23.3
1957	Bobby Joe Conrad	4-149	37.2
1956	Jack Pardee	7-218	31.1
1955	John David Crow	7-129	18.5
1954	Don Watson	8-197	24.6
1953	Don Ellis	9-178	19.8
1952	Don Ellis	17-413	24.3*
1951	Billy Tidwell	7-211	30.1
1950	n/a		

1949	Glenn Lippman	12-308	25.7*
1948	Bob Goode	16-407	25.4*

PUNT RETURNS

Year	Player	RT-YDS	AVG
1995	Ray Mickens	24-281	11.7
1994	Billy Mitchell	26-203	7.8
1993	Aaron Glenn	17-339	19.9*
1992	Derrick Frazier	29-301	10.4
1991	Kevin Smith	19-275	14.5
1990	Shane Garrett	21-196	9.3
1989	Shane Garrett	21-146	6.4
1988	Rod Harris	37-235	6.4
1987	Rod Harris	37-391	10.6
1986	Rod Harris	42-345	8.2
1985	Jimmie Hawkins	39-331	8.5
1984	Jimmie Hawkins	33-298	9.0
1983	Billy Cannon	26-260	10.0
1982	Billy Cannon	31-280	9.0
1981	Billy Cannon	29-109	3.8
1980	David Scott	33-121	3.7
1979	David Scott	46-318	6.9
1978	Darrell Smith	23-132	5.7
1977	Mike Williams	21- 72	3.4
1976	Darrell Smith	28- 75	2.7
1975	Carl Roaches	38-238	7.0
1974	Carl Roaches	27-177	6.6
1973	Carl Roaches	31-224	7.2*
1972	Carl Roaches	19-287	15.1*
1971	Hugh McElroy	17-138	8.2
1970	Dave Elmendorf	13-130	10.0
1969	Dave Elmendorf	24-215	8.9
1968	Barney Harris	8- 88	11.0
1967	Bob Long	8- 94	11.8
1966	Curley Hallman	7- 47	6.7
1965	Jerry Nichols	20-128	6.4
1964	James Willenborg	8- 52	6.5
1963	George Hargett	11-100	9.1
1962	George Hargett	17-163	9.6
1961	George Hargett	9- 78	8.8
1960	Arthur Sims	9-145	16.1
1959	Bob Sanders	8- 57	7.1
1958	Jon Few	7- 79	11.2
1957	Roddy Osborne	7- 65	9.3
1956	Don Watson	10-118	11.8
1955	Billy Dendy	8- 80	10.0
1954	Don Watson	6-115	19.1
1953	Don Ellis	19-170	8.9
1952	Joe Boring	12-134	11.2
1951	Yale Lary	24-388	16.2*
1950	Yale Lary	9-209	23.2

INTERCEPTIONS

Year	Player	INT-YDS	AVG
1995	Ray Mickens	4- 67	33.5
1994	Dennis Allen	4- 27	6.8
1993	Aaron Glenn	3- 40	13.3
1992	Aaron Glenn	6- 99	16.5 (1)
1991	Patrick Bates	4- 37	9.3
1990	Kevin Smith	7-149	21.3 (2)
1989	Kevin Smith	9- 75	8.3 (1)
1988	Mickey Washington	4- 37	9.3
1987	Kip Corrington	3- 0	0.0
	Adam Bob	3- 0	0.0
1986	James Flowers	5- 73	14.6 (1)
1985	Kip Corrington	5- 68	13.6 (1)
1984	James Flowers	2- 55	27.5 (1)
1983	Jeff Fuller	3- 37	12.3
1982	Jeff Fuller	4- 23	5.7
1981	Bobby Strogen	5	n/a
1980	Leandrew Brown	5- 44	8.8
1979	John Dawson	4- 14	3.5

1978	Kenneth Taylor	3- 0	0.0		1963	Mike Pitman	4- 40	10.0
1977	Mike Williams	4- 49	12.3		1962	Jerry Hopkins	3- 4	1.3
1976	Lester Hayes	8- 87	10.9		1961	Travis Reagan	4- 72	18.0
1975	Lester Hayes	6-102	17.0 (1)		1960	Randy Sims	2- 18	9.0
1974	Pat Thomas	6- 85	14.2 (1)		1959	Robert Sanders	3- 28	9.3
1973	Pat Thomas	3- 81	27.0 (1)		1958	Jon Few	2- 14	7.0
1972	Grady Hoermann	3- 42	14.0		1957	John David Crow	5- 39	7.8
1971	Lee Hitt	6- 85	14.2		1956	Jack Pardee	3- 50	16.7
1970	Dave Elmendorf	6- 87	14.5		1955	Roddy Osborne	3- 68	22.7
1969	Dave Elmendorf	5- 0	0.0		1954	Joe Schero	2- 3	1.5
1968	Ross Brupbacher	3- 98	32.7 (1)		1953	Don Ellis	3- 86	28.7
1967	Billy Hobbs	7-162	23.1 (2)		1952	Joe Boring	8- 67	8.4
1966	Curley Hallman	5- 92	18.4		1951	Bill Ballard	3- 17	5.7
1965	Jim Kauffman	3- 0	0.0		1950	Yale Lary	5- 78	15.6
1964	Mike Pitman	2-100	50.0		1941	Bill Sibley	9- 57	6.3

HONORS

A&M ALL AMERICANS

(First team selections only)
1936 Joe Routt, OG.
1937 Joe Routt, OG.
1939 Joe Boyd, OT; John Kimbrough, RB.
1940 John Kimbrough, RB; Marshall Robnett, OG.
1950 Bob Smith, RB.
1951 Jack Little, OT.
1952 Jack Little, OT.
1956 Dennis Goehring, OG; Charlie Krueger, OT; Jack Pardee, FB.
1957 John David Crow, RB; Charlie Krueger, OT.
1966 Maurice Moorman, OT.
1967 Bill Hobbs, LB.
1968 Bill Hobbs, LB; Rolf Krueger, DT; Tommy Maxwell, FS; Steve O'Neal, P.
1970 Dave Elmendorf, FS.
1974 Pat Thomas, CB.
1975 Garth Ten Naple, LB; Ed Simonini, LB; Pat Thomas, CB.
1976 Tony Franklin, PK; Lester Hayes, FS; Robert Jackson, LB.
1978 Tony Franklin, PK.
1979 Jacob Green, DE.
1983 Ray Childress, DT.
1984 Ray Childress, DT.
1985 Johnny Holland, LB; Doug Williams, OL.
1986 Johnny Holland, LB.
1987 John Roper, LB.
1988 Darren Lewis, RB.
1990 Darren Lewis, RB; Mike Arthur, OC.
1991 Kevin Smith, CB.
1992 Partrick Bates, FS; Marcus Buckley, LB.
1993 Sam Adams, DE; Aaron Glenn, CB.
1994 Antonio Armstrong, LB; Leeland McElroy, RB/KR.
1995 Leeland McElroy, RB/KR; Ray Mickens, DB.

ALL SWC PLAYERS

1915 John Garrity, end; N.M. Braumiller, guard.
1916 Newt Settegast, tackle; Jim Crow, tackle.
1917 Tim Griesenbeck, end; Ox Ford, tackle; E.S. Wilson, guard; Rip Collins, back; Jack Mahan, back.
1919 E.S. Wilson, guard; W.E. Murrah, guard; C.R. Drake, tackle; R.G. Higginbotham, halfback; Jack Mahan, fullback; Scott Alexander, end.
1920 W.E. Murrah, end; C.R. Drake, tackle; R.G. Higginbotham, halfback; Jack Mahan, fullback; T.F. Wilson, end.
1921 Sam Sanders, back; T.F. Wilson, end; W.E. Murrah, guard.

1922 W.D. Johnson, guard; T.F. Wilson, end.
1923 A.J. Evans, end; W.D. Johnson, guard.
1924 W.W. Wilson, back; Neeley Allison, end.
1925 Joel Hunt, halfback; L.G. Dietrich, tackle; W.M. Dansby, guard; Barlow Irvin, tackle; W.W. Wilson, back.
1926 Joel Hunt, halfback; L.G. Dietrich, tackle; J.A. Tektorik, guard; J.B. Sikes, end; C.D. Watts, center .
1927 Joel Hunt, quarterback; J.V. Sikes, end; J.G. Holmes, guard; A.C. Sprott, tackle; E.E. Fegari, guard; W.S. Lister, tackle.
1928 Z.W. Bartlett, center; H.E. Burgess, fullback; S.J. Petty, end.
1929 Tommy Mills, quarterback; Charlie Richter, guard.
1930 Adrain Tracey, end.
1931 Carl Moulden, guard; Cliff Domingue, quarterback; Charlie Malone, end.
1932 Willis Nolan, center; Charley Cummings, tackle.
1933 Ted Spencer, fullback; Ray Murray, end; W.T. Jordan, tackle.
1934 John Crow, guard.
1936 Joe Routt, guard; Charles DeWare, center; Roy Young, tackle.
1937 Joe Routt, guard; Roy Young, tackle; Dick Todd, halfback; Virgil Jones, guard.
1938 Dick Todd, halfback; Joe Boyd, tackle.
1939 Joe Boyd, tackle; John Kimbrough, fullback; Marshall Robnett, guard; Herb Smith, end; Jim Thomason, halfback.
1940 James Sterling, end ; John Kimbrough, fullback; Marshall Robnett, guard; Jim Thomason, halfback; Ernie Pannell, tackle.
1941 Derace Moser, running back; James Sterling, end; Bill Sibley, center; Martin Ruby, tackle.
1942 Bill Henderson, end; Felix Bucek, guard; Cullen Rogers, back; Leo Daniels, back.
1943 Marian Flanagan, back; M.E. Settegast, end; Goble Bryant, tackle; Jim Hallmark, back.
1944 Monty Moncrief, tackle; Clarence Howell, end; Paul Yates, fullback.
1945 Monty Moncrief, guard; Grant Darnell, guard; Preston Smith, halfback; Bob Goode, halfback.
1946 Monty Moncrief, tackle.
1947 Jim Winkler, tackle.
1948 Jim Winkler, tackle; Bob Goode, halfback; Odell Stautzenberger, guard; Andy Hillhouse, end.
1949; Bob Smith, fullback.
1950; Bob Smith, fullback; Max Greiner, tackle; Andy Hillhouse, end; Carl Molberg, guard.
1951; Jack Little, tackle; Glenn Lippmann, back;

Hugh Meyer, center; Yale Lary, back; Billy Tidwell, back.

1952 Jack Little, tackle; Ray Graves, quarterback; Joe Boring, safety.

1953 Don Ellis, quarterback.

1954 Elwood Kettler, quarterback; Bennie Sinclair, end.

1955 Gene Stallings, end; Dennis Goehring, guard.

1956 Jack Pardee, fullback; Lloyd Hale, center; Dennis Goehring, guard; John David Crow, halfback; John Tracey, end; Charlie Krueger, tackle; Roddy Osborne, quarterback.

1957 John David Crow, halfback; Charles Krueger, tackle; Bobby Marks, end.

1958 Charles Milstead, quarterback; John Tracey, end.

1960 Sam Byer, fullback.

1961 Jerry Hopkins, center.

1962 Jerry Hopkins, center.

1963 Ronney Moore, guard.

1964 Ray Gene Hinze, offensive tackle; Mike Pittman, defensive halfback.

1965 Ken (Dude) McLean, offensive end; Joe Wellborn, linebacker.

1966 Maurice Moorman, offensive tackle; Gary Kovar, offensive guard; Wendell Houseley, offensive halfback.

1967 Edd Hargett, quarterback; Bob Long, offensive end; Tommy Maxwell, safety; Rolf Krueger, defensive tackle; Bill Hobbs, linebacker; Grady Allen, defensive end; Larry Stegent, offensive halfback; Steve O'Neal, punter; Dan Schneider, offensive tackle.

1968 Edd Hargett, quarterback; Steve O'Neal, punter; Rolf Krueger, defensive tackle; Bill Hobbs, linebacker; Mike DeNiro, defensive end.

1969 Larry Stegent, tailback; Lynn Odom, defensive guard; Dave Elmendorf, safety; Mike DeNiro, defensive end; Ross Brupbacher, end.

1970 Homer May, end; Dave Elmendorf, safety.

1971 Leonard Forey, guard; David Hoot, safety; Boice Best, defensive tackle; Grady Hoermann, linebacker; Buster Callaway, tackle; Mark Green, halfback.

1972 Grady Hoermann, linebacker; Boice Best, defensive tackle; Robert Murski, cornerback; Ed Simonini, linebacker.

1973 Ed Simonini, linebacker; Don Long, defensive end; Skip Walker, halfback.

1974 Pat Thomas, cornerback; Ed Simonini, linebacker; Tim Gray, cornerback; Warren Trahan, defensive tackle; Bubba Bean, offensive halfback; Randy Haddox, place kicker; Glenn Bujnoch, offensive tackle; Garth TenNapel, linebacker; Mark Stanley, punter.

1975 Ed Simonini, linebacker; Pat Thomas, cornerback; Garth TenNapel, linebacker; Bubba Bean, halfback; Edgar Fields, defensive tackle; Blake Schwarz, defensive end; Jimmy Dean, defensive tackle; Jackie Williams, safety; Lester Hayes, safety; Richard Osborne, tight end; Glenn Bujnoch, offensive tackle; Tank Marshall, defensive end; Bruce Welch, offensive guard; Robert Jackson, linebacker.

1976 Jimmy Dean, defensive tackle; Edgar Fields, defensive tackle; Tony Franklin, kicker; Gary Haack, tight end; Lester Hayes, safety; Robert Jackson, linebacker; Tank Marshall, defensive end; Frank Myers, tackle; Dennis Swilley, guard; George Woodard, fullback.

1977 Mark Dennard, center; Frank Myers, offensive tackle; Cody Risien, offensive tackle; Carl Grulich, safety.

1978 Curtis Dickey, tailback; Tony Franklin, kicker; Jacob Green, defensive end; Russell Mikeska, tight end; Cody Risien, offensive tackle.

1979 Jacob Green, defensive end; Gerald Carter, split end ; Ed Pustejovsky, offensive guard.

1980 No selections from A&M.

1981 No selections from A&M.

1982 Domingo Bryant, defensive back; David Hardy, kicker.

1983 Rich Siler, tight end; Ray Childress, defensive end/tackle.

1984 Ray Childress, defensive end/tackle.

1985 Johnny Holland, linebacker; Doug Williams, offensive tackle; Kevin Murray, quarterback; Domingo Bryant, defensive back; Anthony Toney, fullback; Jeff Nelson, flanker; Rod Saddler, defensive end; Randy Dausin, offensive guard.

1986 Kevin Murray, quarterback; Rod Bernstine, tight end; Johnny Holland, linebacker; Roger Vick, fullback; Keith Woodside, halfback; Scott Slater, kicker; Jay Muller, defensive end; Kip Corrington, defensive back; Louis Cheek, offensive tackle; Terrance Brooks, defensive back.

1987 Rod Harris, split end; Louis Cheek, offensive tackle; Matt Wilson, center; Scott Slater, kicker; Sammy O'Brient, defensive guard; John Roper, linebacker; Kip Corrington, free safety.

1988 Darren Lewis, running back; Jerry Fontenot, guard; Matt McCall, tackle; John Roper, linebacker; Aaron Wallace, linebacker ; Mickey Washington, cornerback.

1989 Mike Jones, tight end; Kevin Smith, defensive back; William Thomas, linebacker; Aaron Wallace, linebacker; Richmond Webb, offensive tackle.

1990 Darren Lewis, running back; Mike Arthur, center; Matt McCall, offensive tackle; William Thomas, linebacker; Kevin Smith, cornerback.

1991 Kevin Smith, cornerback; Bucky Richardson, quarterback; Quentin Coryatt, linebacker; Greg Hill, running back; Keith Alex, offensive tackle; Marcus Buckley, linebacker; John Ellisor, offensive tackle; Patrick Bates, free safety.

1992 Marcus Buckley, linebacker; John Ellisor, guard; David Davis, punter; Patrick Bates, free safety; Greg Schorp, tight end; Aaron Glenn, cornerback; Chris Dausin, center; Terry Venetoulias, placekicker; Greg Hill, running back; Sam Adams, defensive end.

1993 Sam Adams, defensive end; Jason Atkinson, linebacker; Calvin Collins, offensive guard; Chris Dausin, center; Eric England, defensive end; Aaron Glenn, cornerback; Tyler Harrison, offensive guard; Greg Hill, running back; Jason Mathews, offensive tackle; Leeland McElroy, kick returner; Ray Mickens, cornerback; Greg Schorp, tight end; Antonio Shorter, linebacker; Lance Teichelman, noseguard; Rodney Thomas, running back; Dexter Wesley, offensive tackle.

1994 Antonio Armstrong, linebacker; Calvin Collins, offensive line; Leeland McElroy, kick returner; Ray Mickens, cornerback; Brandon Mitchell, defensive line; Rodney Thomas, running back.

1995 Reggie Brown, linebacker; Albert Connell, wide receiver; Hunter Goodwin, tight end; Donovan Greer, cornerback; Leeland McElroy, running back/ kick returner; Ray Mickens, cornerback; Brandon Mitchell, defensive line; Keith Mitchell, linebacker

LETTERMEN

A Abbey, Dan R. '29, '30; Abbott, John A. '39; Abraham, Arthur A. '44, '45; Adair, Chad '86, '87; Adamek, Jody '90; Adami, Buster '67, '68, '69; Adams, Brent (Manager) '87, '88; Adams, Darrell '79, '80, '81, '82; Adams, Jimmy '67, '68, '69; Adams, Kent '80, '81; Adams, Sam '91, '92, '93; Aday, Temple '78, '79, '80, '81; Alex, Keith '88, '89, '90, '91; Alexander, Al (Manager) '74; Alexander , Scott '17, '18, '19; Allen, Corey '86; Allen, Dennis '92, '93, '94, '95; Allen, Grady L. '65, '66, '67; Allison, Bill '84; Allison, J. Neely '23, '24; Alsabrook, O.D. '27, '28, '29; Altgelt, George A. '10, '11; Anderson, Gary Lee '50; Anderson, George D. '17; Anderson, Gerald R. (Manager) '53; Anderson, Percy J. '47; Andricks, Dennis B. '41; Andrus, Jason '92, '94, '95; Angermiller, Roy L. '59; Anglin, M.H. '20; Anthony, Shane '93; Appleby, David '76, '77, '78, '79; Armbrister, Gary '69; Armstrong, Adger '75, '76, '77, '78; Armstrong, Antonio '91, '92, '93, '94; Armstrong, Coy (Manager) '90, '91, '92; Arndt, Charles '73, '74, '75; Arnold, D.C. '26; Arnold, W.J. '13; Arthur, Mike '87, '88, '89, '90; Arthur, Tom '83, '84; Asberry, Wayne '82, '83, '84, '85; Aschenbeck, Harvey '66, '67, '68; Ashley, Mike '81, '82, '83; Askey, N. '19; Astin, Erwin H. 1896, '97, '98, '99; Aston, James W. '30, '31, '32; Atkinson, Jason '90, '91, '92, '93; Audish, William '37, '38, '39; Austin, Darrell '82, '83, '84, '85; Axcell, Matt (Trainer) '95.

B Bairrington, David '75; Baker, Keith '75, '76 ; Baker, Paul (Manager) '74; Balcar, Danny '85, '86, '87; Baldwin, Keith '79, '80, '81; Balenti, Michael R. '09; Ballard, William R. '51; Ballentine, John R. '45, '46, '47; Bandy, David '79, '80, '81; Barfield, R.E. '31; Barhorst, Warren '87; Barker, John (Manager) '89; Barker, William O. '65; Barnes, George W. '09, '10, '11; Barnett, Billy Bob '69; Barnett, Robert W. '65, '66; Barnett, Van '79, '80, '81, '82; Barrett, James '83, '84; Barrett, Ralph '77; Barrett, Ray R. '52, '53, '54; Barry, Mark '90; Bartlett, Z.W. Jr. '26, '27, '28; Bartley, Arthur N. '02; Bartley, Tony '86, '87; Barton, Dorbandt J. '49, '50; Bateman, A.R. '10, '11; Bates, Gus '39; Bates, Larry E. '64; Bates, Patrick '91, '92; Bates, Robert G. '48, '49, '50; Batiste, Dana '85, '86, '87,'88; Batts, Marcus '92, '93; Baty, Robert B. '46, '47, '48; Baum, Spencer '86; Baumgarten, Charles 1897, '98; Bayless, Frederick '32; Beal, David '77, '78, '79, '80; Beam, Winston '67, '70; Bean, Earnest (Bubba) '72, '73, '74, '75; Beard, Glenn G. '45; Beasley, Wyatte G. '10, '11, '12, '13; Beavers, Robby '80; Beck, Kenneth '56, '57, '58; Beeman, Del S. '04; Beesley, Ben B. '21; Beesley, E.G. '43; Beilharz, William '01, '02; Beirne, Kevin '93, '94; Belcher, Raymond '78; Bell, Charles '75, '76; Bell, Jim (Trainer) '79, '80; Bell, Luther E. '31; Bell, Tyree L. '10, '11, '12, '14; Bellar, Mike '69, '70, '71; Belville, Vernon R. '42 ; Benjamin, Joseph W. '02, '03; Bennett, Gary L. '62; Bennett, James '93, '94; Bennett, Phil '76, '77; Bernard, Eric '95; Bernay, Camp L. '03; Bernstine, Rod '83, '84, '85, '86; Berry, Dean '85, '86, '87; Berry, Greg '80, '81, '82, '83; Berry, Murry P. '58, '59, '60; Berry, R.H. '24, '25; Best, Boice Watts '70, '71, '72; Best, Bruce Allen '70; Beutel, H.W. '24, '25; Bevans, Tom '83, '84; Bible, Hollis U. '28; Bickford, Lee (Manager) '95; Biggens, Wilbert '91, '92, '93, '94; Billingsley, Charles '71; Bird, Max Dwayne '70, '71, '72; Birdwell, Russ '87; Bitters, Bob (Trainer) '81, '82; Black, Jayson '87, '88,

'89, '90; Black, Marc '69, '70, '71; Blackburn, George S. (Manager) '39; Blair, W.G. '52; Blake, Robert E. '05; Blake, Thomas M. '01, '02, '03; Blalock, Travis '90; Blankenship, Tony '74, '75; Blavier, Steve (Manager) '84, '85; Blessing, William '39; Bob, Adam '85, '86, '87, '88; Boettcher, Reinhardt B. 1896, '03, '04; Bolcerek, Tommy '88; Bonner, H.L. '13; Booker, Herbert '79; Booth, Ellison S. '03; Boring, Joseph '52, '53; Boswell, James R. '48; Bouldin, Steve (Trainer) '93; Bounds, James Y. '62, '63, '64; Boutwell, Jeff '86; Bowers, Alvin '72, '73; Bowler, Sam E. '12; Box, Steve '80, '82, '83; Boyce, C. William Jr. '05; Boyd, Hugh F. Jr. '39; Boyd, Joe M. '37, '38, '39; Boyd, Wm. O. Jr. '35, '36; Brack, Vance '67; Bradberry, Ramsey '89, '90, '91; Bradford, J.B. '23; Bransom, George E. Jr. '37, '38; Braselton, J.W. '24 ; Braumiller, N.M. '14, '15; Brawley, Lance (Trainer) '89; Breding, Edward V. '64, '65, '66; Breedlove, H.M. '32, '33; Breihan, Stacy '75, '77, '78; Brice, Ronald G. '60, '61, '62; Britt, A. Rankin '36, '37, '38; Broaddus, Larry G. '59, '60; Brooks, Hugh '14; Brooks, James '94, '95; Brooks, Terrance '84, '85, '86, '87; Broom, Guy '84, '85, '86, '87; Brothers, David '76, '77, '78, '79; Brotherton, John R. '62, '63, '64; Broussard, Fred E. '53; Browder, Harris M. '39; Brown, Billy '82, '83; Brown, Charles W. '14; Brown, Chris '81; Brown, Darrell W. '54, '55, '57; Brown, J.E. '28, '29; Brown, J.S. '09; Brown, Leandrew '77, '78, '79, '80; Brown, Quinton '94, '95; Brown, Reaville M. 1900, '01, '04; Brown, Reggie '92, '93, '94, '95; Broyles, Marc '95; Brupbacher, Ross '67, '68, '69; Bruton, Alfred L. (Manager) '54; Bruton, Mike '73; Bryant, Domingo '82, '83, '84, '85; Bryant, Goble W. '43; Bryant, Kyle '94, '95; Bucek, Felix A. '41, '42; Bucek, Roy E. '39, '40, '41; Buchanan, A.B. '39, '40; Buckley, Marcus '90, '91, '92; Buckman, Tom '66, '67, '68; Buckner, F.K. '21; Bujnoch, Glenn '73, '74, '75; Bull, A.C. '15; Bullard, Steve '90; Bullitt, Jerry '80, '81, '82, '83; Bullitt, Steve '83, '84, '85, '86; Bulovas, John '89; Bumgardner, Tom '83; Bunger, Mike '69, '70, '71; Buntin, R.F. (Manager) '42, '47; Burditt, Jesse N. '43, '44, '45, '46; Burger, George '74; Burgess, Edwin B. 1894; Burgess, Herschel E. '26, '27, '28; Burks, Steve '69, '70, '71; Burleson, Russell W. 1894; Burney, John W. 1894; Burnett, John '87 ; Burns, Darrace B. '14, '15, '16; Burns, Dennis '83; Burrell, Charles '91; Burton, Alan M. (Manager) '51; Burchofsky, R.L. '43, '44, '45; Butler, Marvin N. '14; Byer, Sam A. '60, '61, '62.

C Caffey, Kenneth D. '64, '65, '66; Caffey, Kevin '94; Caffey, Lee Roy '60, '61, '62; Callahan, A. Paul '34; Callaway, David Earl '70, '71, '72; Calcott, George V. (Trainer) '62; Callcott, Wm. H. (Trainer) '64, '65; Callender, Richard '48, '49; Caldwell, Fred '80, '81, '82; Campbell, Dan '95; Cambell, Henry '88; Campbell, Jerry '66, '67, '68; Cangelose, Marty (Manager) '79, '80; Cannon, Billy '80, '81, '82, '83; Capt, Louis E. '52, '53; Cardwell, John E. '13; Carlin, William J. '09; Carlson, Gray (Manager) '94, '95; Carlton, Lawton '77; Carmody, T.J. '80, '81; Carpenter, Brian '89; Carpenter, Miles 1899, 1900, '01; Carpenter, Ronnie D. '61, '62, '63; Carr, Chuck '77, '78, '79; Carr, Doug '77, '78, '79, '80; Carrero, B.J. (Manager) '95; Carroll, Mike (Trainer) '88; Carruth, Dennis Paschall '70, '71, '72; Carruthers, B.V. '05; Carruthers, R.L. '19, '20, '21; Carson, C. 1894; Carter, Doug '89, '90, '91, '92; Carter, Gerald

'78, '79; Casas, René '88, '89; Case, Frank '84, '86; Case, Stormy '93, '94, '95; Cashion, James T. '44, '45, '46, '47; Caskey, Robert D. '60, '61; Caswell, Mike '67, '68, '69; Cauble, Richard C. III (Trainer) '71; Cauthorn, Sidney W. '58; Cavanaugh, Bill '86, '87, '88; Cawthon, Frank W. '14 ; Chaffee, Tom '67; Chaney, David (Trainer) '84, '85; Chapin, R. Tuck '48, '49, '50; Chatham, Kefa '90, '91, '92, '93; Cheek, Louis '84, '85, '86, '87; Childress, Jay 1894; Childress, Ray '81, '82, '83, '84; Childress, Trent '88, '89; Chiles, H.T. 1894; Choyce, Ken '81; Christensen, John L. '49; Christian, J.P. '29, '30, '31; Christner, Tom '83; Christopher, Todd Dennis '70, '71, '72; Church, Warren E. '37; Clare, Gary (Trainer) '83, '84; Clark, Gregory '77; Clark, Henry F. '55; Clark, Michael V. '60, '61, '62; Clark, Stuart '81; Clark, Willard W. '39; Clay, Hayward '92, '93, '94, '95; Clendennan, Robert J. '55, '56; Coady, Rich '95; Cole, Leon '87, '88; Coleman, Wiley L. '14; Colgin, P.C. '26; Collins, Bubba J. '64, '65; Collins, Calvin '93, '94, '95; Collins, H.W. '16, '17; Collins, Melvin '86, '87; Collins, Ray (Manager) '78; Collins, William A. '14, '15; Colon, Chris '92, '93, '95; Conatser, William E. '38, '39, '40; Connell, Albert '95; Connelley, R.E. '32; Conoley, Odell M. '33, '34; Conover, Brooks W. '28, '29; Conrad, Bobby J. '55, '56, '57; Cook, Greg '91, '92; Cooley, Arthur '67, '68; Coolidge, David '86; Cooper, Brad '92; Cooper, Jeff (Trainer) '72; Cooper, John '88, '89; Copeland, Cedric D.K. '48, '49; Cornell, Albert L. '05, '06, '07; Corona, Craig (Manager) '86, '87; Corrington, Kip '84, '85, '86, '87; Cortez, Roberto '65, '66, '67; Coryatt, Quentin '90, '91; Costar, Gary '87, '88; Coston, F.M. '36, '37, '38; Coulter, Hiram T. 1894; Couser, W.L. '33, '34; Cousins, R.W. 1898; Cover, Robert J. '03; Crowley, Brad '94, '95 ; Cowley, Harold E. '39, '40, '41; Cox, Jessie '90, '92; Cox, Truman D. '42; Cox, William E. 1896; Craig, George W. '60, '61; Craig, James, W. Jr. '62, '63; Cretcher, J.C. '08, '09, '10; Crooms, Chris '88, '89, '90, '91; Crossman, Jerry M. '50, '51, '52; Crouch, Robert '84; Crow, Floyd A. '14; Crow, J.W. '32; Crow, John David '55, '56, '57; Crow, M.O. '34, '35; Crutsinger, Larry L. '61; Cummings, Charley M. '31, '32, '33; Cummings, Leslie L. '34, '35, '36; Cunningham, Pat '88, '89; Curbello, Jimmy (Trainer) '79; Cure, Wayne O. '42; Curington, Lloyd D. '64, '65, '66; Cushman, Cecil A. '12; Cuthrell, J.H. '28.

D Dale, Ivan '06, '07; Dale, Jay '77, '79; Dale, Jesse D. '05, '06, '07; Daniel, Edwin R. '46, '47, '48; Daniel, Thomas C. '44, '45; Daniels, James '73, '74; Daniels, Leo H. '41, '42, '46; Dansby, M.W. '24; Dansby, N.J. '23, '24, '25; Darbyshire, Russell O. '08; Darnell, Grant S. '43, '44, '45; Darwin, Matt '81, '82, '83, '84; Darwin, William B. '57, '58, '59; Dausin, Bryan '79, '81, '82; Dausin, Chris '91, '92, '93; Dausin, Randy '83, '84, '85; Davis, Alan (Trainer) '91, '92; Davis, Dan '78, '79, '80, '81; Davis, David '91, '92; Davis, James M. '02; Davis, Jeff (Trainer) '81; Davis, Jewel '19; Davis, Robin '69; Davis, W.E. '27, '28; Davis, W.E. '30, '31; Dawkins, Marvin H. '63, '64; Dawson, John '78, '79, '81; Dawson, Oran '31 ; Dawson, William H. '38, '39, '40; Dean, Don '72; Dean, James S. (Manager) '05; Dean, Jeff (Trainer) '93; Dean, Jimmy '73, '74, '75, '76; Deaton, Thomas Weldon '70; Debenport, Dan '89; DeBusk, Kelly S. '64; Decker, Jack (Trainer) '68; Deere, Donald R. '43; Deffebach, J.A. '26, '27; Delery, H.B. '28, '29; DeLong, Raleigh '14; Dendy, Billy G. '55; Dennard, Mark '75, '76, '77; Denton, Dean M. '45; Descant,

Dennis '89; DeSilva, Jim '81; Devine, Michael D. '64; Dew, Bobby W. '47; DeNiro, Mike '68, '69; DeWare, Charles A. Sr. '05, '06, '07, '08; DeWare, Charles A. Jr. '34, '35, '36; DeWare, Robert R. 1899, 1900, '01; DeWitt, Bernard John III '70; DeWitt, Mike (Manager) '73; Dickey, Curtis '76, '77, '78, '79; Dickey, Leonard M. '41, '45, '46; Dickie, Byron H. '14; Dickson, Preston '77, '78, '79; Dieterich, A.F. '20, '21; Dietrich, L.G. '24, '25, '26; Dillon, Greg '84, '87; Dillon, Paul G. '62; Dittman, Henry '37, '38; Dixon, Robert H. '51, '52; Dockery, Seth '88, '89, '90, '91; Dollar, Roy I. '52; Dominque, G.C. '31, '32, '33; Donahue, Johnnie '76, '77, '78; Dorsey, R.R. '27, '28, '29; Doucet, Raymond L. '57, '58; Dowell, David '82, '83, '84, '85; Dowell, George S. 1897; Drake, C.R. '18, '19, '20; Dreiss, Ed Jr. '10, '11; Drennan, James L. '62, '63, '64; Driver, Trent '94, '95; Dubcak, James Louis '70, '71; Dubisson, Lydia (Manager) '95; DuBois, H.V. '21, '22, '23; Dudley, Edward R. '55, '58 ; Duncan, William M. '38, '39 ; Dunn, Ralph B. '03; Dupree, Calvin R. '47, '48; Dusek, Ed D. '42, '46, '47; Dusek, John Bradley '70, '71, '72; Dwoskin, Blake '87; Dwyer, W.F. 1897, '98; D wyer, Tom J. '08, '09, '10.

E Easley, Robert, A. Jr. '53, '54; Eberle, A.A. '43, '44; Ebrom, Edwin '69, '70, '71; Eddington, Ashley '84, '85; Edmondson, Larry '81; Edwards, Brian '87, '88; Edwards, Bryan '88; Eenigenburg, Todd '90; Eillers, Joseph A. '60, '61; Eitt, Henry W. '22; Elam, John '87; Elam, K.C. '17, '18; Elder, Jim M. '02; Elkins, John '81, '82, '84; Elledge, Jerry R. (Trainer) '61; Elliott, Jay '91, '92; Ellis, Cedric '81; Ellis, Donald E. '52, '53; Ellis, Herbert W. '44, '45, '47, '48; Ellis, J.P. (Manager) '66; Ellis, Kevin '89, '90; Ellis, Larry '71, '72, '73; Ellis, Oscar L. '07; Ellisor, John '88, '90, '91, '92; Elmendorf, Dave '68, '69, '70; Emerson, Steve '92, '93, '94; Endsley, Lindon C. '64; England, Eric '90, '91, '92, '93; Engle, William F. '45; Erhard, Earl 1900; Erickson, Jalmer L. '61, '62; Ermis, Harvey J. '64; Eschenberg, Arthur C. '14, '15; Esquivel, Carlos '56, '57; Estes, Teddy J. '58, '59, '60; Evans, A.J. '21, '22, '23; Evans, David (Trainer) '77; Evans, Greg (Manager) '89, '90; Evans, Rick (Trainer) '73; Evans, Robert D. '61, '64; Evans, Scott (Manager) '90, '92, '93; Everett, G. Dudley '12, '13, '14; Ewell, W.L. '28.

F Faber, Benny H. '14; Farr, Reso 1896, '97 ; Farrar, Jeff '80, '81, '82; Farrar, Troy (Trainer) '88; Few, Jon W. '58, '60; Figari, E.E. '27; Fields, Edgar '74, '75, '76; Fields, Mike '69, '70; Finley, Bruce Kent '70, '71, '72; Fischler, Chris '90; Fisher, Donnie '80, '82; Fisher, Franklin C. '60, '61; Fister, Lynn '67, '68; Flanagan, Marion D. '43, '46; Fletcher, Pierce H. '63, '65, '66; Flinchem, James M. '07, '10; Flinn, Pat '79, '80; Flournoy, James '90; Flowers, James '83, '84, '85, '86; Flowers, James L. '48, '49, '50; Floyd, Mike '74, '75; Floyd, J.G. '28, '29, '30; Foldberg, Henry C. '42; Foldberg, John D. '45; Fontenot, Jerry '85, '86, '87, '88; Foote, J.M. '11, '12; Force, Henry H. '39; Ford, Bobby (Manager) '95; Ford, Chris '85, '86; Ford, Ken '83, '84; Ford, M.H. '17; Ford, William J. '62, '63, '64; Forey, Leonard '69, '70, '71; Forgason, J.Y. '22, '23, '24; Forgsard, Charles H. '09; Foster, Edmund J. '02, '03, '04, '05; Foster, H. 1899, 1900; Foster, John (Trn.) '79, '80; Foster, Kermit '80, '81, '84; Fowler, E. Odell '32, '34; Fowler, James B. '49, '50, '51; Franklin, Carter L. '58, '59, '60; Franklin, Eric '84, '85; Franklin, Tony '75, '76, '77, '78; Francis, Keith '90; Frazee, Dick '77; Frazelle, Billy J.

(Trainer) '51; Frazier, Derrick '89, '90, '91, '92; Freeman, Matt '74, '75, '76; Freiling, Wayne E. '59, '60, '61; Frey, Richard H. '50, '51, '52; Fronk, Dave '88; Fry, David '87; Frymire, Tom (Manager) '87; Fuller, Jeff '80, '81, '82, '83.

G Galloway, Gerald '78; Galloway, Scott (Trainer) '95; Gantt, Greg (Manager) '80, '81; Gardemal, Richard D. '49, '50, '51; Gardner, John '69, '70, '71; Garner, Robert A. '58; Garrett, Shane '88, '89, '90; Garrett, T.H. 1897, '98, '99, 1900; Garrison, Chris '85, '86; Garrity, John '13, '14, '15; Garth, J.W. '18; Gary, R.J. '43, '44, '46, '47; Gay, Richard C. '56, '57, '58; Gebhart, P.C. 1899, 1900; Geer, Carl E. '39; Geer, W.E. '43, '44, '45; Gerasimowicz, Robert W. '70, '71; Gerrity, Johnny '13, '14; Gibson, Charles B. '43; Gilbert, John R. '55, '56, '57; Gilbert, O'Neill '85, '86, '87, '88; Gilbert, Warren A. (Manager) '07; Gilbert, Warren A. Jr. '46, '47; Gilby, John '90; Gilfillan, Max D. '14, '15, '16; Gill, E. King '22, '23; Gillar, George E. '55, '56; Gillmore, L.M. '17; Gillis, Alton '91; Gillum, Lee (Trainer) '87, 88; Gilman, Greg (Trainer) '82, '83; Glenn, Aaron '92, '93; Glendenning, Craig '73, '74, '75, '76; Glenn, Ronnie '85, '86, '87; Godwin, W.G. '33; Godwin, Willis H. Jr. '57, '58, '59; Goehring, Allen G. '57, '58, '59; Goehring, Dennis H. '54, '55, '56; Goff, Robert E. '44, '48, '49; Golansinski, Joe A. '32; Golson, Kyle '77, '78, '79; Goode, Robert L. '45, '46, '47, '48; Goodwin, Hunter '94, '95; Goodwin, Tommy '70, '71; Gosney, Robert R. '53; Gouger, G. Bryan '17, '19, '20; Gough, Carl '67, '68; Graham, M.C. '16; Graham, Mark '83; Graham, Reggie '91, '92, '93, '94; Graham, Thomas '81, '82; Granger, Jeff '91, '92; Grant, Donald G. '55; Graves, Henry L. '31, '32; Graves, Ray D. '51, '52 ; Gray, Frank M. 1900, '02; Gray, George W. '44, '45; Gray, George William '58; Gray, Tim '73, '74; Greene, Taylor H. (Manager) '54; Green, Jacob '77, '78, '79; Green, Mark '71, '72; Greeno, David '73, '74, '75; Greer, Donovan '93, '94, '95; Gregory, Thomas '76, '78, '79; Gregory, J.C. '33; Greiner, Max G. '47, '48, '49, '50; Griesenbeck, C.T. '17; Griffin, Mike (Trainer) '74; Grimmer, Gib (Manager) '79, '80; Grissom, Roy J. '10; Groce, Clif '91, '92, '93, '94; Gruben, Gary '68; Grudt, Darren '88, '89; Grulich, Carl '76, '77, '78, '79; Gunnels, Roy '67; Gurley, Matt '86, '87, '88; Guseman, Oliver J. '31; Guthrie, Keith '80, '81, '82, '83; Guthrie, Zach '76, '78, '79, '80; Gwin, Clinton D. '50.

H Haack, Gary '74, '75, '76; Haas, Raymond A. Jr. '52; Hackradt, Koby '94, '95; Haddox, Bennie R. '72, '73, '74; Hagerty, Paul '78; Hail, George (Trainer) '59; Hale, Gordon '83; Hale, Lloyd R. '54, '55, '56; Hall, Charles L. '52, '54; Hall, Luther H. '58; Hall, Robert L. '38; Hallman, Curley '66, '67, '68; Hallman, Leroy '83; Hallmark, James L. '43, '46; Hallmark, Kenzy D. '50; Haltom, Bart U. '48; Haltom, Guy V. '04, '05; Hamilton, Jimmy '76, '77, '78, '79; Hamilton, Louis A. '06, '07, '08, '09; Hamner, Stayton W. '02, '03; Hampton, Gary Wayne (Manager) '77; Hampton, Keith (Manager) '83; Hampton, Neil (Manager) '79; Hand, Floyd '42; Hanick, C.F. '05 ; Hanna, Howard E. '03, '05; Hanna, T.W. '22, '23; Hanson, Allan '68, '69; Hardeman, D'Andre '95; Hardin, Eddie '75, '76, '77; Hardman, J.J. '22; Hardy, David '79, '80, '81, '82; Hargett, Edd '66, '67, '68; Hargett, George W. '61, '62, '63; Harper, James L. '60, '61, '62; Harris, Barney '67, '68, '69; Harris, David B. (Manager) '05, '09; Harris, Joey '83; Harris, Rod '85, '86, '87, '88; Harris,

Jay (Trainer) '81; Harrison, R.H. Jr. '18, '19; Harrison, Tony '90, '91, '92, '93; Harrison, Tyler '91, '92, '93; Hart, Lilliard D. '45; Hart, William T. '45; Hartley, Wally '86, '87, '88, '89; Hartman, Jim '73, '74, '75; Harvey, Karl '83; Harvey, Randy '77, '78, '79; Hauerland, Leroy '67, '68; Hauser, Henry '38, '39, '40; Haverda, Lance '83, '84, '85, '86; Hawkins, Donte '95; Hawkins, Jimmie '82, '83, '84, '85; Hayes, Lester '73, '74, '75, '76; Haynes, Marlin '90, '91; Hays, Scott '79, '80; Heard, Marcus '94, '95; Heath, David (Trainer) '75; Heath, Eddie '76, '77, '78; Heaton, Robert (Trainer) '85, '86, '87; Heck, David (Trainer) '89, '90, '91, '92; Hector, Johnny '79, '80, '81, '82; Heidelberg, Frank T. '07, '08; Heimann, Chester E. '39; Henderson, Daniel E. '55; Henderson, Mike (Manager) '91, '92; Henderson, Robert W. '40, '41, '42; Hendricks, Michael '91, '92, '93, '94; Hendrickson, Glenn '83, '85; Henke, Charles E. '38, '39, '40; Henry, Patrick '89, '91; Henry, Peter C. '39; Herman, Odell C. '38, '39, '40; Hernandez, Frank P. (Manager) '58; Herold, Brian (Manager) '90; Herr, Joey '69, '70, '71; Herring, Julian C. '50; Herrold, Brian (Manager) '89; Hewitt, W.W. '30, '31, '32; Higginbotham, G.H. '12; Higginbotham, Roswell G. '17, '19, '20; Higgins, Norton '44, '45, '46, '47; Hill, Carl R. '49 ; Hill, David '79, '80, '81; Hill, Greg '91, '92, '93; Hill, Russell E. '59, '60, '61; Hill, Walter R. '50, '51, '52; Hillhouse, Andy L. '48, '50; Hillje, Bubba '88, '89; Hinnant, Barb '69, '70; Hinze, Ray G. '62, '63, '64; Hitt, Lee Ellison '70, '71; Hobbs, Bill '66, '67, '68; Hodge, Charles H. '50, '51; Hodges, Gene (Trainer) '71; Hoermann, Grady '70, '71, '72; Hogan, George A. '60, '61; Hohn, Caesar '09, '10, '11, '12; Hohn, Charles M. '43; Holder, Leonard D. '41; Holditch, Murry W. '49, '50; Holdman, Warrick '95; Holland, Johnny '83, '84, '85, '86; Holley, Jeff '83, '84, '85, '86; Holliday, T.C. '11; Hollmig, Stanley E. '46, '47; Holmes, Doug '77, '78, '79; Holmes, J.G. '27; Holmes, R.C. (Manager) '47, '48; Honeycutt, Lynn '78, '79; Honore, Jerry '73, '74; Hood, Billy (Trainer) '83, '84; Hooker, Roger M. '07, '08, '09; Hooper, Clarence D. '50, '51, '52; Hoot, David '69, '70, '71; Hope, George N. '02; Hopkins, Jerry W. '60, '61, '62; Horn, Shun '95; Hornsby, H.R. '30, '31; Horton, Larry '87, '88, '89, '90; Housley, Wendell '66, '67, '68; Houston, Brandon '95; Howard, Albert L. '64, '65, '66; Howard, Thomas V. Jr. '56, '57, '58; Howard, Todd '83, '84, '85, '86; Howell, John C. '44, '46, '47; Howse, James '85, '86; Hoyl, Basil L. (Manager) '42; Hubby, Ronnie G. '72, '73, '74, '75; Huddleston, Billy P. '53, '54, '55; Hudeck, Russell R. '49, '50, '51; Hudgins, Charles M. '50; Huff, Jeff '87, '88; Huff, Leslie N. (Manager) '07; Huggins, Alan K. '60, '61; Huggins, Harold '87 ; Hullin, Paul '72, '73, '74; Hull, Burt E. (Manager) '04; Hundl, Philip '90; Hunnicutt, Jesse '74, '75, '76; Hunt, O. Joel '25, '26, '27; Huntington, Bobby N. '60, '61, '62; Hyde, Walter 1900, '01.

I Irby, Jimmie '95; Irvin, Barlow '23, '24, '25; Irwin, B.M. '32; Ivy, Kyle '90.

J Jackson, Basil '85, '86, '87, '88; Jackson, Earnest '79, '80, '81, '82; Jackson, Lance '83, '84, '85; Jackson, Larry '91, '92, '93, '94; Jackson, Robert '75, '76; James, Arlis '78, '79, '80; James, Lex Forrest '70, '71, '72; James, Ronnie '79; Janner, Calvin F. '61; Jasper, Edward '94, '95; Jay, Mike '73, '74, '75; Jay, Monte '85, '86; Jeffrey, William M. '38, '39, '40; Jeffries, Craig '92; Jenkins, Jerry S. '60, '61; Jenkins,

Joseph S. (Manager) '64; Jennings, Curtis '77, '78; Joeris, Leonard '39, '42; Johnson, A.L. '16; Johnson, B.L. '46; Johnson, Chris '69, '70, '71; Johnson, F.S. (Manager) '03; Johnson, George R. '55; Johnson, Harry '85; Johnson, Joe '87, '88; Johnson, Joe B. '60; Johnson, Larry '76, '79; Johnson, Larry '83, '84; Johnson, Scott (Trainer) '79; Johnson, William D. '22, '23; Johnson, Wilbur, G. '45; Joiner, David '86; Jones, Albert '87, '88, '89, '90; Jones, Don '80, '81, '82, '83; Jones, Donald (Manager) '89, '90; Jones, Donald H. (Manager) '60; Jones, Gary '86, '87, '88, '89; Jones, Ivan '66, '67, '68; Jones, Jeff '91, '92, '93, '94; Jones, Michael '88, '89; Jones, Tony '86, '87, '88; Jones, Toya '95; Jones, Troy '86; Jones, Virgil B. '36, '37 ; Jordan, Jim '82, '83; Jordan, W.T. '32, '33, '34.

K Kachtick, Jerry V. '63, '64, '65; Kachtik, Edward D. '52, '53, '54; Kahler, Mike (Manager) '78; Kallus, Kerri (Trainer) '94; Kamp, Charles H. '70; Kapchinski, Karl (Trn.) '78; Kauffmann, James H. '65; Kazmierski, Jim '68; Keeling, Thomas D. '60, '61; Keen, L.S. '21, '22; Keese, Mike '73, '74; Keith, Robert D. '54, '55, '56; Kellen, John '82, '83; Keller, James L. '61, '62, '63; Kelley, Victor M. '05, '06, '07, '09; Kelm, Larry '83, '84, '85, '86; Kemph, Gary S. '65; Kenderdine, J.M. '33; Kendrick, J.M. '15; Kendrick, Robert T. '04, '05; Kennedy, Kevin '80; Kenney, Steve '91, '93, '94; Kennon, Paul A. '54; Kern, R.A. '10, '12; Kern, Ryan '91, '93, '94; Kesey, David A. (Statistician) '69; Kettler, Elwood N. '53, '54; Kidwell, Richard (Manager) '85, '86; Kildow, P.C. 1899; Killion, Reed '82; Kimbrough, Jack C. '39, '40; Kimbrough, John A. '38, '39, '40; Kimbrough, William R. '33, '34; King, Joe Mac '69, '70, '71; Kipp, Kenneth W. '60, '61, '62; Kirby, Selmer M. '34, '35; Kirchmer, John T. '64; Kirk, Kenny '76, '77; Kirkpatrick, Roy '69; Kishi, Taro '24, '25; Kitchens, Gary '67; Klein, Terry (Manager) '77; Knickerbocker, A.G. '19; Knickerbocker, H.W. '22, '23; Knight, Charles J. '64; Kocurek, Jimmy '76, '77; Koehn, Donald W. '64, '65, '66; Kohlman, Joe M. '62, '64; Kotch, Jim (Trainer) '74 ; Kovar, Gary W. '64, '65, '66; Kovar, Jack '67, '68, '69; Krahl, Shane '88, '89, '90; Kramm, Raymond E. '62; Krenek, Benedict J. '60, '61, '62; Krueger, Charles A. '55, '56, '57; Krueger, Rolf '66, '67, '68; Krug, William 1894; Kubala, Raymond G. '61, '62, '63; Kubecka, Bill '67; Kubiak, Gary '80, '81, '82; Kubesch, Raymond A. '62; Kuehn, Russell '71, '72.

L Labar, Harry W. '58, '59, '60; LaBauve, Dwight '71, '72; LaGrange, Charles R. '63, '64, '65; LaGrone, Walter A. '60, '61; Lakin, Greg '88, '89, '90, '91; Lambert, H.G. '10, '11, '12; Lamkin, Kenneth A. '64, '65, '66; Lammers, Chris '83; Lamp, Ted '73, '74; Land, Marshall '86; Land, Mike (Trainer) '81, '82; Landrum, Tim '85, '86, '87; Langford, Alvin L. '50, '51, '52; Langston, James E. '56; Lark, Scott '85, '86, '87, '88; Lary, Robert Y. '49, '50, '51; Latham, Joel P. '60, '61, '62; Lawrence (Trainer) '94, '95; Lawson, Bruce '82, '83; Lawson, Clarence O. '49; Lawson, Doug '89; Lazarine, Marshall M. '50; League, Thomas '44; LeBouef, Gordon E. '57, '58, '59; Ledbetter, Harry L. '65, '66; Ledbetter, Ronald P. '60, '61, '62; Lednicky, Kyle '95; Lee, Larry L. '65, '66; Lee, Robert G. '63; Leggett, Charles W. '09; Lehrer, Robert (Trainer) '86, '87; Leiper, Sam E. '22; Leisner, Lane (Manager) '82, '83; Lemmons, Bernard '50; Lemmons, Kevin (Manager) '95; Lemons, Billy '73, '74, '75, '76; Lemons, Frank '76, '77; Lewis, Darren '87, '88, '89, '90; Lewis, Mark '80, '81, '82, '84 ;

Lewis, Steve '79; Lewis, Trent '89, '90, '91; Leyendecker, Dan '88; Liles, Ike '83, '84; Lillard, Steve T. '09; Lindsey, Ernest M. '35; Lindsey, Glynn '64, '65, '66; Lindsey, Ronald L. '64, '65, '66; Linnstaedter, James A. '61, '62, '63; Linscombe, Corry '84, '85; Lippman, Glenn E. '49, '50, '51; Lister, W.S. '26, '27; Littig, Michael '83; Little, Jack H. '50, '51, '52; Little, Mike '78, '79, '80, '81; Little, Thomas '95; Litterst, Frank C. '16; Lockett, Bobby J. '56; Lofton, Steve '89; Long, Bob '66, '67, '68; Long, Don '72, '73, '74; Long, Eldon W. '43; Lopez, Ricky '81; Lord, George P. '30, '31; Lord, Mike '69, '70, '71; Love, Andrew C. 1894, '98; Love, J.N. '33; Love, Richard L. '59; Loving, James W. '04; Lowery, Gene '93, '94, '95; Luebbehusen, Steve '69, '70, '71; Luethy, Don R. '42; Luna, Otie C. '57, '58; Lutrick, J.A. '11; Lyles, John V. '12.

M Maddox, Randy '69; Magourik, Conrad W. '51, '52, '53; Magrill, O.B. '29, '30, '31; Maham, Scott '87, '88; Mahan, Jack '17, '19, '20; Mahone, Matt '94; Malone, C.C. '30, '31; Malone, Grant (Manager) '89, '90, '91; Malone, Tyronne '90; Maltz, Hershel (Manager) '47; Manning, Waylon E. '35, '36; Maples, Weldon L. '41, '42; Marcus, James '87, '89; Marks, Jared '84, '85, '86; Marks, Robert E. '55, '56, '57; Marquette, Leo J. '52; Marshall, Mike '82 ; Marshall, Tank '73, '74, '75, '76; Martin, G.W. '18, '19, '20; Martin, Gary Wayne '70; Martin, Harry 1894; Martin, John '88; Martin, Sidney T. '34; Massey, Chris (Trainer) '78; Masterson, L. '02; Matthews, Mason L. '44, '45; Mathews, Jason '91, '92, '93; Mathews, Ryan '91, '92, '93, '94; Mathison, Todd '91, '92, '93, '94; Maughmer, Lynn '78; Mauk, Albert '03, '05; Maxfield, Kyle '91, '92, '93, '94; Maxwell, David '94, '95; Maxwell, Stapp N. '32; Maxwell, Tommy '66, '67, '68; May, Homer H. '70, '71, '72; Mayeaux, Hayden E. '51, '52; Mayfield, J.D. Jr. (Manager) '49, '50; Mazur, John '83, '84; McAfee, Keith '88, '89, '90, '91; McAllister, G.T. '43, '44; McAnelly, Phil '68; McArthur, O.A. '12; McCaffrey, Gary '70; McCall, Mark (Trainer) '89, '90, '91, '92; McCall, Matt '87, '88, '89, '90; McCarley, Robert E. '52; McClatchy, Scott (Trainer) '89, '90, '91; McClelland, Don A. '57, '60; McClelland, H.W. '22; McClintock, J.R. '17; McCoy, Joe (Manager) '89, '90, '91; McCoy, Torin '89, '90; McCray, Danny '93, '94, '95; McCrumbly, John '73, '74; McDermott, Pat '70, '71, '72; McDonald, Andy '88, '89; McDonald, Charles N. '49, '50, '51; McDonald, Hugh F. 1894; McDonald, Pace '18; McDonald, William A. '09; McDowell, Charles H. '10; McElroy, Hugh '70, '71; McElroy, Leeland '93, '94, '95; McFadden, P.M. '30, '31; McFarland, Arthur '03, '04; McFarland, H.F. 1893, '94; McFarland, James L. '11; McGinnis, Francis K. 1900; McGonagill, J.D. 1894; McGonagle, Brad '90; McGowan, Billy Joe '52, '54; McGregor, Flint '02; McGuire, Eddy (Trainer) '89, '90; McGuire, Joseph D. '24, '25; McGuire, Trace '85, '86, '87; McIlhany, Joe D. '62, '63, '64; McKaughan, Edward W. '64, '65; McKeehan, James '91, '92, '93, '94; McKinney, Steve '94, '95; McKnight, J.B. '16, '17; McLean, Ken J. '62, '63, '65; McMahan, Billy M. '53; McMahan, James T. '50; McMillan, M. Blaisdale 1894; McMillan, W.G. '21, '22; McMullen, Typail '93, '94, '95; McMurrey, J.D. '17; McNeill, J.C. 1894; McQueen, Mark '81, '82; Meeks, Thomas E. '62, '63, '64; Meitzen, J.B. '24; Mercer, Arthur J. '41, '42; Merka, Jeremiah H. '33; Mertz, Alaina (Trainer) '94; Meyer, D. '02; Meyer, William H. '49, '50, '51; Meyers, Phillip '94, '95;

Mickens, Ray '92, '93, '94, '95; Middleton, Bobby '84, '85, '86; Middleton, Doug '85; Mikeska, Russell '76, '77; Miles, Wadine '77; Miller, A.R. '12; Miller, Eric E. '51, '52, '53; Miller, John '89, '90; Miller, L. '02; Miller, Stephen (Trainer) '93, '94; Miller, T.L. '21, '22; Miller, Thomas B. '39; Miller, Vance W. '12, '13; Milligan, Garry '76, '77, '78; Milligan, Wayne '03, '07; Mills, J. Kenneth '37; Mills, Thomas W. '27, '28, '29; Millsap, Lenard '70; Milstead, Charles F. '57, '58, '59; Minnock, W.A. '37, '38; Mitchell, Billy '90, '92, '93, '94; Mitchell, Brandon '93, '94, '95; Mitchell, Brian '91, '92, '93, '94; Mitchell, Keith '93, '94, '95; Mitchell, Merlin '15, '16; Mohn, Walter '67; Molberg, Carl '48, '49, '50; Moncrief, Monte P. '43, '44, '45, '46; Monk, Kevin '74, '75, '76, '77; Montgomery, J.B. '42; Montgomery, Roark '12; Moon, L.B. '87, '88; Moore, A.A. '30, '31; Moore, Doyle H. '49; Moore, Eric '89, '90; Moore, George F. '07, '08 ; Moore, Kirk (Manager) '90; Moore, Mack '79, '80; Moore, William R. '62, '63, '64; Moore, W. Scott '07, '08, '09, '10; Moorman, Maurice '66; Morgan, Sylvester '84, '85, '86, '87; Morris, A.B. '20, '21, '22; Morris, Alex '85, '86, '87, '88; Morrison, D.E. '12; Morrison, P.M. 1896; Morrow, Johnnie '35, '36; Mortensen, James E. '45; Moseley, Hal 1897, '98, '99, 1900; Mosley, Mike '77, '78, '79, '80; Moser, R. Derace '39, '40, '41; Moses, Sam F. '49, '50, '51; Mossenburg, W.G. 1894; Motley, Larry '86; Motley, Zolus C. '39, '41; Moulden, Carl D. '29, '30, '31; Mudd, Dennis '85; Mulhollan, Ray W. '40, '41, '42; Mullen, Steve '68; Muller, Jay '84, '85, '86; Munson, George (Manager) '72; Munson, Joe U. Jr. '57, '58; Murchison, Phil (Trainer) '93, '94; Murname, T. (Manager) '44, '45, '46; Murphy, A.L. (Manager) '52, '53; Murphy, James L. '59, '60, '61; Murphy, Mike (Manager) '80, '81; Murrah, Thomas F. '63, '64, '65; Murrah, W.E. '18, '19, '20, '21; Murray, Jon '95; Murray, Kevin '83, '84, '85, '86; Murray, Paul '79; Murray, R.L. '32, '33; Murski, Robert '70, '71, '72; Myers, Frank '74, '75, '76, '77; Myers, O.W. 1897, '98, '99.

N Naiser, Derek '88; Nakos, Alex (Manager) '88, '89; Nakos, Spiro (Manager) '90, '92, '93; Nasser, Al '78; Nealy, Otis '89, '90, '91, '92; Neece, Clarence M. '08, '09; Neely, Roy G. '22, '23; Neff, Asa J. '02; Nehib, Greg '88; Nelms, Milton R. '12; Nelson, Freddie A. '65 ; Nelson, Jeff '82, '83, '84, '85; Neill, Doug '69, '70, '71; Nesrsta, J.O. '35, '36, '37; Netardus, Jaro G. Jr. '49, '51; Nettles, Rusty '81, '82; Neville, Henry A. '43; Newton, Keith '83, '84; Nguyen, Dat '95; Nicholas, Don R. '49; Nichols, Jerry D. '64, '65; Niland, Thomas K. '51, '52; Nilson, John H. '63, '64, '65; Noble, Elton 1899, 1900; Nohavitza, Elo E. '49, '50, '51; Nolan, Willis '30, '31, '32; Nolen, Lockhart (Manager) '48; Northup, Roy F. '58, '59, '60; Novosad, Steven (Trainer) '95.

O O'Brient, Sammy '84, '85, '86, '87; Ochterbeck, W.J. '24, '25; Odom, Lynn '67, '68, '69; Odom, Van '69, '70, '71; Ogdee, Edward '42; Ohlendorf, Norbert K. '52, '53, '54; Olbrich, Alvin P. '38; Oliver, Aaron '95; Oliver, Gale G. '57, '58, '59; Oliver, Gary '87, 88, '89, '90; O'Neal, Hardy E. '02; O'Neal, Steve '66, '67, '68; Osborn, John '79, '80; Osborne, Carl R. '55, '56, '57; Osborne, Richard '72, '73, '74, '75; Osgood, Chris '88, '89; Overly, Charles R. '43, '46, '47; Overly, James A. (Trainer) '48, '49; Overshiner, E.M. 1896; Overton, Andrew J. '63, '64; Owens, Bob (Manager) '73; Ozee, Kevin (Manager) '93.

P Page, Sean '87; Paine, Jeff '80, '81, '82, '83; Palasota, Vince '88; Pannell, E.W. '38, '39, '40; Pappas, Mike '87, '89, '90; Pardee, John P. '54, '55, '56; Parish, Joseph M. '39; Park, Mike '70, '71, '72; Parker, James H. (Manager) '39, '40; Parker, Jim '68, '69, '70; Parker, Sirr '95; Parker, William E. '08, '09, '10, '12 ; Parmer, James R. '44; Patterson, Cornelius '88, '89, '90; Pavlas, Lance '87, '88, '89, '90; Payne, Brian '89, '90, '91; Payne, H.B. (Buddy) '57, '58, '59; Payne, Lawrence J. '45; Payne, Rick (Manager) '76; Payne, W.O. '42; Pearson, Henry A. '57; Pender, Paul '79, '80, '81, '82; Peoples, Dan '71; Perkins, Frank D. 1894, '96, '97; Persons, David H. '13; Peter, Philip '61; Peterson, Alcie '94, '95; Petty, Kent '89, '90, '91, '92; Petty, S.J. '26, '27; Peveto, Cal '78, '79; Philley, Andy '69, '70, '71; Phillips, David '84; Phillips, H.D. '30; Phillips, James D. '60, '61, '62; Phillips, Michael L. '64; Phillips, Robert H. '59, '60; Phythian, Walter R. '35, '36; Pickard, Billy (Trainer) '78; Pickett, Tom B. '41, '46; Pierce, J.A. '18, '19, '20; Pierce, Kirk '88; Pillans, Ryan '95; Pinson, C.T. '23; Pinson, Harry T. '21; Piper, Jim '67, '68, '69; Piper, Paul K. '59, '60; Pirie, James E. '01, '02, '03; Pirtle, David (Trainer) '76; Pitman, Mike J. '62, '63, '64; Pitner, H.M. '34, '35, '36; Pittman, Lee (Manager) '81, '82; Pizzitola, Michael J. '61, '62; Polasek, Billy Joe '69, '71; Polk, Scott '80, '81, '82, '83, '84; Pollacia, Tony '85; Pollard, Dan '86; Pollock, Oscar L. '47; Polocheck, Layne '85; Pool, Rusty '71; Porter, Greg '81, '82, '83; Poss, John M. '65, '66; Powell, Jack E. '53, '55; Powell, Louis H. '14 ; Powell, William D. '54, '55, '56; Power, Robert (Manager) '67; Power, Richard S. (Manager) '69; Price, C. Walemon '37, '38, '39; Price, Harold L. '56; Price, Michael '95; Price, P.M. '25; Price, Terry '86, '87, '88, '89; Prokop, Merl A. '47; Puckett, Felix S. '05, '06; Puckett, John W. '02, '03; Pugh, Marion C. '38, '39, '40; Pullig, Corey '92, '93, '94, '95; Pustejovsky, Ed '76, '77, '78, '79; Pyburn, Jack H. '64, '65, '66.

R Ragsdale, Robert 1897, '98; Rahn, Leon F. '39, '40; Raiford, Aubrey '81; Randle, Floyd '77, '78; Ransby, Felton '88, '90; Ransom, Dennis '87, '88, '89, '90; Rau, Tim (Manager) '88, '89; Rawlins, Harry E. 1897; Ray, Tom '85; Reagan, Travis H. '61, '62, '63; Red, Darrell '91, '92, '93; Redus, James '79; Reed, Roderick '76, '77; Reed, Roman '83; Rees, W. Nelson '31; Reeves, John R. '39, '40; Reeves, Ken '81, '82, '83, '84; Reid, Steve (Manager) '83, '84; Reinarz, Cole '92, '93, '94; Rektorik, J.A. '26; Resley, George '68; Restivo, Brian (Manager) '95; Reynolds, James '68; Reynolds, John W. '65; Reynolds, Ron '84; Reynolds, Shawn '95; Richard, John '92, '94; Richardson, Bucky '87, '88, '90, '91; Richardson, Lester S. '39, '41; Richardson, Rod '82; Richenstein, Charles A. '05; Richey, Derrick '87, '88, '89; Richter, Charles E. '27, '28, '29; Ricke, Mike (Trainer) '80, '81; Rickman, Ricky (Manager) '68; Ridenhower, Ray '01, '02; Riggs, Charlie '66, '67, '68; Rion, Dennis '83; Risien, Cody '76, '77, '78; Risien, Flint '80, '81, '82 ; Roach, James B. '33; Roaches, Carl '72, '73, '74, '75; Robbins, Cooper P. Jr. '52, '53; Robbins, Donald '55; Robbins, Doug '70; Robbins, Mike '79, '81, '82; Roberts, F.A. (Manager) '13; Roberts, William C. '08; Robertson, Art Mitchell '70, '71; Robertson, John E. '31, '33; Robinson, Jeroy '86, '87, '88, '89; Robison, Tommy '80, '81, '82, '83; Robnett, Edward '39; Robnett, Marshall F. '38, '39, '40; Rockhold, Jason '89, '90; Roepke, Robert E. (Manager) '61; Rogers, Cullen J. '39, '41, '42; Rogers, Gary '82; Rogers, Gerald G. '61, '62, '63; Rogers, Joe

C. '15, '16; Rogers, Owens A. '36, '37, '38; Rollins, Gerald D. (Manager) '56; Rollins, John W. '14, '15, '16; Rollins, Zerick '95; Roper, James S. '58; Roper, John '85, '86, '87, '88; Roquemore, Michael A. '62; Ross, Brian '86, '87, '88, '89; Ross, James B. '06, '07; Rothe, Joe H. '39, '40; Rother, Randy '82; Routt, Joe E. '35, '36, '37; Routt, William A. '38, '39, '40; Royalty, Charlie A. '48, '49; Ruby, Martin O. '39, '40, '41; Rudder, James Earl '31; Rugel, Dan F. '07, '08, '09; Ruhman, Chris '94, '95; Rush, Marshall N. '51, '52; Rush, William T. '49, '50, '51; Rushing, Eli '37, '38; Rylander, W.E. '15.

S Sacra, Joseph R. '44, '46, '47; Sacra, Joseph R. Jr. '70, '71, '72; Saddler, Rod '83, '84, '85, '86; Sagraves, Steven '90, '91; Sallee, Bill D. '65, '66, '67; Salyer, Johnny A. '51, '52, '53; Sammons, Thomas B. '04; Sams, Bucky '73, '74, '75; Sanders, Chris '91, '92, '94, '95; Sanders, Eugene '76, '77, '78 ; Sanders, Robert W. '57, '58, '59; Sanders, S.H. '21; Sanders, Scot '91; Sanders, Thomas '80, '81, '82, '84; Sarkissian, Steve '89; Sawyer, Buzzy '81; Sawyer, Randy '82; Saxe, Augie W. '50, '51; Saxe, Charles S. '51, '52; Scarborough, J.S. '08; Schaedel, Charles T. '10, '11; Schero, Joe E. '52, '53, '54; Schmid, Joe H. (Manager) '57; Schmidt, Hubert '06, '07; Schmidt, Pat (Trainer) '95; Schneider, Daniel W. '65, '66, '67; Schorp, Greg '90, '91, '92, '93; Schroeder, Bruno E. '35, '37, '38; Schroeder, William H. '53, '54; Schultz, Earl 1900, '01, '02, '03; Schwarz, Blake '72, '73, '74, '75; Scoggins, Phillip C. '64, '65; Scott, David '79, '80; Scott, Herbert B. '52; Scott, Johnny D. '52, '53; Scott, Joseph O. '44, '46; Scott, Richard E. '49; Scott, Verne A. '14; Scovell, J. Field '28; Scudder, Carl F. '18, '19, '20; Seago, H.W. '36; Seeker, Ricky '72, '73, '74; Seely, Bill '68, '69; Selby, Tommy (Manager) '94, '95; Self, Rocky '69; Settegast, Marion E. Sr. '14, '15, '16; Settegast, Marion E. Jr. '43; Shaeffer, Robert J. '49, '50, '51; Shanks, Jeff '88, '89; Shaw, Joe '69; Sheffield, Corky '69, '72; Sheffield, Jimmy '68, '69, '70; Shefts, Morton '44, '46; Shelton, J. Howard '39, '40; Shiller, Steve '83; Shipman, David '74, '75, '76; Shippix '09; Shira, Charles N. '43, '44; Shockey, Jacob C. '35, '36, '37; Sibley, William R. '41, '42; Sikes, Delmar D. '50; Sikes, Jules V. '25, '26, '27 ; Siler, Rich '83, '84, '85; Simmons, A.L. '56, '57; Simmons, Elvis A. '40, '41, '42; Simmons, J.A. '26; Simmons, Melvin D. '62, '63, '64; Simmons, Randy '88, '89, '90, '91; Simmons, Wayland A. '59, '60, '61; Simon, Burnis '80, '81,'82, '83; Simonini, Edward '72, '73, '74, '75; Simpson, J.V. '02, '03, '04; Simpson, O.M. 1897, '98, '99; Simpson, Phillip '77, '78, '79; Sims, Arthur R. '58, '59, '60; Sims, J.P. (Trainer) '88, '89; Sims, M.W. 1894; Sinclair, Bennie C. '53, '54; Singleton, James M. '65, '66; Singleton, Percy '92; Sipe, Brent (Trainer) '89; Skinner, Ben S. (Manager) '52; Slater, Scott '85, '86, '87, '88; Slaton, Tony '82, '83, '84; Slaughter, Marion P. '42; Slocum, Shawn '84; Smelser, Dennis '73, '74, '75; Smith, Alan '80, '81, '83, '84; Smith, Bland '70, '71; Smith, Brent '85, '86, '87, '88; Smith, Darrell '76, '77, '78; Smith, Darrell '82, '83, '84; Smith, Detron '92, '93, '94, '95; Smith, Don G. '56, '57, '58; Smith, Earl L. '39, '40; Smith, George '82, '83; Smith, Gilbert '66; Smith, H.E. '37, '38, '39; Smith, Kevin '88, '89, '90, '91; Smith, Langston M. '14, '15; Smith, M.V. '20, '21; Smith, Preston W. '45, '46, '47, '48; Smith, Ralph W. '58, '59, '60; Smith, Randy (Trainer) '82, '83; Smith, Robert L. '49, '50, '51; Smith, Ted '69, '70, '71; Smitham, Verner R. (Manager) '14; Snow, Dion '88, '89; Solari, Steve '91, '92, '93; Sooy, Tom '67, '68, '69;

Sorrell, Gary '87, '88, '89; Spadora, Joseph (Manager) '65; Spake, W.E. '12; Speed, Carleton D. '25 ; Spencer, Michael F. '49, '50; Spencer, Oliver E. '14; Spencer, Rick '71; Spencer, Ted L. '31, '32, '33; Spikes, Cameron '95; Spiller, Derrick '95; Spires, Truman E. '45; Spitzenberger, Steve '75, '76, '77; Spivey, Marshall '39, '40, '41; Sprott, Alton C. '26, '27; Stabler, James M. '64, '65; Stach, Stanfield A. '33, '35; Stages, William E. '36; Stahr, Richard (Trainer) '89; Stallings, Eugene C. '54, '55, '56; Stallings, Rusty '68, '69; Stanley, James L. '55, '56, '57; Stanley, Mark '73, '74, '75; Stansberry, Robert '69; Stautzenberger, Weldon O. ; '46, '47, '48; Steadman, Nate '82, '83, '84; Steen, Elroy '77, '78, '79; Steffens, Karl K. '38; Stegent, Larry '67, '68, '69; Stephenson, Phillip (Manager) '80, '81; Sterling, James R. '39, '40, '41; Sterns, James B. 1896, '97, '98; Steymann, Walter R. '42; Stinson, Mike '68, '69; Stiteler, Robert H. '30; Stoss, Robert '79, '80, '81, '82; Stratton, Carl K. '72, '73, '74; Street, Gus C. 1899, '01, '02, '03, '04; Street, Robert L. (Manager) '48, '49; Stringfellow, Jack C. '33; Strogen, Bobby '79, '80, '81, '82; Stuard, Kyle '80, '81, '82, '83; Stump, Craig '84, '85, '86, '87; Sturcken, Edward B. '42; Suggs, Tommy '82; Sullivan, Mike '89; Surovik, John H. (Manager) '52, '53; Svatek, Johnnie '77, '78, '79; Swan, Michael K. '63; Swedeen, John '70; Swilley, Dennis '73, '74, '75, '76; Symes, Clarence '06, '07.

T Talbot, Layne '87, '88, '89, '90; Taliaferro, Darrell '73; Tankersley, Rick '85, '86; Tassos, Damon G. '43, '44 ; Tate, Marvin P. '52, '53, '54; Taylor, Anthony '86, '87; Taylor, Arthur W. '08, '09; Taylor, Kenneth '77, '78; Taylor, Loyd F. '55, '56, '57; Teague, Doug '76, '77, '78, '79; Teague, Foster S. '53; Teague, Sammie R. (Manager) '59; Teal, Jimmy '82, '83, '84; Teate, Randall '76; Teichelman, Lance '90, '91, '92, '93; TenNapel, Garth '73, '74, '75; Terry, Sean '94, '95 ; Tewell, Dennis (Trainer) '67; Thelen, David '89, '90; Theriot, Sidney J. '52, '53, '54; Thomas, Clifford '69; Thomas, Clifton '70; Thomas, Edwin W. '13, '14; Thomas, Patrick S. '72, '73, '74, '75; Thomas, Rodney '91, '92, '93, '94; Thomas, William '88, '89, '90; Thomason, James N. '38, '39, '40; Thompson, George E. '80; Thompson, Kyle (Trainer) '95; Thompson, Nash O. '34; Thompson, Thomas E. '09; Thompson, Tony '85, '86, '87; Thompson, William '73, '74, '75, '76; Thornton, Penn B. '16; Thrower, John D. 1899, 1900; Thurmond, Albert N. '72, '73, '74; Tidwell, Billy R. '49, '50, '51; Todd, Dick S. '36, '37, '38; Tolleson, Mike '86; Toney, Anthony '84, '85; Torno, Frank V. '46; Tracey, John '56, '57, '58; Tracy, Carroll A. '28, '29, '30; Tracy, Henry C. '72, '73, '74, '75; Tracy, H.H. 1897; Trahan, Warren '73, '74; Trammell, Bud '73; Trimble, Murry H. '55, '56; Trimmier, Tim '73; Trew, Robert L. '13; Trott, Bobby (Trainer) '66; Tschantz, Todd '84, '85, '86; Tucker, Kevin '89, '90; Tucker, Lanning (Trainer) '85, '86; Tucker, M. Dwayne '48, '49, '50; Tucker, Rex '95; Tulis, Robert F. '41, '46, '47; Turley, Herbert E. '43, '46, '47, '48; Turner, J.G. '37; Turner, Lafayette '86, '87, '88 ; Turner, Stanley S. '43; Turney, John '68.

U Ullrich, Charles E. '33; Underwood, James '90; Uriegas, Alberto (Trainer) '84; Utay, Joe '05, '06, '07; Uzzell, William J. '63, '64.

V Vaden, Frank S. (Manager) '55; Valentine, Ira '82, '84, '85, '86; Vandervoort, A.S. '18, '19; Van Dyke, Lewis E. '60, '62; Van Pelt, Thomas E.

(Trainer) '60; Van Sant, Jon '80, '81, '82; Van Zandt, Roscoe L. '28, '30; Vassar, William C. (Manager) '63; Vaughn, John (Manager) '81, '82; Vaughn, Tommie '38, '39, '40; Veckert, Harman H. 1896, '97; Vela, Javier '67, '68; Velasquez, Joe '81, '82, '83, '84; Venetoulias, Manoli '95; Venetoulias, Terry '90, '91, '92, '93; Vesmirovsky, E. '10, '11, '12, '13; Vick, Richard P. '54; Vick, Roger '83, '84, '85, '86; Vincent, Kary '90, '91; Vitek, Richard D. '35, '36, '37; Vordenbaumen, Tim '93, '94; Voss, Kenneth R. '48.

W Waddle, Percy '87, '88, '89; Waguespack, Keith '94; Walker, Alvin (Skip) '72, '73, '74, '75; Walker, Bill '86; Walker, David '73, '74, '76, '77; Walker, Elvis '82; Walker, George '66; Walker II, Larry '93, '94, '95; Walker, L.E. '18; Walker, Shawn '83, '84; Walker, Shea '83, '84, '85, '86; Walker, Weldon F. '35; Walker, William E. '44; Walker, William T. '02, '03, '04, '05; Wallace, Aaron '86, '87, '88, '89; Wallace, Larry '91, '93; Ward, Arland L. '09; Ward, Brandon '94; Ward, C.E. '09, '10; Ward, Tim '79, '80, '82; Ward, Waylon O. '63, '64; Ward, William R. '63; Ware, Derek '90; Warnke, Carl '73, '74, '75; Washington, Mickey '87, '88, '89; Washington, William H. '12; Watkins, Ronald '81 ; Watson, Donald A. '54, '55, '56; Watson, Matt (Manager) '94; Watson, Steve '83; Watts, Arthur P. 1894; Watts, Claude D. '25, '26; Watts, Dale '68, '69; Waugh, C.A. '23, '24; Weaver, Mark '66, '67; Webb, Duncan '83, '84, '85; Webb, James '88, '89, '91; Webb, Richmond '86, '87, '88, '89; Webster, J.D. '40, '41, '42; Weghorst, Allan (Manager) '85; Weinert, Arthur 1900, '08; Weir, David (Trainer) '87, '88; Weir, H.B. '17; Weir, W.C. '19, '20, '21; Weiss, Joe H. '64, '65, '66; Welch, Bruce '73, '74, '75; Welch, F. Barney '42, '46, '47; Wellborn, Joseph H. '63, '64, '65; Wells, Gaddy '67; Wendt, F.T. '21; Wesley, Dexter '90, '91, '92, '93; Wesson, T. Euel '39, '40, '41; West, Donald E. '64; Westbrook, Wm. A. (Manager) '62; Westerberg, Tom (Manager) '84; Westerfield, Ira Dan '64, '65, '66; Whatley, Richard E. '63, '64, '65; Wheat, Shannon (Trainer) '84, '85; Wheat, Wayne '69; Wheeler, Lee (Manager) '82, '83; Wheeler, Mark '90, '91; White, Finis L. '39; White, Joe R. '37, '38, '39; White, Junior '91, '92, '93, '94; White, Oscar M. '45; Whitehead, Gary '71, '72; Whitfield, Calvin '84, '85, '86; Whitfield, John T. '35, '36; Whitmore, Jack '67, '68, '69; Whittaker, Wray W. '46, '47, '48, '49; Whitwell, Mike '78, '79, '80, '81; Whyte, James A. '10; Wickerhan, James B. '64; Wiebold, Bill '71, '72; Wiley, J.E. '43; Wilkerson, Grady '73, '74, '75, '76; Wilkins, W. Taylor '34, '35; Willenborg, James C. '62, '63, '64; Williams, Andre '93, '94, '95; Williams, Anthony '89, '90; Williams, Brandon (Trainer) '95; Williams, Cedric '93; Williams, Doug '84, '85 ; Williams, George '39; Williams, Greg '80, '81, '82; Williams, Jackie '73, '74, '75; Williams, Jimmie '80, '81, '82, '83; Williams, J. Maurice '39; Williams, Lee (Manager) '95; Williams, Michael '75, '76, '77; Williams, Pat '95; Williams, Reggie '73, '74; Williams, Robert H. '41, '42; Williams, Sammy '68; Williams, T.J. '05; Williams, W.B. '31, '32; Willis, Nicholas W. '34, '35; Willoughby, Jack (Manager) '71; Wilson, E.S. '16, '17, '18, '19; Wilson, Fay '23, '24, '25; Wilson, Matt '84, '85, '86, '87; Wilson, Richard O. '22, '23; Wilson, Robert '88, '89, '90; Wilson, Roy D. (Trainer) '63; Wilson, Sean '87, '88, '89, '90; Wilson, T.F. '20, '21, '22, '23; Wilson, W.W. '24; Winkler, Andrew 1897, '98; Winkler, James C. '45, '46, '47, '48; Winkler, Lawrence E. '52, '53, '54; Winn, W.E. '21; Withers, John '82; Wolf, Herbert J.

'54, '55; Wolf, William M. '30; Wood, Frank M. '39; Wood, Joe '66; Wood, Kristen (Trainer) '95; Woddard, George '75, '76, '77, '79; Woodard, Mike (Trainer) '76; Woodfin, Jim (Manager) '86, '87, '88; Woodland, Sully '32, '33; Woodman, Cony N. '04, '06; Woodman, James O. '30; Woodman, V.W. '25, '26; Woodside, Keith '83, '85, '86, '87; Work, Chris '88; Worthing, Evan E. '01, '02; Wright, Charlie E. '43, '46, '47, '48; Wright, Don '77, '78; Wright, Fred G. '35; Wright, James '55, '56, '57; Wright, Larry '73; Wright, R.C. '43, '46; Wright, Richard H. '32; Wright, Will '79, '80, '81, '82 ; Wurzback, Mark '84, '85, '86; Wyatt, Sherrod '94; Wylie, H.P. '26; Wylie, Randy '83, '84, '85.

Y Yates, Paul T. '44; Yeargain, C.W. '44, '45; Yeoman, William F. '45; Yocum, Gill '71; Young, Gary '76; Young, Roy O. '35, '36, '37.

Z Zachery, James '77, '78, '79; Zachry, Ben '84, '85; Zapalac, Willie F. '41, '42, '46; Zarafonetis, George H. '28, '29; Zedler, Otto F. (Manager) '16; Zuch, Howard W. '51, '52.

TRIVIA ANSWERS

1. Eight. An 11-0 victory in 1902 broke the ice and also put the Aggies' first points on the board. Until then they were 0-6-1 against the Longhorns and were outscored 152-0.

2. 1917, 8-0-0, under coach D. X. Bible.

3. 1939, 11-0-0, under coach Homer Norton.

4. 1948, 0-9-1, under coach Harry Stiteler.

5. Texas, 14-14, A&M's first non-loss ever in Memorial Stadium at Austin.

6. Oklahoma, 14-7, in College Station, 1951.

7. Texas Tech, 38-9, in Lubbock, 1975.

8. Texas, 28-24, in Austin, 1988.

9. .875 (63-9-2)

10. Tony Franklin against Baylor in College Station, 1976.

11. Zero.

12. 1950, twice. Glenn Lippman (8 carries, 124 yards) and Billy Tidwell (6-103) in a 48-12 win over Nevada, Tidwell (14-114) and Bob Smith (19-111) against Oklahoma (28-34).

13. Gary Kubiak to Don Jones, 92 yards against Louisiana Tech, 1981.

14. Tight end Rod Bernstine, 65 in 1986.

15. Split end Bob Long, 19 touchdowns in 1966-68.

16. 1956, 9-0-1 under coach Bear Bryant.

17. Daniel Baker, 110-0, 1920.

18. Texas, 48-0, 1898.

19. Richard Copeland Slocum.

20. Guard Joe Routt, 1936.

21. Most rushing yards by a quarterback, 180 on 20 carries, vs. Southern Cal in the 1977 Bluebonnet Bowl.

22. Fewest first downs allowed (1) and fewest first downs rushing (0).

23. Alabama 29, Texas A&M 21.

24. 12 (seven interceptions, five fumbles).

25. Hunt accounted for four touchdowns, intercepted four passes and punted eight times for a 43-yard average.

26. LSU and Georgia.

27. J.V. "Pinky" Wilson, while standing guard on the Rhine with the AEF after World War I.

28. Eight.

29. Pardee made both football All-America and academic All-America teams.

30. Hall didn't letter.

31. In the Sugar Bowl vs. Tulane on Jan. 1, 1940, Kimbrough gained 159 yards on 25 carries, scoring two touchdowns in a 14-13 victory.

32. John Tarleton Agricultural College.

33. A&M quarterback Branndon Stewart led Stephenville High School to the 1993 Texas Class 4A football championship.

34. Assistant coach Elmer Smith, who recruited and signed Crow for A&M in the spring of 1954 after joining new Aggie coach Bear Bryant's staff.

35. As an Army Air Corps pursuit pilot in World War I.

36. 7,000.

37. 1942.

38. Hooper, who played end and quarterback in 1950-52, won the silver medal in the shot put at the 1952 Helsinki Olympics.

39. Defensive coordinator.

40. .615

41. .325

42. Atlanta Falcons.